Aim High

Student's Book 5

Susan Iannuzzi   Paul Kelly

OXFORD
UNIVERSITY PRESS

CONTENTS

THIS UNIT INCLUDES ●●●●
Vocabulary • holidays • onomatopoeia • idioms with *on* and *off*
Grammar • stative verbs • simple and continuous forms
Skills • describing holidays and places
Writing • a persuasive essay

Getting away

BEFORE READING

Discuss the questions.

1 Describe the best or worst holiday you have ever had. Why do you feel this way about it?
2 What is your idea of an ideal holiday?

READ

1 Read the *Reading tip*. Look at the text. What might be a typical holiday at each destination?

Reading tip

An article separated into sections may have sub-headings. Read the first paragraph and the sub-heading of each section to understand what the main topic is, before reading in detail.

Unusual holidays

Some people dream of their next holiday – a week at the beach or some relaxation in the mountains. However such ordinary holidays do not appeal to everybody. Some crave something unusual.

A Hitting the slopes... in Dubai

Dubai's summer temperatures routinely surpass 40°C and snow has never been recorded in the history of the city. Understandably, it is not the typical place for a skiing holiday, but in Dubai meteorology can be overcome. Since 2005, it has been possible to enjoy five ski runs, a snowboarding area, and an ice cave. This unexpected attraction, which is a marvel of modern engineering, is called Ski Dubai.

Ski Dubai is an indoor facility that is part of the Mall of the Emirates, the largest shopping centre outside the USA. With over 6,000 tonnes of snow scattered across a 22,500 square metre space, Ski Dubai is the world's third largest indoor skiing facility. Holidaymakers can purchase an all-inclusive snow pass which offers jackets, trousers, boots, and disposable socks, but due to health concerns, hats and gloves are not provided. Black, knee-length padded coats are available to guests who prefer to wear traditional clothing during their visit. However, skiing in traditional clothing is strictly banned for safety reasons. Those who just want to watch the activities can sit in a Swiss-style chalet, enjoying fondue, hot chocolate, and other tasty warm treats.

B Being funny on stage... in Spain

Imagine a stay in a remote stone farmhouse in the mountains of Catalonia, in north-eastern Spain. The summer temperature is comfortable, around 25°C, the sunlight shimmers on the rivers in the valley, and the air smells sweet and unpolluted. Tiny villages dot the landscape in the distance, and the only sound is the rustling of the leaves in the surrounding trees.

The Spanish countryside has beautiful scenery that thousands of tourists flock to for a relaxing and refreshing holiday. However, it may also be the perfect holiday destination for those who are interested in fulfilling their ambition of making people laugh.

For seven days, small groups of holidaymakers come to this farmhouse to do something unusual – to learn the art of stand-up comedy. A professional comedian leads them in a series of workshops that cover the entire stand-up comedy process from writing to performing. The participants learn to write gags and humorous dialogue. They also develop their ability to speak in front of an audience by first practising in small groups and then performing for everybody. Those who are interested in acting are encouraged to create characters and portray them for the others.

2 Read the text. Which holiday description (A–C) contains the following information? More than one answer may be possible.

1 Weather. A, B, C
2 Length of the holiday.
3 Teaching or instruction.
4 Something to do for those not interested in the unusual activity.
5 Length of time the unusual holiday has been available to holidaymakers.

3 🎧 (1.02) Read the text again. Choose the best answers.

1 The attractions inside Ski Dubai do not include
   a an ice cave.
   b ski runs.
   c a snowboarding area.
   d a shopping centre.

2 The snow pass offers
   a traditional clothing.
   b knee-length padded coats.
   c ski wear and boots.
   d hot chocolate and warm treats.

3 The location of the stand-up comedy holiday is in
   a a popular Spanish tourist destination.
   b the Spanish mountains.
   c a Spanish city.
   d a quiet seaside town.

4 The comedy workshops
   a are taught by a group of actors.
   b teach participants how to write and tell jokes.
   c help participants stand up in front of others.
   d encourage participants to explore their acting ability.

5 The best time to see animals in their natural habitat is when
   a a lion or cheetah is near.
   b the temperature is at its highest.
   c they cool down near water.
   d they are being hunted.

6 One of the goals of the art safari is to teach artists
   a about the local customs of the Kenyan people.
   b how to paint animals that are moving rapidly.
   c how to get close to wild animals.
   d how to photograph wildlife and landscapes.

UNDERSTANDING IDEAS

Answer the questions. Look at the text, and use your own words and ideas.

1 Would you like to go on any of these holidays? Why or why not?
2 Which holiday idea is the most unusual in your opinion? Why?
3 Which, if any, of these unusual holidays will still be popular in twenty years? Why?

VOCABULARY

Unusual holidays

Match the highlighted words in the text with these definitions.

1 Positions from which you can watch something.
2 People who are visiting a place.
3 To have a strong desire for something.
4 The sound of light, dry things moving together.
5 A wonderful or surprising thing.
6 A house traditionally made of wood, built in the mountains.
7 An animal that hunts and kills other animals.
8 Shines with a soft light that seems to be moving.
9 An entertainer who makes people laugh.
10 Exceed, be greater than.
11 A very large number of people or things.
12 To gather somewhere in large numbers.
13 Jokes or funny stories.
14 Having a pleasant environment.
15 The science of the Earth's atmosphere, used in forecasting the weather.

(●●○○ Workbook: page 4)

C *Painting the perfect picture... in Kenya*

Kenya is a wildlife lover's paradise. There is a multitude of animals to observe in their natural habitat. The best time to view them is in the early morning or evening when the temperatures, about 25°C, are more hospitable. Gazelles, giraffes, and hippos gather at the watering holes to drink or bathe. They scatter only when a predator, such as a cheetah or a lion, approaches.

Most holidaymakers come to Kenya for a safari to photograph this amazing wildlife from the safety of a jeep. However, those who are intent on a more unusual experience can go on a ten-day art safari and paint the animals from some frighteningly close vantage points. The goal of this is to help artists improve their ability to depict moving animals.

In addition to the artistic opportunities, highly-trained guides accompany all participants and provide information on the wildlife, landscape and local customs. In this way, non-painting holidaymakers will never be bored or excluded from activities.

VOCABULARY

Unusual holidays

ACTIVATE

Complete these sentences with the correct form of the words from the box.

> chalet comedian crave flock gag holidaymaker
> hospitable marvel meteorology multitude predator
> rustling shimmer surpass vantage point

1 It was a cool evening on the banks of the river Nile. The light of the moon was _____ on the water and, with the _____ of the palm trees in the breeze, it was perfect.

2 From our _____ at the top of the tower, we could see the entire valley.

3 Some children _____ attention so much that they cry until their mothers come to them.

4 We stayed at a _____ in the Swiss mountains for our holiday last year.

5 London is the perfect place for an art holiday – there is a _____ of museums and art galleries. The collection at the National Gallery _____ any other in the world!

6 The advantage of staying in a small village or town is that the people tend to be more _____ than they are in cities, where most people are too busy to welcome tourists.

7 Many tourists on safari in Africa are disappointed if they don't see a large _____ , like a lion, catching its prey.

8 Scientists in the field of _____ are researching the interaction between weather and ocean levels.

9 Spain is a popular holiday destination for British _____ . Many families _____ to Spanish beaches and cities every summer.

10 It was his first show as a stand-up _____ . Unfortunately, the audience didn't find his _____ very funny, so he wasn't invited to perform again.

11 The Burj Khalifa is a _____ of architecture, construction and design.

EXTEND

Onomatopoeia

> Onomatopoeia refers to words imitatating the noise they describe. They can make a description more interesting or lively.

1 🎧 (1.03) Read the *Look out!* box. Match the words with their descriptions. Say the words out loud. Then listen and check.

1	rustling	a a sound like a long 's'
2	clatter	b a sound of hard objects knocking together
3	creak	
4	screech	c a squeaky noise, like the sound of a rusty hinge
5	gurgle	
6	hiss	d the sound of light, dry things moving together, like paper
		e a shrill piercing noise or cry
		f the sound of bubbling liquid

2 Look at the pictures. Choose the onomatopoeic word that best describes the picture.

1 a clatter	2 a gurgle	3 a creak
b hiss	b hiss	b rustle
c screech	c ping	c ping

4 a clatter	5 a creak	6 a clatter
b gurgle	b hiss	b creak
c whoosh	c rustle	c gurgle

3 Write a sentence for each picture. Some of the words can be used as a noun or a verb.

The screech of the tyres frightened us. The car screeched to a halt.

Idioms with *off* and *on*

4 Look at the idioms in bold in the sentences (1–8) and match them with their definitions (a–h).

1 This may sound like an **off the wall** idea, but if you try it, you'll see that it works. *c*

2 This is completely **off the record**: I think the new student representative is not doing the job very well, but he's a friend of mine so I don't want to complain.

3 Maggie is always **on the go**. She's got three jobs!

4 The film was full of action and suspense, and we were **on tenterhooks** until the end.

5 The press is keeping the scandal **on the boil**. There are several articles about it in the papers.

6 I could tell you what I think **off the cuff**, but I'd prefer to research it some more and give you a more definite answer.

7 **On the off chance** that you're free tonight, I was thinking you might like to go to the pizza place.

8 I read the report **on the hoof**, so I couldn't remember much.

a Speaking without thought or preparation.
b In a state of nervousness or worry.
c Unusual and slightly crazy.
d Not official, not to be made public.
e Being kept very active or intense.
f Possible but unlikely.
g Quickly and without your full attention.
h Being very busy all the time.

> ●●●○○ Workbook: page 5

Stative verbs

EXPLORE

1 🎧 (1.04) **Read and listen to the dialogue. What do the verbs in blue have in common?**

ON HOLIDAY

Andy What's your ideal holiday Mark? Look at this website – it has some great photos.

Mark This beach looks very relaxing and quiet, but personally I prefer somewhere more exciting.

Andy I agree that it doesn't seem very exciting, but I love empty beaches, and the ocean breeze always feels great.

Mark True, and a deserted beach certainly smells better!

Andy What do you think about this beach, then? It's a larger resort, but it's private, so I imagine that it's fairly quiet.

Mark Yes, you're probably right. But it looks expensive. I'm sure it wouldn't be within my budget.

Andy Let's look at the prices. Hmm… it depends on whether you book a sea view or a land view.

Mark I would definitely want a sea view.

Andy OK. A sea view room costs £200 per person per night…

Mark OK. Well in that case, maybe the deserted beach does appear to be more attractive after all.

2 **Read the *Learn this!* box. Put the stative verbs into the table.**

agree believe belong contain feel forget hate hear imagine like look love possess prefer seem smell taste think understand want

Some verbs are almost never used in the continuous form. These verbs describe states, e.g. *have, own, prefer, agree, feel.* They are called stative verbs. They can be classified into four categories.

A	verbs of thinking and perception	1 _____, 2 _____, 3 _____, 4 _____, 5 _____, 6 _____
B	verbs of emotions and feelings	1 _____, 2 _____, 3 _____, 4 _____, 5 _____
C	verbs of having and being	1 _____, 2 _____, 3 _____, 4 _____
D	verbs of senses and appearance	1 _____, 2 _____, 3 _____, 4 _____, 5 _____

(●○○○○ Grammar Reference: page 94)

EXPLOIT

Some stative verbs can be used in the continuous form, but with a different meaning.
I think you're right. (belief)
I'm thinking of going to the cinema. (a plan under consideration)
She has a new car. (ownership)
She's having a wonderful holiday in Turkey. (current state or behaviour that is changeable)

1 **Read the *Look out!* box. Complete the sentences using the simple or the continuous form of the verbs in the box.**

see   smell   taste   think   weigh

1 This cheese smells terrible – but it tastes delicious! Can I have some more?
2 James _____ the soup now just to check if it needs more salt.
3 I can't talk to you right now. I _____ the doctor. I'm in the consultation room.
4 It's just my opinion, but I _____ this holiday package is too expensive.
5 If you look very closely, you can just _____ the tower in the distance.
6 The grocer _____ my vegetables now and then I'll be ready to pay and leave.
7 They _____ of going on a cruise, but they haven't made a decision about it yet.
8 My suitcase _____ over 20 kilos. I might have to pay an excess luggage charge.

2 **Correct the errors, if necessary.**

1 Samantha isn't at home right now. She sees the doctor.
Samantha isn't at home right now. She is seeing the doctor.

2 Brian is having a lot of free time these days, so he is studying French.
_____

3 The jeweller is weighing the bracelet now and then he can give you a price.
_____

4 I am preferring holidays at the beach, but I'm having great fun in the city this time.
_____

5 Hurry up! I see the train on the platform! The engines are starting.
_____

6 As my mother ages, she is forgetting more and more.
_____

(●●○○○ Grammar Builder: page 95)

(●●●○○ Workbook: page 6)

Feeling at home

VOCABULARY

1 Look at the hotels in photos (A–C). Use three adjectives in the box to describe each one.

> atrocious   charming   cosy   dreadful   enchanting
> extravagant   five-star   frosty   homely   lavish
> luxuriant   opulent   sparse   stark   unassuming
> uninviting

A Ice hotel	B Seven-star hotel	C No-star hotel
_____	_____	_____
_____	_____	_____
_____	_____	_____

A

B

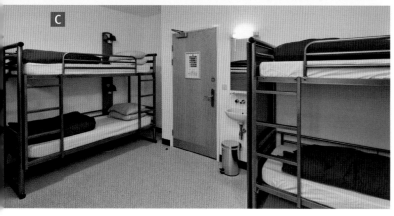

C

2 Look at the photos of different types of travellers (1–4). Decide which hotel they might choose to stay in. Make alternative suggestions if necessary. Explain why.

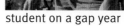

student on a gap year   travel journalist

retired couple   businessman

(●●●●● Workbook: page 7)

LISTEN

1 🎧 (1.05) Listen to the dialogue. Which hotel do you think Jamie would prefer to stay in?

2 🎧 (1.05) Listen again and complete the table.

	Ice hotel	Seven-star hotel	No-star hotel
Location			
Attractions			
Cost			

SPEAK

Which hotel would you like to stay in? Think of reasons why, and discuss with a partner. Use the vocabulary from Vocabulary exercise 1 to help you.

> I'd like to stay in the ice hotel. It looks quite cosy.

> I don't think so. It seems a bit uninviting. I'd prefer ...

Expressing trends with simple and continuous forms

EXPLORE

1 Read the interview. Who does the travel industry cater for today: the backpacking set or the upmarket traveller?

What trends are we seeing in the travel industry these days?
It's very interesting. We're actually seeing two very different trends. On the one hand, customers are becoming more interested in finding bargains. They are trying to make their travel budgets go further. On the other hand, luxury hotels are also growing in popularity.

Aren't those two trends incompatible?
Not really. The travel industry is huge, and these trends are affecting different market segments. For example, in the 1990s Prague was becoming the fashionable destination for the backpacking set, and the upmarket traveller was almost ignored. But some travel companies realized there was more to Prague than budget travel. Now luxury travellers can stay in five-star hotels and dine at extravagant restaurants. Prague has turned into a destination with something for everyone.

Can you give examples of the trend in bargain hunting?
Absolutely. Air travel is a good example. It has been changing dramatically. In the mid-1990s, the demand for business class travel was increasing. Several business-only airlines began flying between London and New York. However, by the end of the decade, almost all of these companies had stopped their services. Low cost airlines are dominating the market now, and they are even appealing to business travellers.

2 Read the interview again and find examples of the present continuous, the past continuous, and the present perfect continuous. Then complete the *Learn this!* box with the names of the tenses.

The ¹_____ is used to describe current trends. These trends can change.
The ²_____ is used to describe trends that have been halted or reversed. They are no longer happening.
The ³_____ is used to describe a trend that began in the past but is still happening, or the results of which are relevant at the time of speaking.

⬤◉◌◌◌ Grammar Reference: page 94

EXPLOIT

LOOK OUT!

When describing trends, the present perfect simple and continuous can often be used interchangeably. We may choose the continuous form to emphasize a change that is progressive, rather than completed.

1 Read the *Look out!* box. Complete the sentences with the present continuous, past continuous, or present perfect continuous form of the verbs in brackets.

1 The number of people using travel agencies _____ (get) smaller over the past ten years, as more people have booked holidays online.
2 Currently, the number of budget travellers headed for Europe _____ (not increase), but as more airlines expand their routes, this may change.
3 Space travel _____ (turn into) an interesting prospect for billionaires before the cutback on space missions.
4 Many of our country's hotels _____ (not respond) quickly enough to the needs of more sophisticated guests. This is starting to change now, however.

2 Look at the diagrams. Complete the sentences with the present continuous, past continuous or present perfect simple or continuous form of one of the verbs below.

decline   decrease   increase   stabilize   stop

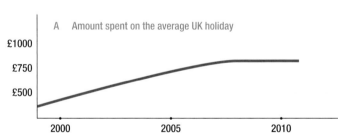

In the early 2000s, the amount spent on the average holiday ¹_____ . However, this trend ²_____, and the amount spent on the average holiday ³_____ at this time.

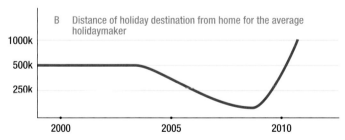

In the early 2000s, the average distance the typical holidaymaker travelled from home ⁴_____ but it ⁵_____ either. Around 2004, the distance ⁶_____, but this trend ⁷_____ now, although we are not sure it will continue to do so.

⬤◉◌◌◌ Grammar Builder: page 95
⬤◉◌◌◌ Workbook: page 8

A persuasive essay

READ

Read the essay and complete the sentences with information from the text.

1 In paragraph A, the writer introduces the opinion that Paris
_____ .

2 In paragraph B, the writer's first reason for having this opinion is _____ .

3 In paragraph C, the writer's second reason for having this opinion is _____ .

4 In paragraph D, the writer _____ the opinion about Paris.

August: the best time to visit Paris

A Paris is a fabulous city. Whether your interests lie in art and architecture or fine cuisine and fashion, there is something for everyone. Most people visit Paris in the spring. While this is a beautiful time in the city, the best time to get the full effect of the city is in August, at the height of a steamy summer. Paris in August offers a wide variety of memorable experiences for the adventurous tourist.

B Firstly, the atmosphere and pace of Paris are extremely relaxed in August. Most Parisians have left the city for the beaches or mountains. As a result, there is significantly less traffic on the roads, which makes cycling, rollerblading, and walking all pleasant activities. Although the metro may be extremely hot, the people crowded onto it are typically not rushing to get anywhere.

C In addition to the relaxed pace, August is the ideal time to experience the River Seine and its offerings. Explore the river or the canals on a cruise. Having a relaxing meal gliding along the Seine is a memory of a lifetime. You can also enjoy the beach in August. Each summer, three spots along the Seine are turned into beaches, each sporting a different theme. The beaches have something for everyone, including swimming pools suspended over the Seine, boardwalks to stroll along, or concerts on a summer's evening.

D To conclude, a visit to Paris is always a treat, but visitors to Paris should plan their trips for August, taking advantage of the relaxed atmosphere and special activities offered in this hot summer month.

PREPARE

> ### Writing tip: using a mind map
>
> A mind map is a useful way to prepare an essay. By making an outline of the content of your essay, you can organize your ideas into paragraphs. This helps to make your arguments clearer and makes the writing process smoother.

1 Read the *Writing tip*. Read the essay again and complete the mind map below with the writer's arguments.

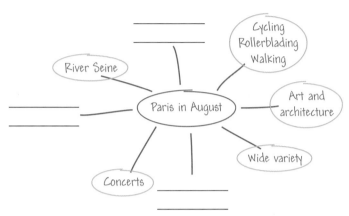

2 Read the following examples. In which paragraph would each example best fit: paragraph A, B, C or D?

1 Kayaking on the Seine is also possible in August.
_____

2 Parisians are friendlier because many of them are not going to work in August. _____

3 Cruises on the Seine are a good way to see the city and avoid the summer heat. _____

4 Fewer people and cars on the road make the city less stressful. _____

WRITE

1 When is the best time to visit your country? Why? Organize your arguments, using a mind map.

2 Write a persuasive essay on the best time of year to visit your country. Write 200 words and use the paragraph plan to help you.

Introduction	Opinion
Paragraph 2	Main argument
Paragraph 3	Supporting argument
Conclusion	Repeat opinion

●●●●● Workbook: page 9

The great escape

LANGUAGE SKILLS

1 🎧 (1.06) Complete the dialogue with the words from the box. Then listen and check your answers.

> clatter   hear   imagine   luxurious   means   off the wall
> recommend   rustling   sounds   sparse

Maria How was your holiday?

Sally It was … interesting. We went camping in the mountains. The mountain scenery was enchanting, but unfortunately the campsite facilities were quite ¹_____ and the cooking areas were very basic. It was my brother's idea to go camping. His ideas are a bit ²_____ and he always wants to do something different. Personally, I prefer beach holidays. Staying in a ³_____ hotel and relaxing to the sound of ⁴_____ palm trees is my idea of an ideal holiday.

Maria Well, staying in the mountains ⁵_____ very relaxing too.

Sally Yes, but not this place. The campsite was next to a small factory and we could ⁶_____ the ⁷_____ of machinery all night long. I didn't sleep a wink!

Maria Oh, poor you. I ⁸_____ you won't go there again.

Sally No, definitely not. But there is one advantage of camping. It doesn't cost a fortune, so it ⁹_____ we can afford a city break later in the year, too.

Maria Well, for a city break, I really ¹⁰_____ Vienna. It's wonderful in winter.

2 Answer the questions.

1 Why did Sally go on a camping holiday?
2 What was wrong with the campsite?
3 What kind of holiday does Sally prefer?
4 What was good about Sally's holiday?
5 Which holiday destination does Maria recommend?

3 Choose the correct answer.

1 That TV screen _____ about 10 kilos. It's huge!
  a weighs   **b** is weighing   **c** both are possible
2 You've definitely burnt the steak. It _____ awful.
  a smells   **b** is smelling   **c** both are possible
3 I _____ English much better than before.
  a understand **b** am understanding **c** both are possible
4 Where are you going on holiday this year? We _____ of taking a cruise up the Nile.
  a think   **b** are thinking   **c** both are possible
5 The dentist _____ a patient now. You can't go in.
  a sees   **b** is seeing   **c** both are possible
6 We _____ a wonderful time on holiday! Wish you were here.
  a have   **b** are having   **c** both are possible

American English vs. British English

1 Use your dictionary and look at the entries for *holiday*, *sea* and *underground*. Answer the questions.

1 What is the American English word for *holidaymaker*?
  vacationer
2 What is the American English word for *holiday*? When is this word used in British English?
3 What does *holiday* mean in American English? What is this called in British English?
4 What is the typical American English word for *sea*?
5 What do speakers of American English say for a *holiday by the sea*?
6 What is *the underground* called in American English?
7 What other names are used for the underground systems in Washington D.C. and London?

2 Look up the words in bold and find their equivalents in American English.

1 This restaurant has definitely gone **downmarket** – it used to be much better.
2 We can get to the top floor using the **lift**.
3 We lost our **luggage** at the airport.
4 The **taxi rank** is just outside the airport.
5 This is certainly a hotel that will be popular with **upmarket** travellers.

I CAN ...

Read the statements. Think about your progress and tick (✓) one of the boxes.

| ✷ | I need more practice. | ✷✷ | I sometimes find this difficult. | ✷✷✷ | No problem! |

	✷	✷✷	✷✷✷
I can understand a magazine article about holiday destinations.			
I can use stative verbs in the present simple or present continuous tense correctly.			
I can understand and discuss information about hotels.			
I can use the present continuous to describe trends.			
I can use a mind map to prepare ideas for a persuasive essay.			

(●●○○○   Workbook: Self check pages 10–11)

Talking the talk

Inventing words

BEFORE READING

1 Which language do you think these English words come from? Complete the table.

> avant-garde ~~cotton~~ gazelle hamburger judo kindergarten tsunami unique

Arabic	French	German	Japanese
cotton	1 _____	2 _____	3 _____
4 _____	5 _____	6 _____	7 _____

2 Are there any words in your language that come from other languages? What are they?

Where do words come from?

How do new words enter a language? Who coins new words? Sometimes the inspiration for a word is obvious. For example, in the 1960s, *calculator* made its first appearance in everyday English. Its name was based on its apparent function: to calculate.

Sometimes a word or name is eponymous. This means that it takes its name from the person who discovered or invented the object. The radioactive element *Einsteinium* is an example of an eponymous word, taking its name from the famous scientist Albert Einstein. Other words are toponymous; they take their name from the place where they were invented or made famous. An example of a toponymous word is *tangerine*, which comes from the city of Tangiers in Morocco, where the fruit is abundant. Another example is the word for the material *denim*, which originated in Nîmes, France. The material was said to be 'de Nîmes' or 'from Nîmes'.

Sometimes people simply invent words. Milton Sirotta is documented as the youngest person ever to coin a word that is in use today. He coined the words *googol* and *googolplex* when he was nine years old. Sirotta's uncle was a mathematician called Edward Kasner. Kasner wanted to find a name for an extremely large finite number – the number 1 followed by 100 zeroes. One day in the late 1930s, Kasner asked his nephew Sirotta for some ideas about a name. Sirotta thought about it for a moment and then suggested *googol*.

READ

Kasner was delighted. He had finally found a name he liked. Sirotta also suggested the term *googolplex* for the number 1 followed by zeroes until a person got tired of writing them. Kasner appreciated the boy's ingenuity, but pointed out that no two people would tire at precisely the same moment. As a result, Kasner defined the googolplex as the number 1 followed by a googol of zeroes. This made googolplex a finite number, although it was unimaginably large. The terms *googol* and *googolplex* first featured in Kasner's 1940 publication *Mathematics and the Imagination*.

It's highly unlikely that Sirotta or Kasner ever imagined what would happen to the words they coined so many decades ago. What is more intriguing about Sirotta and Kasner's story is that their creations are, in a way, now known by millions, if not billions, of people around the world.

In 1996, two computer science graduate students at a California university created a new search engine. After working

1 Read the *Reading tip* then read the text quickly. Put the main ideas below in the order they appear in the text.

The youngest person to coin a word ___
Types of names for new words ___
The origins of the name 'Google' ___
How words enter a language ___

2 🎧 (1.09) Read the text again. Choose the best answers.

1 The word *calculator*
  a is an example of an eponym.
  b is an example of a toponym.
  c is both an eponym and a toponym.
  d is derived from the purpose of the object it names.

2 According to the article, *tangerine* derives its name from Tangiers, Morocco because
  a there are a lot of tangerines in Tangiers.
  b the best tangerines come from Tangiers.
  c the people of Tangiers make their living from the fruit.
  d the person who discovered the fruit was from Tangiers.

3 The word *denim*
  a is based on the French word for material.
  b originated in Morocco.
  c is an eponym.
  d originally referred to a place.

4 A *googolplex*
  a is a word that means infinity.
  b was based on a word in the 1940 publication *Mathematics and the Imagination*.
  c is the number 1 followed by zeroes until a person gets tired of writing.
  d was identified as a number more than 70 years ago.

5 The creators wanted to call the new search engine 'googol' because
  a they were not good at spelling.
  b it reflected the massive amount of data that a search engine could organize.
  c it was based on a word coined by a nine-year-old boy.
  d they hadn't been able to come up with a name in over a year.

6 The spelling of *Google*
  a was coined by Kasner.
  b is the result of a spelling mistake.
  c is an abbreviated form of the word *googolplex*.
  d first appeared in the book *Mathematics and the Imagination*.

3 Look at the text again. Explain the following sentences in your own words.

1 The radioactive element *Einsteinium* is an example of an eponymous word, taking its name from the famous scientist Albert Einstein.

2 It's highly unlikely that Sirotta or Kasner ever imagined what would happen to the words they coined so many decades ago.

3 What is more intriguing about Sirotta and Kasner's story is that their creations are, in a way, now known by millions, if not billions, of people around the world.

4 They wanted a name related to the indexing of a colossal amount of data, so someone suggested 'googol'.

UNDERSTANDING IDEAS

Answer the questions. Look at the text, and use your own words and ideas.

1 What types of words do you think are passed from one language to another?

2 Do you think Google will still be used 25 years from now? Why? Why not?

3 Have you ever searched for your own name on Google? Are there many other people with your exact name? Where are they? What do they do?

VOCABULARY

Where do words come from?

Match the highlighted words in the text with these definitions.

1 Happened or appeared for the first time.
2 Extremely large.
3 Recorded or verified in writing.
4 To name or invent a new word.
5 Something obvious, easy to see or to understand.
6 Creativity or inventiveness.
7 A lot; plentiful.
8 A word or group of words having a particular meaning.
9 Unusual, not typical.
10 Thinking about something to generate a lot of possible ideas.
11 The origin of a new exciting idea from something you see or hear.
12 Died.
13 Something that's very interesting or fascinating.
14 Original or new.
15 Limited, with an end.

for more than a year to perfect it, the students and several of their fellow officeworkers had a number of brainstorming sessions to find the right name for this innovative tool. They wanted a name related to the indexing of a colossal amount of data, so someone suggested 'googol'. One of the students liked the idea, and asked his friend to check if the name was available for a web address. According to the story, although the students were brilliant computer scientists, they were bad at spelling, and instead of searching for 'googol.com', they searched for 'google.com'. They found that this web address was available. They realized their error, but they preferred the unconventional spelling, so they registered the web address www.google.com.

Unfortunately, neither Kasner nor Sirotta lived to see the internet age. Kasner died in 1955 and Sirotta passed away in 1980. Neither of them found out how the word they had coined inspired the name of the most popular search engine in the world.

(●●●) Workbook: page 12

Where do words come from?

ACTIVATE

Complete these sentences with the correct form of the words from the box.

> abundant apparent brainstorm coin colossal
> document finite ingenuity innovative inspiration
> intriguing originate pass away term unconventional

1 It became _____ that the students had not understood the science lesson when they all failed the test.
2 The detective novel was so _____ that I read it from cover to cover in one night.
3 Through research on the extent of global warming, scientists have _____ an increase in temperatures in the Arctic.
4 She thought her logic was perfect, but she has made a _____ miscalculation.
5 Only a small percentage of new words which are _____ every day end up in the dictionary.
6 Jane writes her numbers in an _____ way: she writes them from bottom to top.
7 Please note that we have only got a _____ amount of time to review the results, so we need to hurry.
8 There are some really _____ ideas coming from young computer scientists in India and China.
9 Bananas are so _____ in the winter that prices tend to be low.
10 The author says that things which happen in his life are the _____ for his stories.
11 Our teachers expect us to use some _____ to find our own solutions to problems.
12 I'm not familiar with those technical _____ . Could you explain it in simpler language?
13 We should _____ some titles for your new novel.
14 My grandfather _____ more than ten years ago, but I still miss him.
15 It is likely that coffee _____ in East Africa and spread throughout the world from there.

EXTEND

Collocation

1 Some words are frequently used together and some are never used together. Decide which verb is never used with the word in italics.

1	a coin	b invent	c ~~do~~				*a word*
2	a have	b make	c take				*a holiday*
3	a open	b switch on	c turn on				*a light*
4	a care for	b like	c care about				*some tea*
5	a make	b get	c collect				*data*
6	a get	b have	c make				*an idea*
7	a turn off	b turn out	c shut down				*the computer*
8	a investigate	b search	c explore				*the internet*

Computing words

2 Match the words (1–8) with the definitions (a–h). Which words are illustrated in the pictures below?

1 malware
2 podcast
3 to digitally enhance
4 data-mining
5 webinar
6 wiki
7 phishing
8 social networking

a to alter a digital image on the computer with software
b a live online presentation in which participants can ask questions
c using websites to communicate with friends or people with similar interests
d software designed to harm a computer or its normal function
e to attempt to get digital information such as passwords by trickery
f a website where people post or contribute information
g a program in digital format for downloading over the internet
h to search massive amounts of computerized data to find a pattern

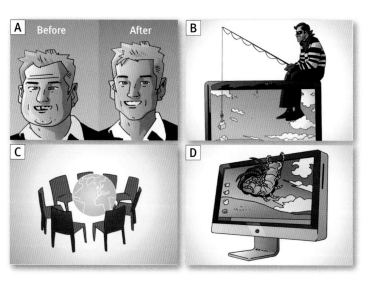

3 Complete the sentences (1–8) with the correct form of the words from exercise 2.

1 I must tell you about a great _____ I downloaded from Radio 4 about the history of photography.
2 Colin _____ some images of himself so that he looked younger – they were hilarious!
3 Be suspicious of any email with urgent requests for your financial information, as _____ is on the increase.
4 My son does all his _____ via his computer and hardly ever goes out except to go to school.
5 _____ is the biggest threat to both large and small businesses that are dependent on computers.
6 I took part in a _____ for the first time last night. It was weird talking to complete strangers in real time.
7 Jenny asked the school headmaster if they could set up a school _____ to post messages and share information.
8 _____ is a popular technique used in market research.

(●●●●● Workbook: page 13)

Past tenses for distancing

EXPLORE

1 🎧 (1.10) Read and listen to the dialogues. What tenses are the words in blue?

1 At the local café

Waitress Hi Nancy! What can I get for you?
Nancy Can I have an orange juice please?
Waitress Sure. Are you having anything to eat with that?
Nancy Have you got any snacks?
Waitress You name it. Do you want something sweet?
Nancy No, I fancy something savoury.
Waitress We've got crisps.
Nancy Sounds good!
Waitress What flavour do you fancy?

2 At the hotel

Receptionist Good morning sir, welcome to the Grand Hotel. Did you have a reservation?
Guest Yes, the name is Wilson. I made a reservation for three nights, but I was hoping to change it. I was thinking of extending my stay.
Receptionist Let me have a look for you. How many days were you thinking about staying, Mr Wilson?
Guest I wondered about staying an extra two nights.
Receptionist Certainly sir. You have reserved a double room, haven't you?
Guest Yes, but I was wondering if the executive suite is available?
Receptionist Yes, of course, no problem at all.

2 Answer the questions about the dialogues. Then read the *Learn this!* box.

1 Which time is being spoken about in both conversations?
2 Which verb tenses are used in the dialogue at the café?
3 Which verb tenses are used in the dialogue between the guest and the receptionist at the hotel?
4 Why do you think we use different tenses in these dialogues?
5 What is the effect of using the past tense?

Distancing is a technique used to create a more polite tone in more formal situations, such as speaking to people in a position of authority or when speaking to guests or customers. It is achieved by using the simple past tense for questions and requests. For example:
Friend to friend: *How much **do** you want to spend on your mother's gift?*
Shop assistant to customer: *How much **did** you want to spend on your mother's gift?*
We can also use the past continuous to make questions and requests more polite. This often involves the verbs *wonder*, *think*, and *hope*. For example:
I was wondering about making a reservation.

●●○○○ Grammar Reference: page 96

EXPLOIT

1 🎧 (1.11) Listen to the dialogues. Which dialogue is informal?

1 A I was hoping to buy a gold necklace for my wife.
   B How much did you want to spend?
   A I was wondering if you had something nice for £500.
2 A Did you enjoy your time here in New York?
   B Yes, we had a terrific time.
   A We were very pleased to have you in our hotel.
3 A Do you have a table for two available?
   B Do you want to sit inside or outside?
   A We want to sit outside.
4 A Victor and I were thinking of inviting you to dinner.
   B Great. When did you want to meet up?
   A We were hoping to see you next week.

2 Rewrite the informal dialogue using distancing.

3 Complete the dialogues with verbs from the box. More than one verb may be possible. Use distancing techniques, and *wonder*, *think*, or *hope*.

1 A I was hoping to order some tea please. (hope, order)
   B Did you want to order some food with that? (want, order)
2 A I _____ a ticket for the 10 o'clock train. (hope, buy)
   B I'm sorry. That train has been cancelled. _____ a seat on the 11.30 train? (want, book)
3 A I _____ with someone in the admissions office. (wonder, speak)
   B No one is available now. _____ a message? (want, leave)
4 A I need to schedule an important meeting for tomorrow.
   B Very good, Ms. Carter. _____ the large meeting room? (want, reserve)
5 A I have an important essay to hand in tomorrow. _____ your notes? (wonder, borrow)
   B Sorry. I've already lent my notes to Phillip.

●●○○○ Grammar Builder: page 97

●●○○○ Workbook: page 14

Words about words

VOCABULARY

1 Read the example sentences (a–e). Match the words in bold with definitions (1–5).

a **acronym:** There was some news about NATO and the UN on the BBC website today.

b **alliteration:** Four figs fell from the fat fig trees.

c **anagram:** orchestra = carthorse; listen = silent

d **cliché:** There's no place like home.

e **simile:** The cat stalked the mouse like a detective with a magnifying glass.

1 __ A word or phrase made by rearranging letters from another word or phrase.

2 __ A saying or expression that has been used so often it has lost its effect.

3 __ A comparison using *like* or *as*.

4 __ Repetition of the first consonant sounds of words in a sentence.

5 __ A word, phrase or name formed with the initial letters of the words it includes.

2 Look at the pictures and solve the anagrams.

1 curt poem *computer*   2 give a demo

3 Note! Is live!   4 aim fly

5 A stew, sir?   6 a fluid star

3 Write your own example of each of the following.

1 alliteration: _____

2 acronym: _____

3 simile: _____

4 anagram: _____

⬤⬤⬤◦◦ Workbook: page 15

LISTEN

1 You are going to listen to an interview with a teacher of creative writing. What do you think 'creative writing' is?

1 Writing about art and music

2 The same as academic writing

3 Writing that expresses thoughts and feelings in an imaginative way

2 🎧 (1.12) Listen to the interview. What does Meryl do in her workshops?

3 🎧 (1.12) Listen again. Choose the correct answers.

1 The workshops are for
   a young people
   b old people
   c both young and old people

2 Meryl finds the material she reads interesting because
   a people write about topics she chooses
   b people often write about personal experiences
   c her students often use acronyms

3 The OAU means the organisation of
   a African Unity
   b Asian Unity
   c American Unity

4 The cliché Meryl mentions is
   a as green as an emerald
   b as green as grass
   c as green as a palm tree

5 According to Meryl, alliteration is suited to
   a dialogues
   b factual texts
   c descriptive passages

SPEAK

Ask and answer the questions in pairs.

1 Look at the following acronyms. What do you think they stand for?

BBC FBI OPEC ~~OUP~~ UAE UN UNESCO

OUP stands for Oxford University Press.

2 Look at some typical similes. What do you think they mean?

a He's as strong as an ox.

b I slept like a log last night.

c She's as quiet as a mouse.

d My brother is like a bull in a china shop.

Modals for distancing

EXPLORE

1 🎧 (1.13) Read and listen to the dialogue. Which emoticon (A–D) are they talking about?

A

};-)

B

=|:)=

C

:-)

D

5:-)

Anna	Professor Smith, ¹could you possibly tell me what this emoticon means?
Smith	Yes, of course. It's supposed to look like the US president, Abraham Lincoln.
Anna	Ah, I've heard of him, but I've never seen him. ²Might you be able to explain how this looks like him?
Smith	Certainly. He was known for his long beard and tall hat, but ³I would think that you have seen him. He is on the US five-dollar bill.
Anna	Oh, yes! The equals sign is a hat, but Lincoln isn't wearing a hat on the bill. Emoticons are very clever!
Smith	Yes, they are. Might you be interested in learning the history of emoticons? They were actually first used to communicate amongst professors at an American university.
Anna	I didn't know that. It's difficult to imagine a time when emoticons weren't popular.
Librarian	Pardon me, but we would ask that you keep talking to a minimum in the library. ⁴Might you continue your discussion elsewhere?
Smith	So sorry. Yes, of course.

2 Read the dialogue again and find the modal verbs. Do you think they make the language more or less polite?

LEARN THIS!

We can use the modals *would*, *could* and *might* in questions and requests to make our speech more tentative.
Would you like to come with me?
[Do you want to come with me?]
Could you tell me where the nearest train station is?
[Where's the nearest train station?]
We can also use *could…possibly*.
Could you possibly lend me £10?
[Can you lend me £10?]
Might you be interested in learning about the history of the emoticon?
[Are you interested in learning about the history of the emoticon?]
We can also use *would* before verbs of thinking, saying or instruction, to make a statement more tentative and a command less direct.
I would think that emoticons are sometimes overused.
[In my opinion, people overuse emoticons.]
We would ask that you keep talking to a minimum in the library.
[Keep talking to a minimum in the library.]

3 Read the *Learn this!* box. Rewrite the sentences in blue in the text in a less formal way.

○●○●○ Grammar Reference: page 96

EXPLOIT

1 Choose the correct modal verb.
1 Could / (Might) you need some assistance with your application?
2 I **could** / **would** ask that you switch off the computers now.
3 I **would** / **could** think it's about six o'clock.
4 We **would** / **might** ask that you don't open that door.
5 **Could** / **Would** you possibly show me where the library is?
6 **Would** / **Might** I request that you lower the TV volume?

2 Rewrite the sentences using *would*, *could / could possibly*, or *might*. More than one answer may be possible.
1 Do you want some help you with that?
2 Is this seat free? Can I sit here?
3 Tell me where the exit is.
4 Does he need a recommendation letter from the professor?
5 Don't remove the equipment from the lab.
6 Don't leave valuables lying around on the desks.
7 Are you interested in joining the local history preservation society?
8 In my opinion, people are less careful about spelling in an email.

○●○●○ Grammar Builder: page 97

○●○●○ Workbook: page 16

An opinion essay (1)

READ

Read the essay and answer the questions.

1 What words does the author want deleted from the dictionary?
2 What reason does the author give to support this?
3 What additional reason does the author give for the second word to be deleted?

As technology advances, dictionary entries should keep up

Dictionary entries should reflect the world in which we live. They should not contain useless or old-fashioned words that most of the population will never hear or read. Furthermore, words that no longer play an important role in society should be removed from dictionaries. With regard to obsolete technology, the words *telex* and *word processor* should be deleted from the dictionary. Telex machines have been replaced by fax machines, and almost no one uses a word processor any more.

Telex was once the most-used written telecommunication system in the business world. In the 1990s, it was used in more than 190 countries. Although telexes are still available, albeit in very few shops, the widespread use of fax machines, electronic mail, and the internet has made the telex of limited use. Considering that the telex is on its way to extinction, its entry should be deleted from the dictionary.

The word processor's only function is to write documents; hence, the invention of word processing programs for computers. It is nearly impossible to buy a word processor in a shop today, and the replacement parts for existing models are quite hard to find. The machine will be extinct in a few short years. The term *word processor*, nevertheless, can still be understood without a dictionary because the term *word processing* is still used in the computer software field. This means that speakers and learners of English can understand the meaning of *word processor* without looking it up.

Therefore, words that are rarely used such as *telex* and *word processor* should be deleted from the dictionary to create room for new words entering the English lexicon.

PREPARE

Writing tip: formal linking words

Formal linking words are often used in academic writing. They can make writing more authoritative, professional and polished.

1 Read the *Writing tip*. Complete the table with the linking words that are underlined in the text.

Reference	Contrast	Consequence
With regard to	_____	_____
_____	_____	_____

2 Complete the sentences with a suitable linking word from the table in exercise 1.

1 Extremely obscure words are not useful; _____, they should be deleted from the dictionary.
2 Susan Brown's second novel was a colossal failure; but _____ she continued to write.
3 The school authorities agreed, _____ with some reluctance, to allow students to use electronic dictionaries.
4 Tuesday 11th of March is a public holiday; _____, all interviews will take place on Wednesday 12th.
5 _____ the true origin of the word was unknown before the 1990s, this article from the 1960s makes some insightful observations.
6 English has some sounds that speakers of different languages find difficult. _____ Arabic speakers, the most difficult sounds are usually *p* and *ch*.

WRITE

Choose one of the titles about the best way to learn a language and write an opinion essay. Use the writing plan to help you. Write 200–250 words and use formal linking words.

> The best way to learn a language is to learn ten words a day from a dictionary.

> The best way to learn a language is to read a lot of novels in the language.

> The best way to learn a language is to look online for news articles written in the language.

Paragraph 1	Explain how the method works.
Paragraph 2	Explain the first reason why it's effective.
Paragraph 3	Explain the second reason why it's effective.
Paragraph 4	Conclude your essay.

●●●●● Workbook: page 17

Talking the talk

LANGUAGE SKILLS

1 🎧 (1.14) **Complete the dialogue with the words from the box. Then listen and check your answers.**

> acronym cliché hoping ingenuity innovative
> inspiration malware social networking software would

Interviewer My guest today is 16-year-old Darren Black from East London, the computer genius who created the highly ¹_____ computer program, PSC. Would you be able to tell us more about it, Darren?

Darren Yes, it's a program to eliminate any ²_____ from your computer. PSC is an ³_____ that stands for Premium System Clearing.

Interviewer And could you possibly tell us why the program is so successful?

Darren Well, it's the only piece of ⁴_____ that acts instantly as soon as a threat enters your computer system. There's no need to scan, as the program takes care of everything.

Interviewer That's absolutely amazing. And what do your friends at school think about you being the whizz-kid of the decade?

Darren Oh, I think that's a bit of a ⁵_____. There are lots of kids my age who have the ⁶_____ to create complex programs.

Interviewer I understand that you are working on a new ⁷_____ site just for teenagers. We were ⁸_____ you could tell us something about it?

Darren It's still in development but I can tell you that the text writing function will have a menu with a lot of colourful new emoticons.

Interviewer Finally, would you mind telling us where you get the ⁹_____ for these ingenious projects?

Darren I just love technology. I wanted to come up with an invention to change everything!

Interviewer Judging from your success to date, I ¹⁰_____ say that you will! Thank you for speaking to us.

2 **Answer the questions.**

1 What is special about Darren Black?
2 What did Darren invent to become so well known?
3 What features does his program have that make it unique?
4 How does the interviewer describe Darren? Does Darren agree with this description?
5 What is Darren's current project?
6 How is Darren motivated in his work?

3 **Rewrite the questions and requests using modals or past tenses for distancing.**

1 Are you planning to get married soon?
2 Do you want to order now?
3 How many days do you want to stay in the hotel?
4 Do you want to reserve a separate room for the children?
5 Can you lend me five hundred pounds?
6 How much do you want to spend on a new car?

Expressing amounts

1 **Look up the words in the box to find their meaning as an amount. Write them in the correct columns.**

> couple   hundred and one   mass   pinch   touch   ton
> trace   zillion

large amounts	small amounts
_____	couple
_____	_____
_____	_____
_____	_____

2 **Are the words in exercise 1 usually used as a singular or plural noun, or both? Look at the example sentences in the dictionary and complete the sentences.**

1 This soup is not very tasty. It could do with a pinch of salt.
2 My maths teacher gives us _____ of homework. There's no time for other subjects.
3 Do you have _____ of minutes to answer this question?
4 I'm not feeling well. I think I have _____ of the flu.
5 The investigators found _____ of poison in the bottom of the glass next to the bed.
6 I have _____ little jobs to do this week. I don't know where to start.
7 There were _____ of people waiting to see the football match.
8 There must be _____ of grains of sand on this beach.

I CAN ...

Read the statements. Think about your progress and tick (✓) one of the boxes.

	✴ I need more practice.	✴✴ I sometimes find this difficult.	✴✴✴ No problem!

	✴	✴✴	✴✴✴
I can understand a text about the origins of words.			
I can use polite distancing language.			
I can talk about words and brainstorm acronyms.			
I can use distancing language in formal situations.			
I can write an opinion essay using formal linking words.			

(●●●●● Workbook: Self check pages 18–19)

Leisure
by William Henry Davies

WHAT is this life if, full
of care,
We have no time to stand
and stare?
No time to stand beneath
the boughs,
And stare as long as sheep
and cows:
No time to see, when
woods we pass,
Where squirrels hide their
nuts in grass:
No time to see, in broad
daylight,

Streams full of stars, like
skies at night:
No time to turn at
Beauty's glance,
And watch her feet, how
they can dance:
No time to wait till her
mouth can
Enrich that smile her eyes
began?
A poor life this if, full of
care,
We have no time to stand
and stare.

Biography

William Henry Davies was born in 1871 in Wales. He spent his early adulthood travelling throughout the United Kingdom, Canada, and the United States before becoming one of the most popular poets of his generation. He published his first book of poetry in 1905, and soon caught the attention of literary critics, publishers, and other writers. He went on to write numerous poems that centred on themes of nature and the hardships of life. He died in 1940.

1 🎧 (1.17) Read the poem. According to the poem, what is the poet's definition of 'leisure'?

a a time to relax with friends
b a time to reflect on life
c a time to go walking in the countryside

2 Read the poem again. Choose the best answer.

1 The poet thinks that sheep and cows **are / are not** worthy of imitation.
2 In the poem, 'Beauty' is a metaphor for a **dancer / nature**.
3 The poet's ideal way of spending leisure time is **with other people / alone**.
4 The phrase 'streams full of stars' is an example of **alliteration / a cliché**.

3 Answer the questions. Look at the poem and use your own words and ideas to explain your answers.

1 This poem was written more than 75 years ago. Do you think the message of the poem is still true today? Why or why not?
2 The poet mentions several animals in the poem. Are there any animals that you find interesting to watch? Do they make you feel relaxed?
3 The poet gives human characteristics to the concept of beauty. What metaphor would you use to describe beauty – honesty or patience?

4 Look at the two photos on this page. Which is closer to your idea of a perfect place to spend your leisure time? Why? Write a short paragraph explaining your opinion. Include references to things you see in the photo you choose.

Language and literature

READ

1 Read the text. Who was Chyngyz Aitmatov?

Chyngyz Aitmatov

Kyrgyzstan is a mountainous country of incredible natural beauty and strong nomadic tradition. Located in central Asia with a population of just 5.4 million, Kyrgyzstan is a small county with very powerful neighbours: China in the south-west and Russia to the north-east. For over a hundred years, Kyrgyzstan had been struggling for independence from Russia, which was finally achieved in 1991, with the collapse of the former Soviet Union. However, Russian is still an official language of the country, along with Kyrgyz. Kyrgyz is also widely spoken both in Kyrgyzstan and in neighbouring countries such as China and Kazakhstan.

The word 'Kyrgyz' is believed to have originated from the word 'forty', and also means 'immortal' and 'unconquerable'. According to legend, the word refers to the forty tribes that were united by the Kyrgyz hero Manas to fight off their common enemies in the 9th century. The heroic deeds of Manas were recorded in an epic poem, which, with over half a million lines, is one of the longest poems in world literature.

In more contemporary times, one of Kyrgyzstan's greatest writers is Chyngyz Aitmatov. Not only did he write in his mother tongue, but he also preserved the rich legends, folklore and landscapes of his native land in his novels. Aitmatov was born in 1928, and he began to write short stories in Kyrgyz while studying agriculture. In 1956 he went to study at the Maxim Gorky Literature Institute in Moscow. Just two years later, *Jamila* was published in both Russian and Kyrgyz, and was an immediate success. *Jamila* describes traditional Kyrgyz family life in transition, and evokes the concerns of Manas to preserve a sense of national identity. With the translation of *Jamila* into French and other languages, Aitmatov's work became available to a much larger and wider audience.

Throughout his literary career Chyngyz Aitmatov won many awards and achieved a popular following. Like his parents, he also became involved in politics and witnessed the changes that eventually led to the end of the Soviet Union. After independence, Aitmatov served as the ambassador of Kyrgyzstan to France, Belgium, Luxemburg and the Netherlands.

Without doubt, Chyngyz Aitmatov was one of the greatest ambassadors for the Kyrgyz language, literature and people in modern times.

2 Read the text again. Answer the questions.

1 Why is Russian one of the official languages of Kyrgyzstan?
2 What role, according to legend, did Manas play in the history of Kyrgyzstan?
3 What social issues did Chyngyz Aitmatov address in his novel *Jamila*?
4 In what ways was Chyngyz Aitmatov an ambassador for Kyrgyzstan?

3 Answer the questions. Use your own words and ideas.

1 Who are the best known writers in your country in the last 50 years?
2 In your opinion, why was it important for Chyngyz Aitmatov to write in Kyrgyz?
3 What do you think are the problems of translating a novel into a foreign language?

LISTEN

Scotland

TARBERT STORES

1 Look at the photos of Scotland. What do you think Scotland and Kyrgyzstan have in common?

2 🎧 (1.18) Listen to the interview about Scottish Gaelic and decide if the sentences are true or false.

1 Scottish Gaelic originated in the islands of the Hebrides.
2 The Scottish Parliament passed legislation in 2005 to make Scotland bilingual.
3 Scottish Gaelic is used by members of the European Union.
4 There has been a sharp increase in the number of people studying Gaelic.

3 🎧 (1.18) Listen again. Which initiatives to protect and promote Scottish Gaelic are mentioned?

1 Compulsory bilingual education for young children.
2 Broadcasting in Gaelic on TV and radio.
3 New legislation from the European Union.
4 A new Scottish Gaelic online dictionary.
5 Qualifications in Gaelic.
6 Road signs in Gaelic and English.

WRITE AND SPEAK

1 Plan a short presentation about either the language or literature of your country. With a partner, prepare the key points for the presentation. Choose one of the topics below for your presentation:

• Languages and / or dialects spoken in your country
• Characteristics of the language you speak
• The literature of your language
• An important literary figure

2 Using photos and other images or diagrams to illustrate your main points, give your presentation to the class.

3 Eureka!

Making discoveries

BEFORE READING

1 Match the people with their discoveries. Which discoveries were made by accident?

1 Isaac Newton ___
2 Watson and Crick ___
3 William Herschel ___
4 Alexander Fleming ___

READ

Reading tip

When you read a text to check if statements are true or false, start by underlining the key information and identifying the main idea. Find the corresponding sections or sentences in the reading text. Do the ideas in the text and the statements match up? Check names, dates and reasons.

a penicillin

b gravity

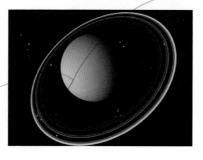

c Uranus

d DNA

THE ORIGIN OF INSPIRATION

How are discoveries made? We can learn a lot about the origins of inspiration from the famous account of Archimedes' Eureka moment in his monumental discovery in 260 BC.

As the story goes, the King of Syracuse had commissioned a goldsmith to make an elaborate golden crown. The goldsmith was known for his great skill, and indeed, he crafted a fine crown for the king. However, the king was suspicious by nature, and he suspected that the goldsmith may have mixed silver with the gold used in the crown. Believing he had been charged too much for the crown, the king asked Archimedes to assist him in proving his case. Could Archimedes confirm the king's suspicions? Archimedes knew that he would be rewarded considerably for finding the answer, and safe from trouble with the king, so long as he did not damage the crown in finding the truth.

The easiest way to prove whether the crown was pure gold would be to melt the crown into a block and measure its density, as gold is more dense than silver, but this was out of the question. Melting the crown would destroy it.

Archimedes was frustrated. He faced setback after setback. He found that constantly thinking about the problem exacerbated his frustration, so he decided to do something different – take a long, warm bath.

Archimedes believed that he could overcome his lack of inspiration, provided that he relaxed and allowed a breakthrough to emerge.

So Archimedes filled his tub with water, and as he lowered himself into it, the water level rose, and some of the water spilled over the top of the tub and onto the floor. In an instant Archimedes realized the significance of this – he could measure the volume of the king's crown by submerging it in a tub of water. When the crown was put in the water, the water level would rise as the crown displaced

1 Read the *Reading tip* and then read the text quickly. Decide if the sentences are true or false.

1 The crown had been a gift to the king from the goldsmith.
2 The king promised to give Archimedes a small reward if he could determine whether the crown was pure gold.
3 Archimedes believed he would get into trouble with the king if he damaged the crown.
4 Silver has a higher density than gold.
5 *Eureka!* means 'I have found the answer'!

2 🎧 (1.19) Read the text again. Choose the best answers.

1 The king thought the goldsmith may have mixed silver with the gold because
  a the king was naturally suspicious.
  b the goldsmith had cheated the king before.
  c the crown didn't look like it had been made of pure gold.
  d the goldsmith had charged too much for the crown.
2 Archimedes didn't melt the crown because
  a he didn't know how to melt the crown.
  b melting the crown would have damaged it.
  c he couldn't have found out if it was pure gold by melting it.
  d he didn't know the density of gold.
3 Archimedes wanted to take a bath because
  a he was dirty.
  b he wanted to relax.
  c he didn't want to think about his problem.
  d he knew that he could solve his problem in the bath.
4 If the goldsmith had mixed silver with the gold, the crown
  a would have been less dense than a crown made of pure gold.
  b would have been more dense than a crown made of pure gold.
  c would have been more valuable than a crown made of pure gold.
  d would have looked different.
5 Archimedes shouted *Eureka!* because
  a he had to report to the king.
  b he had burned himself in the bath.
  c he had finished his bath.
  d he had found the answer to his problem.
6 The author of this text believes
  a Archimedes' discovery was solely due to chance.
  b the role of relaxation is not very important to Archimedes' discovery.
  c almost any intelligent person could have made the discovery that Archimedes made.
  d a combination of knowledge and relaxation led to Archimedes' discovery.

UNDERSTANDING IDEAS

Answer the questions. Look at the text, and use your own words and ideas.

1 Why do you think Archimedes accepted the king's request to find the purity of the crown? Was he motivated by the challenge, the reward, or fear of the king?
2 Have you ever tried to relax so that you could solve a problem or discover something? What did you do? Did this work for you? Why? Why not?
3 Thomas Edison, inventor of the electric light bulb, once said, 'Genius is 1% inspiration and 99% perspiration.' Do you think this is true? Why? Why not?

VOCABULARY

The origin of inspiration

Match the highlighted words in the text with these definitions.

1 Something not important or connected with a situation.
2 Expert knowledge of something.
3 To have a rest or to relax after, or in between activities.
4 The amount of space that an object or a substance fills.
5 Appear or come forward out of nothing.
6 Putting something under water.
7 Moved or shifted something from its normal position.
8 Made something worse.
9 Very much or significantly.
10 The thickness of a solid, liquid or gas.
11 A written or spoken description of something that has happened.
12 Showing distrust.
13 Huge and very important; having a great significance.
14 Made or created something by hand using special skills.
15 To have officially asked someone to do or make something for you.

(●●○○   Workbook: page 20)

it. The shape of the crown was irrelevant, and more importantly, putting the crown under water would not damage it. The submerged crown would displace an amount of water equal to its own volume. Archimedes worked out that by dividing the mass of the crown by the volume of water displaced, the density of the crown could be calculated. If cheaper and less dense metals, such as silver, had been added, the density of the crown would be lower than the density of gold.

In an instant, Archimedes leapt from the tub, shouting, 'Eureka! Eureka!' or 'I've found it! I've found it!'

This incident provides some insight into an important ingredient for inspiration – relaxation. Intelligence alone was not enough to enable Archimedes to solve his problem. He needed something else to make his discovery, specifically the relaxation a warm bath offered. He needed to take a break from thinking.

This story shows that relaxation and knowledge go hand-in-hand when it comes to inspiration. If Archimedes hadn't watched the water flow over the top of his bathtub, he probably wouldn't have realized that he could find the crown's purity by measuring its density. Conversely, someone who did not have Archimedes' mathematical and scientific expertise would have watched the water flow onto the floor without coming to any conclusion at all.

The origin of inspiration

ACTIVATE

Complete the sentences with the correct form of the words from the box.

> account   commission   considerably   craft   density
> displace   emerge   exacerbate   expertise   irrelevant
> monumental   submerge   suspicious   take a break
> volume

1 Joanna is an excellent teacher. Her _____ is widely recognized.
2 The witnesses had to give an _____ of how the accident happened.
3 Our teacher was angry, but John's rude remarks _____ the situation and now she's furious.
4 The _____ of the liquid in this jar is about half a litre.
5 A Mercedes is _____ more expensive than a Fiat.
6 The _____ of some metals make them too heavy for use in planes or helicopters.
7 The committee would like to _____ an artist to create a sculpture for the community centre.
8 I am highly _____ of Sandy's offer to help us. I don't think she actually wants us to succeed.
9 Jack _____ as the star of our singing class with his brilliant performance last week.
10 The goalkeeper's accidental death was a _____ loss to the team.
11 Natural disasters, such as flooding, can _____ thousands of people from their homes.
12 The stolen car was completely _____ in the river, so the police were unable to see it.
13 The jeweller _____ a beautiful necklace, bracelet, and ring for my engagement.
14 I'm exhausted, so I am going to _____ for a while.
15 To win an argument you need to be clear, concise and to the point; don't mention things that are complicated or _____.

EXTEND

Prefixes

1 Match the prefixes (1–5) with their meanings (a–e).

   1 ultra
   2 mal
   3 auto
   4 semi
   5 anti

   a undesirable or bad.
   b far beyond average or to an extreme degree.
   c done or exists only partially.
   d opposing or against something.
   e done by yourself.

2 Complete the sentences with the prefixes from exercise 1. Use a dictionary to check your answers.

   1 Only the ultra-rich can afford a fleet of private planes.
   2 After the accident, she was only _____conscious and couldn't speak, so they took her to hospital for tests.
   3 All the systems went down after the main computer experienced a major _____function. It was a total disaster for the company.
   4 I have an _____graphed book from my favourite author.
   5 Martin doesn't go out much. He's rather _____social.

Phrasal verbs: *break*

3 Read the sentences and match the phrasal verbs in bold with their meanings (1–6).

   a Our bus **broke down** two kilometres from the school.
   b The prisoner **broke away** from the policeman and ran off.
   c I was eating when part of my front tooth **broke off**.
   d The thief **broke into** the jewellery shop on the corner.
   e A fire **broke out** in the factory last night.
   f The workers **broke up** the pavement with a pneumatic drill.

   1 f to break something into smaller pieces
   2 __ to stop working
   3 __ to come off or to come apart
   4 __ to enter by force
   5 __ to start
   6 __ to escape

4 Match the sentences (a–f) in exercise 3 with the pictures below. Then write your own sentences, using the phrasal verbs.

   a–2   If my computer breaks down, I can't work.

> ●●○○○ Workbook: page 21

Conditionals without *if*

EXPLORE

1 🎧 (1.20) **Read the dialogue below. How did George de Mestral invent velcro?**

Teacher The invention of Velcro was the result of an accidental discovery by the Swiss engineer George de Mestral. De Mestral had been hiking when he noticed some seeds stuck to his clothes. The seeds were extremely difficult to remove. In fact, having looked at them under a microscope, de Mestral found that [1]the seeds could only be removed provided they were turned a certain way and pulled hard. Even then, pieces remained attached to his clothing. De Mestral discovered that the seeds had natural hooks which latched onto the material. This inspired him to create the hook and loop fastener that was eventually called Velcro.

Student [2]Supposing de Mestral hadn't been an engineer. He might not have looked at the seeds under the microscope.

Teacher That's a possibility. You or I might not have thought to look at the seeds under the microscope. [3]However, as long as you keep your mind open, you'll stand a good chance of discovering something new.

Student [4]Imagine that Velcro hadn't been invented! Our lives wouldn't be nearly as convenient.

2 **Look at the sentences highlighted in blue in the text. What kind of conditional, 1st, 2nd, 3rd or mixed, is expressed in each sentence? Which words or phrases indicate that it is a conditional?**

	Conditional type	Words or phrases indicating condition
Sentence 1	2nd conditional	provided
Sentence 2		
Sentence 3		
Sentence 4		

LEARN THIS!

Conditions can be expressed without *if*. The phrases **provided (that)**, **on condition (that)**, and **as / so long as** can be used to indicate conditions.
Suppose, supposing (that), and **imagine that** can be used to express unreal conditional sentences.

●●●●●● Grammar Reference: page 98

EXPLOIT

1 **Read the *Learn this!* box. Complete the sentences with the correct form of the verbs in brackets.**

1 I will lend you my MP3 player on condition that you *give* it back before Friday. (give)
2 Suppose you _____ your junk emails! You would never have known about that message. (not check)
3 Susan will come to see our match provided that she _____. (not have to work)
4 Supposing David had finished in fourth place. The coach _____ him to join the national team. (not invite)
5 So long as you try your best, I _____ happy with your performance. (be)
6 Imagine that Arab scholars _____ the zero! Mathematics would be very different. (not introduce)

LOOK OUT!

Conditionals with *suppose*, *supposing*, and *imagine* require two sentences. The sentence with *suppose*, *imagine*, or *supposing* must come first.
If Velcro hadn't been invented, our lives wouldn't be nearly as convenient.
Imagine that Velcro hadn't been invented. Our lives wouldn't be nearly as convenient.

2 **Rewrite the sentences, using the words in brackets.**

1 If we hadn't noticed the water dripping from the ceiling, we would've had a flood in our flat. (suppose)
Suppose we hadn't noticed the water dripping from the ceiling. We would've had a flood in our flat.
2 You wouldn't have been able to attend that university if you hadn't applied on time. (imagine)
3 I'll work next weekend if you agree to work this weekend. (on the condition that)
4 The object will float if it is lighter than water. (so long as)
5 They didn't mind my singing if they couldn't hear it! (provided that)
6 We would've missed the plane if we hadn't been on time. (supposing)

3 **Correct the errors.**

1 Suppose I hadn't done well in the exam, I wouldn't have passed the course!
Suppose I hadn't done well in the exam. I wouldn't have passed the course!
2 I will ring you later provided that my phone will work.
3 We would never have met up! Imagine that you'd lost my phone number.
4 Supposing our team hadn't won last night. We have been miserable.
5 So long as I tried my best, my parents would've been pleased with my progress.

●●●●●● Grammar Builder: page 99

●●●●●● Workbook: page 22

Success versus failure

VOCABULARY

1 Words can suggest a positive or negative idea or feeling. Check the meaning of the words and put them in the correct place.

aggravate	breakthrough	enable	frustrate	overcome
persevere	setbacks	struggle		

Positive	Negative
_____	aggravate
_____	_____
_____	_____
_____	_____

2 Complete the paragraph with a word from exercise 1.

Even the most intelligent inventor will ¹struggle and fail at something, but it is important not to get angry and allow failures to ²_____ you! Every inventor faces ³_____, but successful inventors will ⁴_____ until they ⁵_____ these obstacles. Of course, repeated failures can ⁶_____ the financial problems that most inventors encounter, but money is available from a variety of sources, from private investors to government funding. Obviously, adequate financial resources ⁷_____ the inventor to conduct further experiments and to be patient until a ⁸_____ occurs. However, this only happens to the lucky few.

(●●●●● Workbook: page 23)

LISTEN

1 Match the photos (1–6) with the words in the box. Which of these do you use regularly?

microwave oven	pre-packaged food	satellite technology
text messaging	satellite navigation device	mobile phone

2 🎧 (1.21) Listen to the dialogue about how inventions have changed our lives. Which three inventions do the speakers discuss?

3 🎧 (1.21) Listen again and answer the questions.

1 Why does Professor Berry think that text messaging has had a negative impact on students?
2 What are the two drawbacks of pre-packaged food?
3 What is the benefit of pre-packaged food?
4 Why does Professor Berry rank satellite technology so highly?
5 In which fields is GPS technology used?

SPEAK

1 List the inventions from Listen exercise 1 in order of importance, with 1 being the most important in your opinion. Why did you rank them in this order?

2 What would your life be like without the inventions in exercise 1?

Supposing we didn't have mobile phones. How would we contact our friends?

3 Which invention do you think the world could do without? Discuss with your partner.

'I think the world could do without mobile phones. We didn't have them twenty years ago so we don't need them today.'
'I don't really agree with you about that. I'd be lost without my phone.'

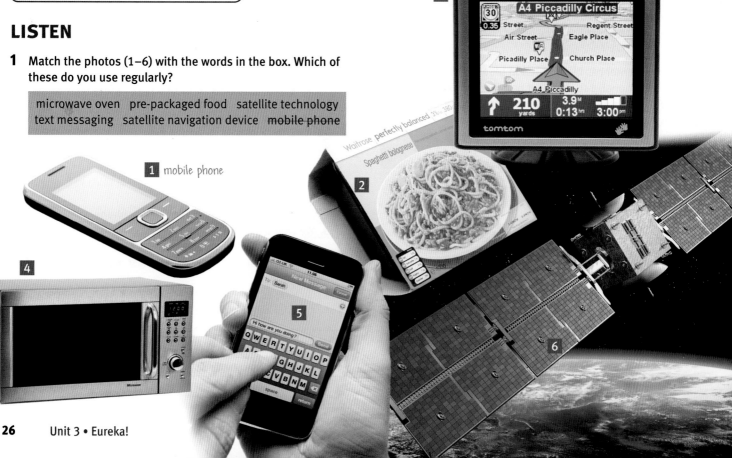

1 mobile phone

GRAMMAR

If only...

EXPLORE

1 Look at the inventions in the pictures. Imagine what life would be like if they hadn't been invented. Read the text and complete the sentences.

1 If the printing press hadn't been invented ...
2 Imagine that there weren't electric light bulbs ...
3 Supposing we didn't have cars ...

The printing press made it possible to produce books in greater quantities. According to most history records, Johannes Gutenberg invented the printing press in the 15th century. However, the printing press was also invented several centuries earlier in China. Many experts speculate that the printing press was not popular in China because Chinese does not use an alphabet. Chinese is written with thousands of characters, making the language too complicated to be used easily in a printing press. If only Chinese were simpler! Chinese might be the language we all speak today.

Although we think of Thomas Edison as the inventor of the light bulb, the first patent for a light bulb was given to Henry Woodward and Matthew Evans. Thomas Edison bought the patent in 1879 and improved the wires inside the bulb so it would last longer. If only Woodward and Evans had seen the potential of their patent for the light bulb! They would have become rich!

In 1885 the first practical automobile was invented by Karl Benz from Germany. His name is still part of the Mercedes-Benz brand. But it wasn't until Henry Ford developed the car manufacturing process in 1913 that car ownership became affordable for many people. In only a few decades, the automobile became extremely popular and the world's need for petrol dramatically increased. If only the world would use a vehicle that didn't need so much petrol! We could live on a cleaner planet.

2 Read the text again. Find examples of *if only* in the text. Then read the *Learn this!* box.

> We can use *if only ...* to express what things would be like if they were different, or to express a wish or desire. When *if only* is used in the first or third person singular with the verb *be*, we often use *were* instead of *was*.
> We can use *if only* to talk about situations in the present, past or future. *If only* can be used in an independent clause.
> *If only I were on holiday now.*
> However, *if only* is often used as a subordinate clause, followed by a comma. Note the tenses used in the main clause.
> *If only* + past simple › talks about the present
> *If only we had money to buy the tickets, we could see the film.*
> *If only* + *would* + infinitive › talks about the future
> *If only they would get here, we could leave soon.*
> *If only* + past perfect › talks about the past
> *If only we had locked the door, the house wouldn't have been burgled.*

●●○○○ Grammar Reference: page 98

EXPLOIT

1 Complete the sentences.

1 If only I _____ German, I would be able to explain the article to you. (read)
2 If only it _____ yesterday, we could have played the match. (not rain)
3 If only she _____ to me, she would find her job much easier. (listen)
4 If only the weather _____ better, we could sit outside for lunch. (be)
5 If only I _____ Liz, you could ask her for help. (know)
6 If only they _____ a new car, they could have come on holiday with us. (not buy)

2 Write sentences with *If only*.

1 I / be / better at science / have / better job opportunities
If only I were better at science, I could have better job opportunities.
2 he / study / more often / become / engineer
3 we / be / at the lecture / learn / so much
4 I / speak / French / understand / French newspapers
5 they / not leave / early / take / James with them
6 she / not be / on holiday / tell us / what to do

3 Complete the sentences, expressing present, past or future situations. Use your own ideas.

1 If only cars hadn't been invented ...
If only cars hadn't been invented, the world would be a cleaner place today.
2 If only space travel ...
3 If only they would invent ...
4 If only scientists ...
5 If only more people ...

●●●●○ Grammar Builder: page 99

●●●●○ Workbook: page 24

An opinion essay (2)

READ

1 Read the opinion essay about what makes an inventor successful. Which sentence (A–D) sums up the author's opinion best?

- **A** A strong academic record is the key to an inventor's success.
- **B** Different types of intelligence are needed to make a successful inventor.
- **C** Hard work can't be overlooked in the successful inventor's life.
- **D** Successful inventors have many characteristics that can't be easily identified.

The mind of a genius

The great inventor Thomas Edison once said, 'Genius is 1% inspiration and 99% perspiration.' Although it is true that hard work, perseverance, and good ideas are essential, there is another factor which cannot be underestimated in achieving success – intelligence.

Intelligence is an important asset that a successful inventor must have. Most people associate intelligence with strong performance in tests or a perfect school record, but this definition of intelligence is too simple. Intelligence isn't limited to academic performance, but also includes the ability to understand social situations and to work well with others. This is a kind of 'people intelligence'. This type of intelligence is important because the best ideas can fail if they aren't presented in the right way. The successful inventor must be able to convince others to believe in his or her idea.

Another type of intelligence that is often overlooked is common sense. This includes skills such as making tools out of common objects, understanding how to solve simple problems, or organizing a work space. Since many extremely gifted academics do not have common sense, this is often a real setback. They are unable to organize themselves, or they become frustrated by their inability to solve the problems of daily life.

Inventors who achieve success have undoubtedly worked extremely hard, but the vast majority of them also possess a significant amount of people intelligence or common sense.

2 According to the author, what is the difference between 'people intelligence' and common sense? Why are they important for an inventor?

PREPARE

1 Read the *Writing tip*. Classify the underlined sentences in the text. Which is the dependent clause in the complex sentence?

Writing tip: using a variety of sentence types

Sentence variety is an important writing technique.
Simple sentences consist of one independent clause. They are good for giving clear information, getting the reader's attention or summing up. Too many simple sentences can make your writing sound immature.
Compound sentences have two or more independent clauses of equal importance, which are joined by a conjunction such as *and*, *but*, or *yet*. A compound sentence is useful to create a balance or contrast between two equally important pieces of information.
Complex sentences have one independent clause and one dependent clause joined by words such as *although*, *before*, *since*, *after*, or *if*. Complex sentences contain clauses which are not equal because one clause is dependent on the other. A complex sentence makes it clear which ideas are more important, and which ideas are secondary or subordinate.

2 Read the sentences. Decide if they are examples of simple, compound or complex sentences.

1 Although the internet gives everyone access to lots of information, quality is more important than quantity.
2 Many websites have a lot of useful free information, and this is useful if you need to carry out research.
3 After I had used the translation site a few times, I felt more confident and independent.
4 The internet is important because it helps connect up people and knowledge across the world.
5 The main benefit is that it gives you quick access to information, but it also organizes information for you.
6 The internet is the greatest discovery of the 20th century.

WRITE

Write an opinion essay about the following statement. Use the writing plan to help you. Write 200–250 words and use different types of sentences.

> The internet provides many educational benefits.

Paragraph 1	Explain your opinion. Introduce the main arguments.
Paragraph 2	Present two points to support your opinion. Give examples.
Paragraph 3	Present a further point to support your opinion. Give examples.
Paragraph 4	Conclude your essay.

●●●●● Workbook: page 25

Eureka!

LANGUAGE SKILLS

1 🎧 (1.22) Complete the dialogue with the words from the box. Then listen and check your answers.

> breakthrough   exacerbate   frustrate   persevere
> setback   so long as   struggling   suppose   were   would

Anna What are you doing?

Martina I'm trying to solve this Sudoku puzzle, but I'm ¹_____ with it at the moment. Something's not right!

Anna Well, I'm sure you can solve it if you ²_____ .

Martina Yes, if I think about it long enough, something will come to me and I'll have a ³_____ . I've never left a puzzle unfinished.

Anna So you must enjoy doing Sudokus, then.

Martina Well, I enjoy them ⁴_____ I'm able to solve them quickly! Otherwise, they just ⁵_____ me, like this one I'm doing at the moment!

Anna Let me take a look. Hmm. Let's change these two numbers, and this one.

Martina Oh, no. Stop! I think you're just going to ⁶_____ the problem.

Anna No, it's just a small ⁷_____ . Now, let's make changes... Here... This number... And this number... Now look! I think that's it!

Martina Wow! I think you're right. Amazing! Thank you! If only I ⁸_____ as smart as you!

Anna ⁹_____ I hadn't been able to help you – you ¹⁰_____ have faced your first puzzle defeat!

2 Answer the questions.

1 Is Martina having difficulty with the puzzle?
2 Does Martina feel confident about being able to solve the puzzle?
3 What frustrates Martina?
4 Does Martina think Anna's first attempts at helping her are positive?
5 How does Martina react to Anna's help?
6 What might have happened without Anna's help?

3 Rewrite the sentences using the words in brackets.

1 We will be on time if you don't delay us any longer. (provided that)
2 If they hadn't spent all their money, they could have bought a new car. (supposing that)
3 You were looking at your phone, so you fell down the stairs. (If only)
4 Supposing you had taken the later flight. You would have missed the game. (If)
5 You can join the team on the condition that your physical examination is acceptable. (so long as)

Compound adjectives: *-proof* and *-free*

1 Check the meaning of the words in the box and complete the sentences.

> childproof   duty-free   foolproof   hands-free
> interest-free   ovenproof   smoke-free   soundproof

1 Please don't leave that bottle of tablets on the table. The lid is not childproof, so Lily may be able to open it.
2 It is very difficult to get an _____ loan in most European countries.
3 You can't bake food in this dish because it's not _____ .
4 In the 1990s people campaigned for _____ working environments.
5 The singer can't hear you unless he's wearing his headphones. He's in a _____ room.
6 When we return from a trip abroad, we always buy something in the _____ shop at the airport.
7 I need to buy a _____ device for my mobile phone so that I can use it more safely while driving.
8 Anyone can use this phone, it's _____ .

2 Complete the sentences with the suffix *-proof* or *-free*.

The suffix ¹_____ means *without something*.
The suffix ²_____ means *resistant to* or *safe from something*.

3 Complete the words with *-proof* or *-free*. Write an example sentence for each one.

1 trouble-free
The operation went very smoothly and was trouble-free.
2 bullet_____   4 water_____
3 tax-_____   5 fat-_____

I CAN ...

Read the statements. Think about your progress and tick (✓) one of the boxes.

| ※ | I need more practice. | ※※ | I sometimes find this difficult. | ※※※ | No problem! |

	※	※※	※※※
I can understand an article about discoveries and inspiration.			
I can use conditional structures without *if*.			
I can talk about the importance of different inventions.			
I can use *if only* to express regret about present, past and future situations.			
I can write an opinion essay, using a variety of sentence types.			

(●●●●● Workbook: Self check pages 26–27)

4 It's a must-have!

THIS UNIT INCLUDES ●●●●

Vocabulary • idioms: marketing • advertising vocabulary • shopping • parts of speech
Grammar • preparatory *there* • perfect, passive and negative gerunds
Skills • reading, listening and talking about shopping habits
Writing • a product description • appositive phrases

Marketing to teenagers

BEFORE READING

1 Look at the photos. What kind of products are being advertised?

2 What kind of advertisements do you see on TV?

3 Do you think advertising works? Why? Why not?

TARGETING TEENAGERS

Adults earn most of the money in the economy, so shouldn't most advertisements be directed at them?

Over a billion pounds is spent every year in order to target teenage customers. It's nearly impossible to visit a shopping centre or switch on the television without finding products and advertisements that many adults may not be interested in or even understand. Why are teenagers, a group with relatively little earning power, such targeted consumers?

Today's teenagers have an unprecedented amount of money to spend on personal items. They have more money to spend than teenagers of any previous generation. Many of them receive money from their parents on a regular basis, and some teenagers earn money from part-time jobs. Around the world, there are millions of teens with a disposable income to spend on clothing, electronics, music, and other items. Because young people make a lot of the purchasing decisions for these objects, companies market them with teenagers in mind.

Another reason teens are so important to marketing departments is that they influence the spending of their families. In some countries, such as the United Kingdom and Canada, teenagers may have an influence on up to 70% of the purchases for the home. Teenagers often have a say in the brands that the family buys, whether the products are food or personal care items like shampoo or soap. In fact, advertisers often market directly to teens because they know that teenagers can be very powerful and persistent about getting their parents to buy things or give them money to buy things themselves.

Marketing departments know that getting people to switch brands can be tough. Therefore, it is important to attract customers who have not yet developed strong brand preferences or brand loyalty. Older teens who are going to leave school and become consumers are a perfect target for marketing companies.

Because of their money, influence and potential, teens are big business for most major companies. As a result, advertisers have many techniques to get teens to buy their products. Here are some of the most popular ones.

A Perfect World
This technique presents an ideal world – everyone is attractive and hip, with the latest fashions and trendiest haircuts. The families are well off. They have expensive cars and homes. Families in these ads are smiling and they get along amazingly well. These ads represent the world that most teens would like for themselves.

B Family Fun
Bringing the family together is the appeal of this technique. Advertisers show a product as something that helps a family overcome struggles with each other or a difficult task. The product is often the reason the family come together; for example, dad brings home dinner from the family's favourite fast-food restaurant and then suddenly the quarrelling brother and sister set aside their differences and enjoy a meal with their parents.

C Bandwagon
Join the crowd! Everyone has one. Don't be left out. This is the strategy of the Bandwagon technique. Advertisers try to convince consumers that they need the product to be trendy. Usually advertisers do this by showing people who are awkward and unpopular. The people try the product and then suddenly become popular and cool.

These are just a few of the techniques advertisers use. There are also many others, including endorsements by star athletes, popular actors, and beautiful models. It is important for all consumers, including teens, to watch adverts critically. In other words, we should all think about whether we really want or need the product promoted in the advert, or whether we are simply responding to the marketing techniques.

READ

1 Read the text quickly and find three reasons why many marketing companies target teenagers.

Reading tip

When dealing with multiple choice options, read the sentence openings and then read the section in the text that it refers to. Try to predict how the sentence will finish. Then read the four options and try to identify the option with the answer you predicted. If your answer is not one of the choices, try to eliminate any answers that are obviously wrong first.

2 🎧 (1.26) Read the *Reading tip*. Then read the text again and choose the best answers.

1 Each year, advertisers spend more than a billion pounds on advertising aimed at
   a consumers who earn a lot of money.
   b consumers who watch TV every day.
   c all consumers.
   d teenage consumers.
2 The amount of money teenagers have today means that they
   a spend more money than their grandparents.
   b have more money than their parents.
   c make decisions about buying household products.
   d are important to advertisers.
3 Teenagers can influence the family's spending by
   a living in Canada.
   b doing the shopping for their families.
   c influencing their parents' purchasing decisions.
   d listening to their parents' opinions about different goods.
4 Advertisers target teenagers because they
   a will be loyal consumers.
   b have more money than their parents.
   c are willing to try different brands.
   d are going to leave school.
5 The techniques to attract teenagers described in this text are
   a the only techniques that actually work effectively.
   b more effective than techniques using celebrities.
   c positive about image and family life.
   d not very popular with most consumers.
6 The author of this article probably wants teenagers to
   a spend more money on products they see in adverts.
   b take this information to create their own adverts.
   c choose the products they buy based on adverts they enjoy.
   d understand how advertising works.

3 Read the descriptions of advertising techniques. Which of the marketing techniques (a–c) from the article do they use?

1 A lonely teenager doesn't have many friends at university. He notices that all of the students who have a certain brand of trainers are popular and athletic. The teenager buys the trainers and suddenly he is invited to play football with a group of students.
2 A family is having a difficult time. The mother is at her office. Her computer has just switched off unexpectedly. The teenage brother and sister have missed their bus home. The father has dropped his briefcase of papers in the mud next to his car. At the end of the advert, we see the family coming out of an expensive clothing store, each of them smiling and carrying a bag.
3 The sun is shining and the sky is blue and clear. A teenage girl is walking down the street. She is beautiful and well-dressed, listening to an MP3 player. As she walks down the street, groups of attractive teenagers, who are also dressed in fashionable clothes, smile and wave at her. They are also listening to the same MP3 player.

UNDERSTANDING IDEAS

Answer the questions. Look at the text, and use your own words and ideas.

1 Do you have a favourite advertisement? What is it for? Why do you like it?
2 Think of some adverts that use any of the three techniques in the text. Describe them.
3 Do you think product endorsements by athletes, models or singers are effective? Why? Why not?

VOCABULARY

Targeting teenagers

Match the highlighted words in the text with these definitions.

1 Not moving in an easy way, uncomfortable.
2 Forget or disregard arguments because something else is more important.
3 Promote and advertise.
4 Arguing.
5 Personal favourites or choices.
6 Never done or known before.
7 Not one of a group, excluded.
8 Aim at or direct at.
9 Money available to spend freely on whatever you want.
10 The ability to make money.
11 Rich.
12 Statements or actions by important or famous people to support something being advertised.
13 Something continual or constant.
14 Have a right or power to influence or make a decision about something.
15 The possibility of something being developed or used.

(●●○○   Workbook: page 28)

Targeting teenagers

ACTIVATE

Complete these sentences with the correct form of the words from the box.

> awkward   disposable income   earning power
> endorsements   have a say   leave out   market   persistent
> potential   preference   quarrelling
> set aside their differences   target   unprecedented   well off

1 Having good exam results does not necessarily lead to higher _____ when you start working.
2 The President's speech at the university was _____. No foreign dignity had ever done that before.
3 I don't believe that product _____ by athletes are effective unless the product is related to sport.
4 Advertisers should not be permitted to _____ unhealthy products.
5 The economy is not very good, so the _____ of many families has decreased.
6 Tom was nervous and his body language was _____ as he entered the gym.
7 Anne has the _____ to be become a scientist in the future.
8 Our new teacher is very supportive. He wants us to _____ in the topic for our class project.
9 Daniel has been _____ of the team for Friday's football match, so he's not happy.
10 The new healthy eating programme _____ school children.
11 They decided to _____ to try to find some compromise through discussion.
12 Some kids were _____ in the playground yesterday. They were extremely noisy.
13 The company had suffered _____ difficulties year after year before finally shutting down.
14 The flats in this neighbourhood are fabulous! Most of the residents are obviously very _____.
15 I don't have a _____ for either restaurant. You choose!

EXTEND

Advertising vocabulary

1 Match the words (1–6) with the definitions (a–f).

1 slogan   a a large display board for advertising
2 jingle   b a sign or symbol of a company or product
3 product   c a short, memorable tune used to promote
  placement   something
4 hype   d a short, memorable phrase used to
                    promote something
5 logo   e exaggerated publicity to excite people
                    about a product
6 billboard   f using brand-name products in TV shows
                    or films

2 Complete the sentences using words from exercise 1.

1 The marketing company for that tea should think up a new slogan. 'The quality tea, QUALITEA.' isn't very catchy.
2 I enjoy this TV show, but I find the _____ is distracting. The actors are always holding soft drinks!
3 Don't believe the _____ about the multi-intelligent vacuum cleaner. It doesn't work that well.
4 I've already seen six huge _____ advertising the new shopping mall. Look! There's one across the street.
5 I can't stop singing the _____ for those chocolate bars!
6 The _____ for my favourite basketball team is a rocket.

Idioms: marketing

3 Check the meaning of the expressions (1–6) and match them with their definitions (a–f).

1 to corner the market   a not as good as it should be
2 to drum up business   b to find new, innovative ideas
3 to think outside of   not used previously
  the box   c to be dominant in an area of
4 not up to scratch   business
5 in the pipeline   d being developed
6 to put sth on the line   e to try hard to generate
                                product interest and sales
                              f to risk something

4 Read the sentences. Replace the words in bold with an idiomatic expression from exercise 3.

1 Although Apple computers are popular, the PC has **dominated the market** to date. cornered the market
2 Celebrities should be careful about which products they endorse because their reputations can be **jeopardized** if the product isn't successful.
3 Market research is essential for companies to discover if their products are **not good enough**.
4 Many new companies spend a lot of money on advertising to **increase their sales**.
5 To come up with a good marketing campaign, you sometimes have to **think in an unconventional way**.
6 Many marketing departments need to plan how to promote their products that are **being developed**.

(●●●●○ Workbook: page 29)

The passive with preparatory *there*

EXPLORE

1 Have you ever bought anything online? What are the advantages and disadvantages of buying these goods online? Which would you prefer to buy in a shop?

1 CDs and books
2 clothes and shoes
3 food
4 plane tickets

In 2009, there were believed to be over 1.8 billion internet users in the world. Of these users, there was estimated to be 85% who had made a purchase through the internet. This represents a 40% increase in the number of online shoppers compared with two years before. The statistics also show that more than 50% of internet users are 'regular online shoppers', in other words, they make an online purchase at least once a month.

So how do businesses attract online shoppers? About 80% of advertising campaigns use the web, but today there are reported to be only 50 sites that attract any significant advertising. These sites, including Yahoo and Google™, attract 96% of the online advertising business. Although it is thought that there is great potential in online advertising, it only accounts for a small percentage of total advertising spending. Most companies spend much more on newspaper and radio advertising.

2 Read the text. Find four sentences that use the passive. Why do you think the writer uses the passive in these sentences? Read the *Learn this!* box to check your answers.

> **LEARN THIS!**
>
> The passive with preparatory *there* is used to make a generalization about an event or give information that comes from a variety of sources. It is often used with verbs such as *say, think, believe, report, presume, estimate,* and *feel*.
> The word *there* acts as the subject of the sentence. The passive verb form agrees with the number of the noun in the noun clause that comes after *to be*.
> *There* + *be* + past participle + *to be* + noun clause
> *There **is** thought to be enormous **potential** in online advertising.*
> Time markers signal the use of the present or past passive.
> *Today, there **are reported** to be only 50 companies that attract any significant spending.*
> *In 2006, there **were believed** to be 627 million internet users in the world.*

(●●●○○ Grammar Reference: page 100)

EXPLOIT

1 Complete the sentences with the correct passive form of the verb in brackets.

1 There _____ to be a higher number of female online shoppers than male. (think)
2 There _____ to be more than 1,000 students on the school's register last year. (report)
3 There _____ to be a better turnout at the staff meetings than last year. (say)
4 There _____ to be more demand for internet access points in the airport. (presume)
5 There _____ to be several possible candidates for the election next year. (think)
6 There _____ to be a cautious attitude to spending money after the the economic crisis. (feel)

2 Rewrite the sentences in the passive with preparatory *there*.

1 People estimate that there are fewer than 500 tigers in the world today.
   There is estimated to be fewer than 500 tigers in the world today.
2 People presume that there is a direct relationship between the price and the quality of a product.
3 People think that there are a number of benefits to the environment if fewer people go out shopping.
4 Scientists say that there are more eco-friendly ways to create electricity.
5 Officials reported that there was a major breakthrough at the climate conference.
6 Customers felt that there were a number of areas for improvement of delivery services.

3 Write sentences about the following topics, using the passive with preparatory *there*. Make guesses if you don't know the exact figures.

1 the amount of money spent on TV advertising every year
   There is estimated to be about £20 million spent on TV advertising every year.
2 the number of households that don't have a computer
3 an increase in the number of school essays downloaded from the internet
4 a fall in the number of science graduates
5 growth in the number of companies providing delivery services
6 new ways to protect credit card details

(●●●○○ Grammar Builder: page 101)
(●●●○○ Workbook: page 30)

Shopping habits

VOCABULARY

1 Do you enjoy shopping? Why? Why not?

2 Look at the pictures (A–C) and match the types of shopper with the descriptions (1–3). What type of shopper are you?

A impulse buyer

C serious shopper

B bargain hunter

1 These shoppers usually go out with a **shopping list**. They are shopping for a specific item, and they are clear about the quality and features it must have. They aren't distracted by **cheap offers,** and they will shop until they find exactly what they want.

2 These shoppers want to get as much as they can for their money. They aren't **wasteful with money**. They are always on the lookout for **terrific deals**. They will shop around, and they know **a good buy** when they see it.

3 These shoppers might go to the shops in search of a new shirt and come home with a pair of boots. They buy without looking at the **price tag**. They often find that those '**must-have' items** often don't get used. This type of shopper loves to go on a **shopping spree**.

3 Look at the words in bold in the descriptions in exercise 2. Match them with the definitions (a–h).

1 must-have items — a the label on a product that indicates how much it costs
2 shopping list — b a note of the essential things you want to buy
3 terrific deals — c spending without care
4 a good buy — d promotions of goods at greatly reduced prices
5 cheap offers — e an item that is good value for money
6 shopping spree — f exceptional bargains
7 wasteful with money — g things that you believe you have to own
8 price tag — h buying a lot of things, often too much, in a short period of time

LISTEN

1 🎧 (1.27) Listen to the market research interviews. What kind of shopper does each person say they are? Write *IB* for impulsive buyer, *BH* for bargain hunter or *SS* for serious shopper.

1 Richard Lewes __ 2 Daphne Smith __

2 🎧 (1.27) Listen again. Answer the questions.

1 What does David Huntley do for a living?
2 How does Richard Lewis describe his attitude to money?
3 What type of items does Richard shop around for?
4 What does Daphne Smith do to prepare for a shopping trip?
5 What happened when she went shopping for a winter coat?
6 What other items has she bought impulsively?

3 According to the shopper descriptions, which of the people interviewed is wrong about what kind of shopper they are?

SPEAK

1 Interview a partner about what kind of shopper he or she is. Use the following questions. Give examples from a recent shopping trip to support your answer.

1 Do you ever make a shopping list? If yes, do you follow it?
2 Is there anything that is a must-have item for you?
3 Do you look at the price tag before you buy something?
4 How many things are in your closet with the price tag still on them?
5 Are you more interested in cheap offers or fine quality items?
6 Are you careful or wasteful with money?

2 Tell the class about the kind of shopper your partner is. Give examples to support your opinion. Use the vocabulary from the shopper descriptions in Vocabulary exercise 2.

> Lisa is a serious shopper. She always makes a shopping list and follows it...

(●●●●○○ Workbook: page 31)

Gerunds: perfect, passive and negative

EXPLORE

1 Read the text. How did the BlackBerry get its name?

Branding companies can help their clients to name new products. In some instances, the inventors have tried to name a product, without **having been** successful. The inventors may be frustrated about **not having come to** an agreement, and they need to consult branding experts. On the other hand, some inventors are not interested in choosing a product name. They are only interested in **being consulted** once there are a few options to choose from.

When Lexicon Branding met with the makers of the device that was eventually called the BlackBerry, they discovered that the inventors were intent on **not giving** the device a name with 'mail' or 'email' in it. Although they knew the device would be popular with people who were obsessed with **being connected**, they didn't want a name that reminded people of work.

The inventors of the BlackBerry participated in a brainstorming session with Lexicon Branding. Because they liked the name of a successful computer brand named after a fruit, the brainstorming focused on names associated with fruits and vegetables. One of the team recalled **having seen** some blackberries recently and observed that the keys on the devices were like the fruit's tiny seeds.

LEARN THIS!

Gerunds are nouns that are formed from verbs, e.g. *the brainstorming focused on...* They are often used after prepositions or prepositional phrases. All gerunds contain a present participle component (*-ing* form). Gerunds in the passive and perfect forms reflect the usage of those verb forms. For example, passive gerunds focus on the receiver of the action, not the actor.
The company are interested in being consulted. [It is unimportant who initiates the consulting.]
Perfect gerunds indicate something happened in the past but still has an impact on the present.
They have tried to name the product, obviously without having been successful. [They tried in the past, and the lack of success has an impact on now.]

2 Read the *Learn this!* box. Look at the gerunds in blue in the text and complete the table. One item fits in two columns. Then complete the rules.

Perfect gerund	Passive gerund	Negative gerund
having been		

A ¹_____ gerund contains not before the present participle.
A ²_____ gerund contains the present participle of the verb be and the past participle.
A ³_____ gerund contains the present participle of the verb have and the past participle.

(●●●●● Grammar Reference: page 100)

EXPLOIT

1 Complete the sentences with the perfect or passive gerund form of the verbs in brackets.

1 The students were angry about *being informed* of the essay title only one day before it was due. (inform)
2 They were charged with _____ a crime. (commit)
3 She insists on _____ every time she visits us. (entertain)
4 Olivia doesn't like _____ in our neighbourhood. (see)
5 Sandra was happy about _____ first prize in the competition. (win)
6 We were shocked at the bus _____ by the falling tree. (hit)

LOOK OUT!

It is not possible to use a contraction in negative gerunds.
Her problem was not paying attention in class.
[NOT: *Her problem wasn't paying attention in class.*]

2 Read the *Look out!* box. Rewrite the sentences, using the negative form of the gerund.

1 Shelly was annoyed about being picked first.
Shelly was annoyed about not being picked first.
2 I'm sorry for having left the stadium half way through the match.
3 He hates being noticed.
4 Our mistake was trusting him.
5 My father regrets buying a flat in London.
6 I felt bad about giving my students extra homework.

3 Find the mistakes in the sentences and correct them.

1 Howard was unhappy about being not given the first choice of the seats in the theatre.
Howard was unhappy about not being given the first choice of the seats in the theatre.
2 Emma felt good for having gaining the highest mark in the end of year test.
3 We were thrilled about having to have the opportunity to meet our favourite actor.
4 He was thrilled about being honour for his research.
5 Michael was embarrassed about having losing his brother's car keys.
6 They were happy about not be seen in their school uniforms.

(●●●●● Grammar Builder: page 101)

(●●●●● Workbook: page 32)

A product description

READ

Read the product description and answer the questions.

1 Where will people wear these screens?
2 What will the screens look like?
3 What will people do with their screens?
4 Why will advertisers be interested in these screens?

Would you advertise a product on your arm?

The wearable screen may be the advertising outlet of the future. It will soon be possible to produce flat, flexible screens which will be worn on the arm. The wearable screen, about 10–15 centimetres long and 6–8 centimetres wide, will enable the wearer to check emails, read the news, and watch films. The screens will be linked to wireless devices which connect them to the internet in the way that our computers and smart phones already do. The screens will be extremely lightweight, and they will be blank when switched off, so they won't be a distraction. Ordinary people interested in earning extra money will be able to wear advertising messages on them.

Gavin Marshall, director of a digital advertising company, thinks the future of advertising will use individuals for marketing. He believes the personal, flexible screen will be used to spread brand messages. He claims many sports fans, keen to support their favourite teams, will be happy to wear the teams' brands or logos. Advertisers see great potential in the wearable screens because they can hire a few popular individuals to reach out to target markets.

PREPARE

1 Read the *Writing tip*. Find three appositive phrases in the text.

Writing tip: appositive phrases

We often use appositive phrases in our writing to make it shorter and to add variety. An appositive phrase is made by omitting the relative pronoun and *to be* from a relative clause. *The wearable screen, about 10–15 centimetres long and 6–8 centimetres wide, will enable the wearer… [The wearable screen, which will be about 10–15 centimetres long…]*

Appositive phrases can be created from passive verb forms. *Personal screens,* ~~which will be~~ *worn on the arm, will be used for advertising purposes.*

Appositive phrases cannot be created from relative clauses that use verbs other than *to be*.
Gavin Marshall, who lives in London, works in advertising.
~~Gavin Marshall, lives in London, works in advertising.~~

2 Rewrite the sentences that can be written using appositives. Two of them cannot be changed.

1 National museums, which are found in major cities all over the world, are popular tourist attractions.
   National museums, found in major cities all over the world, are popular tourist attractions.
2 Mr Maloney, who is my favourite teacher, is from Ireland.
3 Her perfume, which has a jasmine scent, is quite strong.
4 Ms Frost, who is a manager at a major advertising firm, predicts strong sales this quarter.
5 The best sport teams, which will be determined by a survey of sports journalists, will be announced next week.
6 Teenagers, who are a growing consumer group, are targeted by many advertising companies.
7 Micro-computers, which can cost more than £500, are becoming quite popular.
8 The new jingles, which were composed by Victor, are extremely catchy.

WRITE

1 Write a product description for a new product that you would like to see on the market. Think of a product that can be used in one of the following categories.

- something for the house
- something for entertainment
- something for travelling
- something for school

2 Answer the following questions and make notes.

- What will the product do?
- What will it look like?
- How will it work?
- Who will use this product?
- How and where could you advertise this product?

3 Write a product description of 180–200 words, using your notes from exercise 2 to help you. Use appositive phrases.

(●●●●● Workbook: page 33)

It's a must-have!

LANGUAGE SKILLS

1 🎧 (1.28) **Complete the dialogue with the words from the box. Then listen and check your answers.**

| been | have a say | having | impulsive | logo | potential |
| spree | target | terrific deals | wasteful with money |

Katie Hi, Jim. You look happy! What's happened?

Jim I've just heard that the ¹_____ I designed for the school magazine has won the competition. Mr Jones says it's perfect because the magazine is going to ²_____ both students and parents and my design appeals to both generations.

Katie That's great! I always thought you had the ³_____ to be a designer. Your father works in advertising, doesn't he? Did he ⁴_____ in your design?

Jim Of course not! Though ⁵_____ seen a lot of his work, it might have helped. I did have some useful comments from my mum though.

Katie What will you do with the prize money?

Jim Oh, I think I'll go shopping. There are some ⁶_____ in the sales at the moment.

Katie Don't forget that there's a recession on. It's not a good idea to be ⁷_____, and I know you are an ⁸_____ buyer!

Jim It's not that much money Katie! Having ⁹_____ a poor student for so long, I don't think I'm going to go crazy on a shopping ¹⁰_____ with this amount.

2 **Answer the questions.**

1 Why is Jim happy?
2 Why does Mr Jones say his design is perfect?
3 Who helped Jim?
4 Why does Jim want to go shopping?
5 What advice does Katie give Jim?
6 Why isn't Jim going to go on a shopping spree?

3 **Correct the mistakes in these sentences.**

1 There was estimated to be over 900 million internet users in 2010.
2 Michelle is angry about not having being told that her flight was late.
3 My mistake wasn't asking for your permission before I took your phone, and I'm sorry about that.
4 There was reported a 10 per cent increase in the number of TV commercials for laptops last year.
5 My younger brother is persistent about to be included in discussions when my friends visit.
6 There is said to be some new marketing techniques that can target regular online shoppers.

DICTIONARY CORNER

Word stress

Word stress changes when a word is used as a different part of speech. For example, the word *export* can be used as a noun or a verb and its word stress changes accordingly.

1 **Read the sentences. What part of speech is the word in bold? Write noun or verb.**

1 The rise in tax on petrol will **impact** on all manufacturing industries. verb
2 I don't think your absence will have an **impact** on the success of the team.
3 Before choosing a new slogan, a marketing firm needs to **survey** its customers.
4 I was asked to answer a **survey** at the shopping mall.
5 Our teacher won't **permit** us to leave early.
6 We weren't able to get the **permit** to visit the site.

2 **Look up the words in bold in exercise 1 and check which syllable is stressed. Mark the stress in front of the correct syllable. Then complete the rules about stress.**

I im'pact (v)

When the word is used as a ¹_____, it is typically stressed on the first syllable.
When the word is used as a ²_____, it is typically stressed on the second syllable.

3 🎧 (1.29) **Mark the stressed syllables in the words in bold. Practise saying the sentences aloud. Then listen and check.**

1 It's common for teens to **rebel** against their parents.
2 There's a lot of **refuse** in that empty building site.
3 The boy's **conduct** at school has been improving lately.
4 The scientists will **present** their results at a conference next month.
5 I don't **object** to sitting next to him.
6 He hopes to set a **record** for distance running some day.

I CAN ...

Read the statements. Think about your progress and tick (✓) one of the boxes.

※ I need more practice. ※※ I sometimes find this difficult. ※※※ No problem!

	※	※※	※※※
I can understand an article about marketing to teenagers.			
I can use the passive with preparatory *there* to make generalizations.			
I can talk about different types of shoppers and shopping habits.			
I can use perfect, passive and negative gerunds.			
I can write a product description.			

●●●●● Workbook: Self check pages 34–35

The Adventures of Tom Sawyer

by Mark Twain

Biography

Mark Twain was born in 1835 in the state of Missouri in the USA. He began his career as a journalist and also spent some time working as a river-pilot on the Mississippi River. He started writing in 1867 and became famous for being the creator of the well-known characters Tom Sawyer and Huckleberry Finn. His novels were popular because of his humorous writing style, his use of authentic dialogue, and his realistic portrayal of life in the American south in the years just before the American Civil War. He died in 1910.

'Tom!'

No answer.

'Tom!'

No answer.

'What's gone with that boy, I wonder? You TOM!'

No answer.

The old lady pulled her spectacles down and looked over them about the room; then she put them up and looked out under them. She seldom or never looked through them for so small a thing as a boy; they were her state pair, the pride of her heart, and were built for 'style,' not service – she could have seen through a pair of stove lids just as well. She looked perplexed for a moment, and then said, not fiercely, but still loud enough for the furniture to hear:

'Well, I lay if I get hold you I'll—'

She did not finish, for by this time she was bending down and punching under the bed with the broom, and so she needed breath to punctuate the punches with. She resurrected nothing but the cat.

'I never did see the beat of that boy!'

She went to the open door and stood in it and looked out among the tomato vines and "jimpson" weeds that constituted the garden. No Tom. So she lifted up her voice at an angle calculated for distance, and shouted:

'Y-o-u-u Tom!'

There was a slight noise behind her and she turned just in time to seize a small boy by the slack of his roundabout and arrest his flight.

'There! I might 'a' thought of that closet. What you been doing in there?'

'Nothing.'

'Nothing! Look at your hands. And look at your mouth. What is that truck?'

'I don't know, aunt.'

'Well, I know. It's jam—that's what it is. Forty times I've said if you didn't let that jam alone I'd skin you. Hand me that switch.'

The switch hovered in the air—the peril was desperate—

'My! Look behind you, aunt!'

The old lady whirled round, and snatched her skirts out of danger. The lad fled, on the instant, scrambled up the high board-fence, and disappeared over it.

His aunt Polly stood surprised a moment, and then broke into a gentle laugh.

'Hang the boy, can't I never learn anything? Ain't he played me tricks enough like that for me to be looking out for him by now?'

1 Read the text quickly. Which characters are introduced? What is their relationship?

2 🎧 (1.32) Read the text again and answer the questions.
1 Where does Aunt Polly first look for Tom?
2 Where was Tom hiding?
3 What was Tom doing?
4 What does Aunt Polly want to do to Tom when she finds him?
5 How does Tom escape from Aunt Polly?
6 What is Aunt Polly's reaction to Tom escaping?

3 Answer the questions. Look at the text, and use your own words and ideas to explain your answers.
1 What do you think Aunt Polly's character is like? Is she kind? Is she strict?
2 Do you think Tom and Aunt Polly get along? Why or why not?
3 What kind of boy do you think Tom is? Why?

4 The text focuses on Aunt Polly and her actions and feelings. Rewrite the events of the text from Tom's point of view. Include information about the following:
- Where is he?
- What is he doing?
- What does he hear?
- What is he thinking?
- How does he feel about his aunt?

Media

READ

1 How much time do you spend each day using the following electronic devices? Compare your answers with a partner.

1 MP3 player   2 TV   3 mobile phone   4 computer

2 Read the text. How much time do some teenagers in America spend in a day using electronic devices?

Teen Media Usage

How much time do you spend watching TV? Online? Listening to an MP3 player? Suppose you were an average American teenager, the answer would be simple – almost every waking moment outside of school.

According to a 2010 study, Americans aged 8 to 18 spend more than seven and a half hours a day using electronic devices. And that all takes place in addition to the time spent each day going to school, having meals, and sleeping. Researchers were surprised by the results, which show a steady growth in the amount of time teenagers are spending with their electronic devices. After a similar study in 2005, they had believed that there would be little, if any, increase in the number of hours spent using electronic devices simply because there weren't enough hours in the day.

One contribution to the increase may be advances in mobile technology, such as smart phones and notebooks, which are easy for students to carry around, or use in their own rooms. The study also indicated that an average teenager spends an hour and half a day texting and half an hour talking on a mobile phone, which usually happens while he or she is using another electronic device. In fact, this type of multi-tasking is not unusual. Lots of young people who took part in the study listened to music while using the internet, or watched TV while texting friends.

But are there thought to be any long-term issues related to the findings of this study? Are health and education being negatively influenced by such heavy usage of electronic devices? According to these studies, the heaviest users (those who used electronic devices for at least sixteen hours a day) reported a similar amount of exercise and participation in physical activity as the light users. However, there was found to be a negative effect on school marks and exam scores. The light users tended to get better results in school exams than the teenagers using electronic devices from the moment they get up until they go to sleep!

3 Read the text again. Are the sentences true or false?

1 Researchers expected the 2010 usage to be significantly higher than the 2005 usage.
2 In 2010, the average American teenager spent about seven and a half hours a day using their mobile phone.
3 It is common for young people to use two devices at the same time.
4 Those who spent more time using electronic devices were less active than those who used them least.
5 School performance is shown to be affected negatively by frequent usage of electronic devices.

4 Answer the questions. Use your own words and ideas.

1 Do the results of these studies surprise you? Why/Why not?
2 How do you rate yourself – as a 'heavy user' or a 'light user'? Explain your rating.
3 Imagine this study was going to be repeated in 2015. What do you think the results would be? Explain your prediction.

LISTEN

1 🎧 (1.33) Listen to the conversation between two teenagers, John and Carolyn. Is John a typical teenager, according to the information in the reading text?

2 🎧 (1.33) Listen again. Answer the questions.

1 Why is John giving away his computer games and DVDs?
2 What is John not going to give up? Why not?
3 What kind of sports league was Carolyn's brother in? Why did he quit?
4 What does John do at the sports centre?
5 Why is Carolyn going to take a camera to the sports centre next Tuesday?

WRITE AND SPEAK

1 Make a list of your free time activities from the time you leave school until you go to sleep. How much time do you spend:

1 using electronic devices
2 being active
3 studying
4 helping at home
5 helping people in the community
6 doing other things

2 Make a table showing the class results. Do people spend too much time using electronic devices? Discuss the results, positive or negative.

3 Use the results to write a report about the way people in your class spend their free time. Make some suggestions as to how people could improve the way they spend their free time.

You're cured!

Plant medicines

THIS UNIT INCLUDES ● ● ● ●

Vocabulary • alternative medicine • word formation: nouns and verbs • the body and medical conditions • adjectives of sensation
Grammar • preparatory *it* as subject and object
Skills • comparing alternative health remedies
Writing • a blog • using similes and metaphors

BEFORE READING

1 What kind of medicine do you usually take for a headache, a stomach ache, or pain?

2 The plants in the photos are all used to treat illnesses. Do you ever use any plants or herbs when you are unwell?

> **Reading tip**
>
> When scanning a text for specific information, decide what type of information you need to find. If the information you need is a fact, a date, or a name, scan the text for key nouns, usually proper nouns. If the information you need is to identify the cause or the result of something, identify where the key noun of the topic is in the text, then consider carefully the meanings of the adjectives and verbs used around the noun to find your answer.

The healing power of plants

Some of the best known medicines come from a plant. People have used plants to treat illnesses for thousands of years, and scientists today are searching in jungles and tropical rain forests for plants that may contain substances to cure cancer and other serious diseases.

A *Aspirin*: The ancient Greek doctor Hippocrates recorded the use of the bark of the willow tree as an effective remedy for headaches, pains, and fever. Willow bark had been used in this way in many cultures for centuries. In 1829, German scientist Johann Buchner identified the specific pain-relieving substance of willow bark. Buchner found that its special ingredient was an acid, which was extracted and used as a medicine. Unfortunately, the acid upset the stomach, and doctors found that many of their patients couldn't tolerate it.

In 1853, a French chemist called Charles Frederic Gerhard was able to neutralize the acid. He added an ingredient that reduced the irritation caused by the acid. Fortunately, this ingredient did not diminish its healing power, but Gerhard had no interest in marketing his discovery.

In 1899, a German chemist named Felix Hoffmann became interested in the willow bark medicine. Hoffman's father suffered from arthritis, and he found that the acid of the willow bark relieved his pain. Hoffman convinced his employer, Bayer, to market the acid. Bayer agreed, and in 1900, aspirin was patented and sold to the public.

B *Quinine* is found in the bark of the cinchona tree. Since the 1600s, it has been used to treat malaria, a potentially deadly disease carried by mosquitoes.

According to one legend, a Native American with a high fever was lost in an Andean jungle. When he drank from a pool of water, he was surprised by its very bitter taste. Realizing the water had been contaminated by the surrounding cinchona trees, he thought he had been poisoned. However, his fever abated, and he returned to his village to share his experience.

Europeans who visited the Andes in 1630 learned of the Native Americans' treatment for malaria. Soon another legend of the discovery of quinine spread throughout Europe. It involved the Countess of Chinchon, a noblewoman from Spain, who had visited Peru. While in Peru, the countess allegedly contracted a fever which was cured by the bark of a tree. The legend says that she returned to Spain in 1638 with the bark, thereby introducing quinine to Europe. In 1742 a Swedish scientist visited Peru and named the tree 'Cinchona' in honour of the noblewoman. However, the legend is not accurate because the Countess never had malaria and actually died in Colombia before ever returning to Spain.

READ

1 Read the *Reading tip*. Look at the photos and read the text quickly. Which plant (A–C) is used to cure …

1 malaria? ___
2 heart problems? ___
3 headaches? ___

2 🎧 (2.02) Read the text. Which medicine, *aspirin*, *quinine* or *digitalis*,

1 comes from a flower?
2 treats a disease caused by mosquitoes?
3 can be used to treat arthritis?
4 was first used in Peru?
5 was brought to the public by a German company?
6 reduces swelling caused by heart trouble?

3 Read the text again. Then choose the best answers.

1 Johann Buchner discovered that acid extracted from willow bark could relieve pain but also caused
   a stomach ache.
   b headaches.
   c swelling.
   d arthritis.

2 The German company Bayer started selling aspirin to the public
   a when Gerhard discovered how to neutralize the acid.
   b because they realized it was a good product to market.
   c because they wanted to patent it.
   d because the public demanded it.

3 Water with quinine in it
   a is extremely poisonous.
   b causes terrible fevers.
   c cured a noblewoman of malaria.
   d doesn't taste nice.

4 According to the legend, quinine was taken to Europe by
   a Native Americans from the Andes.
   b a noblewoman called the Countess of Chinchon.
   c a Swedish scientist in 1742.
   d Europeans who had visited Peru in the 18th century.

5 William Withering discovered that foxglove
   a could be poisonous.
   b gave the most effective medicine.
   c could be used to treat swelling caused by heart problems.
   d grows best in people's gardens.

6 Today doctors who prescribe digitalis
   a still have difficulty knowing the correct dose.
   b are still researching foxglove to find out how to make it safer.
   c do not have difficulty determining the correct dose.
   d do not give it to people with heart problems.

UNDERSTANDING IDEAS

Answer the questions. Look at the text, and use your own words and ideas.

1 Which of the three medications has been the most important? Why do you think so?
2 What other medical conditions do you know of that can be treated with medicines made from plants?
3 Do you agree with the introduction to the text that there may be cures for other serious diseases from plants found in jungles or rain forests?

VOCABULARY

The healing power of plants

Match the highlighted words in the text with these definitions.

1 Deadly or fatal.
2 To be affected by something without being harmed.
3 Became less strong.
4 An upper-class woman with a special title.
5 A specific amount.
6 To be removed from something.
7 A cure for a disease or illness.
8 Impure, made dangerous because of the addition of another substance.
9 Make something smaller or weaker.
10 Removed or reduced pain.
11 Breaking up something into smaller pieces or powder by pressing hard.
12 Stop something from having any effect.
13 Becomes bigger due to illness or injury.
14 Obtained exclusive rights to use or sell a product or invention.
15 A way of solving a problem using different methods until successful.

(●●○○ Workbook: page 36)

C *Digitalis*: One of the most important heart medications is made from a common flower called foxglove. Many people grow foxglove in their gardens, but it also grows in the wild – along roadsides, and in wooded areas.

In 1775, an English doctor named William Withering heard that a peasant woman was curing the swelling associated with heart problems using the foxglove flower. Withering wanted to learn more, so he visited her. The woman had no idea why foxglove worked, but it was clear that it relieved the swelling.

Withering began studying foxglove. Through trial and error, he learned that an effective medicine could be made from crushing the plant's dried leaves which were picked just before the plant produced flowers. He also discovered that foxglove could be lethal if the patient was given too much. In spite of his warnings about beginning with a low dose, many doctors prescribed the medicine in amounts that were too large and many people died. Today, the medicine, known as digitalis, has been researched very carefully and doctors are knowledgeable about the correct doses.

The healing power of plants

ACTIVATE

Complete these sentences with the correct form of the words from the box.

> abate contaminate crush diminish dose extract
> lethal neutralize noblewoman patent relieve remedy
> swelling tolerate trial and error

1 Many rivers in Europe are _____ with harmful chemical waste products from factories.
2 Oils are _____ from rare plants found in the Amazon jungle to make new medicines.
3 Due to the _____, my eye looks much bigger than normal.
4 The scientist couldn't find the solution to the problem but he solved it eventually through _____ .
5 My grandmother believes that hot lemon with honey is a good _____ for the flu.
6 To season this dish, I always _____ some garlic with salt, pepper and lemon juice before adding it to the mixture.
7 A lot of the world's natural resources are _____ at a much faster rate than ever before.
8 Stop! Don't eat those mushrooms! They are _____ – they look safe, but they are deadly.
9 The Duchess of Alba is a _____ from Spain.
10 The inventor had to _____ his invention to guarantee his rights.
11 If I have a bad headache, I take aspirin to _____ the pain.
12 If you don't feel better, you can take another _____ of medicine in twelve hours.
13 My body can't _____ wheat. I have to have a gluten-free diet.
14 We can't drive home until the sandstorm _____ . It's too dangerous.
15 We must intervene to _____ the dispute between the two governments; we can't have any tension whatsoever.

EXTEND

Word formation

1 Find the noun form of the following verbs taken from the reading text.

> contaminate cure extract neutralize patent relieve
> tolerate treat

2 Complete these sentences with the correct form of the word, noun or verb, from exercise 1.

1 Many cures for fatal diseases and conditions have been discovered in the twentieth century.
2 John goes to see his physiotherapist every Thursday to get _____ for his back injury.
3 Hot water, honey and lemon is good to _____ the symptoms of the common cold.

4 _____ of the earth's oceans is leading to the extinction of many marine species.
5 The police have zero _____ for any crime or violence.
6 The sale or copy of the innovative new device was protected by _____ .
7 Coal _____ in the UK has diminished to the extent that now only a few mines are in operation.
8 To _____ an acid, you need an alkaline.

The body and medical conditions

3 Label the parts of the body.

> appendix brain heart intestines kidney liver
> lungs pancreas spleen stomach

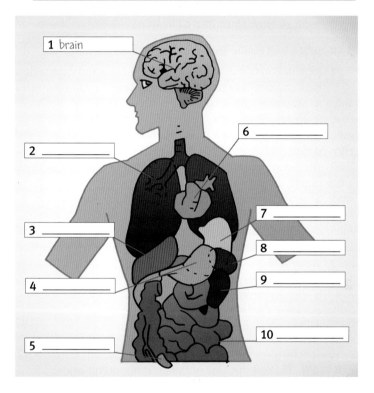

1 brain
2 _____
3 _____
4 _____
5 _____
6 _____
7 _____
8 _____
9 _____
10 _____

4 Match the conditions and diseases with the definitions.

> amnesia asthma cramps diabetes
> high blood pressure stroke tuberculosis ulcer

1 an infectious disease in which swellings appear on the lungs tuberculosis
2 a sore inside or outside the body, typically in the mouth or stomach
3 when blood travels around the body too quickly
4 a condition caused when a blood vessel in the brain bursts or is blocked
5 a brain condition when someone loses part or all of their memory
6 a condition due to a lack of insulin
7 a condition that makes it difficult to breathe
8 severe pains in the stomach or intestines

(●●●○○ Workbook: page 37)

Preparatory *it* as subject

EXPLORE

1 Read the text. What happened to Andrew? How does he stay healthy now?

University student Andrew Rigby tries to find the humour in the world around him. It isn't because he's a particularly funny person; he does it in order to keep healthy. When Andrew was 20, he had a stroke. He was on his way to class when a blood vessel in his brain exploded. Andrew collapsed, and it was fortunate that he was discovered shortly afterwards. It was also lucky that the university hospital was so near. Doctors were able to treat him quickly and save his life. Andrew said afterwards, 'I'd been feeling fine. It's incredible that there weren't any warning signs.'

It's unusual to be struck down by this condition at such a young age. Andrew was in good health, though he had been worried about his exams. He knew that it wasn't a good idea to study for hours on end, but it's very easy to lose track of time. One of his doctors had read about the lethal effects of stress on otherwise healthy people. The research showed that laughter could reduce a person's stress because it released tension. Although initially sceptical, Andrew eventually discovered that he felt less anxious when he was able to see the humorous side of stressful situations. 'It's amazing how much better I feel by laughing more. It sounds odd, I know.' For all the sophistication of the modern world, it's surprising how little we know about the brain.

2 Find three examples in the text of preparatory *it* followed by a clause, and three examples of preparatory *it* followed by an infinitive expression.

(Andrew collapsed, and) it was fortunate that he was discovered shortly afterwards.

3 Read the *Learn this!* box. Find two more examples from the text of preparatory *it* + clause or infinitive expression. Explain how the eight structures from exercises 2 and 3 are different from the other sentences in the text starting with *it*.

⬤⬤○○○ Grammar Reference: page 102

EXPLOIT

Preparatory *it* is generally not used when the subject is a noun phrase. We say:
Her new dress is really beautiful. [NOT *It's really beautiful her new dress.*]

1 Read the *Look out!* box. Then decide which sentence in each pair sounds more natural.

1 A It's great how quickly you picked up French.
  B It's great that quickly you picked up French.
2 A Their new house is wonderful.
  B It's wonderful their new house.
3 A There's a lot of cake left. To waste it is a pity.
  B There's a lot of cake left. It's a pity to waste it.
4 A It was annoying that he didn't recognize me.
  B It was annoying to he didn't recognize me.
5 A It's always strange when hear the sound of your own voice.
  B It's always strange to hear the sound of your own voice.
6 A The old cinema is going to close down.
  B It's going to close down the old cinema.
7 A It's going to rain. It would be a good idea to carry an umbrella.
  B It's going to rain. It would be a good idea that you carry an umbrella.
8 A It's interesting to agree with Peter about this.
  B It's interesting that you agree with Peter about this.

2 Correct each sentence by changing or deleting one word only.

1 The night before an exam, it is advisable that to sleep well.
2 The party was great, so it a pity that Joe couldn't come.
3 It doesn't worry me what that he thinks about the situation.
4 If you want to save money, it's not a good idea you to buy clothes.
5 I think is easy to learn anything if you practise regularly.
6 It's likely to that we'll be away for your birthday.
7 I love this beach. It's nice that see so many people here.
8 It's a strange feeling that when you think you've met someone before.

3 Write sentences from the prompts, using preparatory *it* followed by a clause or infinitive expression.

1 essential / prepare / thoroughly for a job interview
2 incredible / how hot / the weather is at the moment
3 given the day I've had / surprising / I still have / any energy left
4 important / you / take your time when reading the exam questions
5 at this time of day, / unusual / see / so many people around
6 normal / feel / nervous before your driving test
7 on Saturdays / great / have / a lie-in
8 after falling so far, / amazing / she got up / and walked away unhurt

⬤⬤○○○ Grammar Builder: page 103

⬤⬤○○○ Workbook: page 38

Sensations

VOCABULARY

1 Which adjectives from the box would you use to describe the items in the list 1–7 below? Match four of the adjectives with the photos (A–D).

> **Adjectives of sensation**
> aromatic bitter clammy deafening
> mouth-watering scorching slimy

1 damp clothing
2 bright sunshine
3 raw squid
4 strong coffee
5 dried herbs
6 freshly-baked cake
7 crashing waves

2 Read the sentences and study the expressions in bold. Which feelings are they describing? Match the expressions (1–5) with feelings (a–e).

1 Karen **felt lightheaded** when she stood up, so we helped her back into a chair in case she fainted.
2 Shelly **has got butterflies in her stomach** because she's going to give her speech in front of the class.
3 They **were feeling queasy** after eating oysters – perhaps they weren't very fresh.
4 Gavin **was under the weather** yesterday, but he is fine today, so it obviously wasn't anything serious.
5 I need to buy a packet of tissues because **I've got the sniffles**.

a feeling slightly ill   d feeling nauseous
b a runny nose   e feeling dizzy
c feeling nervous

3 Write five questions using the expressions in exercise 2. Ask and answer the questions with your partner.

When do you get butterflies in your stomach?
What makes you feel queasy?

(●●●●● Workbook: page 39)

LISTEN

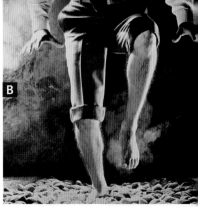

1 What is happening in photos (A–B)? Describe them using words and expressions from Vocabulary exercises 1 and 2. Do you think these activities are good for your health?

2 🎧 (2.03) Listen to the conversation at a health spa describing the therapies shown in photos (A–B). What are the benefits and the drawbacks of each treatment?

3 🎧 (2.03) Listen to the conversation again and answer the questions.

1 What is done to the mud to make it more comfortable?
2 What should you do if you feel faint?
3 Why are companies using spas?
4 What is the challenge in fire walking?
5 What should you do before walking on the coals?

SPEAK

Discuss the following questions with a partner and report your answers to the class.

1 Would you ever try fire walking or a mud bath? Why? Why not?
2 Read the descriptions about two alternative medicines, aromatherapy and acupuncture. With your partner, discuss what you think are the benefits and drawbacks of these alternative medicines.
3 Would you ever try aromatherapy or acupuncture? Why? Why not?

> **Aromatherapy**
> Aromatherapy is an alternative health therapy that uses substances such as plant oils and extracts to help a person's relaxation, powers of concentration and overall health. Depending on the substance, aromatherapy can be administered through infusions, breathing in oils through vapour, or through massages and baths. Typical oils include lemon, eucalyptus and sweet almond. The effectiveness of aromatherapy is still largely unproven by scientific research.
>
> **Acupuncture**
> Acupuncture is a form of alternative medicine that has been practised for thousands of years originating in China. It involves sticking sterilized needles into the body and manipulating them to relieve pain. While it is difficult to research the benefits of acupuncture, some medical authorities believe that there is enough positive evidence to increase the use of this alternative medicine and to encourage further scientific studies.

Preparatory *it* as object

EXPLORE

1 Read the text and identify the two types of doctors that are described. Which type of doctor do you prefer seeing? Why?

HERBAL MEDICINE

A trip to the doctor's surgery can be frustrating for people who believe that herbal medicine can cure a variety of illnesses. Many doctors make it clear that herbal medicine is not part of their treatment plan. Some of these doctors admit that they didn't always feel this way, and they remember their grandparents using plants as medicine. However, these doctors find it problematic to accept these natural remedies after years in medical school.

On the other hand, there are a number of doctors who do use herbal medicines in their treatment. Even after years of medical school, these doctors find it unnecessary to give up these natural remedies. They believe that there should be a balance between herbal medicine and modern medicine. This attitude makes it easier for people to follow a treatment. With a balanced approach, patients feel that they are contributing to both their recovery and well-being.

2 Read the *Learn this!* box and read the text again. Find two sentences in the text using preparatory *it* as the object.

> We can use preparatory *it* to introduce the object of a sentence. The object must be an infinitive or clause.
> We say:
> *Many doctors make it clear that herbal medicine is not part of their treatment plan.*
> [NOT *That herbal medicine is not part of their treatment plan many doctors make clear.*]
> We use: [subject] + [main verb] + [*it*] + [adjective or noun phrase] + [infinitive or clause]
> *I found it hard to follow his speech.*
> [NOT *To follow his speech I found hard.*]
> Note that we generally do not use preparatory *it* when there is no noun or adjective complement after the main verb.
> [NOT *I remember it that the sun always shone when we were young.*]

⬤⬤◦◦◦ Grammar Reference: page 102

EXPLOIT

1 Which sentences need *it*? Add *it* where necessary in these sentences.

1 Many people have made clear that they are unhappy with their medical care.
2 Some people forget that their first visit to a new doctor was a little frightening.
3 A lot of medical students find difficult to believe that alternative medicines can work in some cases.
4 Most doctors expect that traditional medicine will work better than herbal medicine.
5 Some parents find worrying to send their children to school when they are ill.
6 Many teachers accept that they can become ill from the infections that their students bring into class.

2 Complete the sentences (1–6) with the verbs from the box. Decide if the object clause requires *it* or *that*.

admit   believe   ~~find~~   make   recall   think

1 Doctors find it difficult to believe that their patients are knowledgeable about herbal medicines.
2 Older people _____ their diets were poor and lacking in nutrition when they were young.
3 Many experts _____ clear that most people do not know how to look after their health properly.
4 Many scientists _____ some alternative medicines have proven benefits.
5 Many people in China _____ acupuncture can be an effective treatment.
6 Some doctors _____ a waste of time to study alternative remedies such as aromatherapy.

⬤⬤⬤◦◦ Grammar Builder: page 103

⬤⬤⬤◦◦ Workbook: page 40

A blog

READ

1 Read the text. Why does Sally call her blog 'a strange encounter'?

Out and about in Tokyo – a strange encounter

by Sally Smith

12 May 2010

Last week, my family and I visited Japan for the first time. Everything was so different from England – it was like being on another planet. My eyes were like sponges, absorbing new sights with each glance. We went shopping for clothes. The young people we saw were like pictures from a magazine! They were wearing all sorts of fashions and they had obviously put a lot of effort into their hair and make-up. We walked from store to store for a very long time until we had run out of steam. All my energy had completely disappeared.

Then my sister noticed an oxygen bar. We had never seen one before. People were standing around small tanks of water, wearing face masks with hoses attached to the tanks, like some sort of alien creatures from a science fiction film – they were breathing pure oxygen. Apparently, breathing pure oxygen enhances your health and well-being. It can help you overcome stress and increase your energy levels. Although pure oxygen has no taste or smell, this oxygen had been flavoured by bubbling the oxygen through bottles containing aromatic solutions. We decided to give it a try. It was expensive, but it was worth every penny. We chose fruit cocktail – a mixture of apple, peach, lemon and banana. It was like taking deep breaths in an orchard full of fruit. After twenty minutes, with our batteries fully recharged, we were ready for another walk around the shops again!

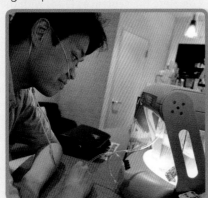

Travel is food for thought and our trip to Japan was no exception. Have any of you out there tried an oxygen bar?

Leave a comment:

2 What do you think about Sally's experience? What comment would you leave on her blog?

PREPARE

We often use metaphors and similes to make our writing more interesting. Similes compare things or people using *as* or *like*:
My eyes were like sponges.

Metaphors describe a thing or person by calling it something else directly.
... we had run out of steam.

1 Read the *Writing tip*. Identify two more similes and two metaphors in the text. Explain why the author has chosen them.

2 Match the beginnings and the ends of the sentences to make metaphors and similes.

1 Her eyes were	**a** as blind as a bat.
2 The children were	**b** like an angry lion.
3 That boring show was	**c** as lively as playful kittens.
4 The room's dust was	**d** as exciting as watching paint dry.
5 Without her spectacles, she is	**e** two blue sapphires.
6 The storm was	**f** a grey blanket of powder.

WRITE

1 Write one simile and one metaphor for each picture. Share your ideas with other people in your class.

2 Imagine you have been to one of the places in the pictures. Write a blog about your experience there. Use metaphors and similes. The title of your blog entry is 'A strange encounter'.

Paragraph 1	Describe the place you visited and what you saw there.
Paragraph 2	Describe a new experience that you had there.
Paragraph 3	Conclusion.

●●●●○ Workbook: page 41

You're cured!

LANGUAGE SKILLS

1 🎧 (2.04) Complete the dialogue with the words from the box. Then listen and check your answers.

> alternative aromatic cure even though neutralize make slimy swelling treatment what

Carol You look great, Tina. What's your secret?

Tina Well, it's this new ¹_____ I'm following for my skin. Although I'm allergic to loads of things, this seems to work. It's mud from the Dead Sea. I put it on my face and neck for 4–5 minutes, like a mask, then just relax.

Carol Mud! That's disgusting, it must be like putting raw squid on your face, really ²_____ and wet.

Tina Not at all. It is really soft, soothing and ³_____ – it smells like deep sea herbs.

Carol I'm sure that's ⁴_____ it says on the label. Tina, don't you read what the experts say? Many scientists ⁵_____ it clear that these ⁶_____ therapies don't work and are not based on any studies, though I must say, your complexion is much better.

Tina Well, actually, the minerals in the mud ⁷_____ the acidity in the skin. If you have a bad skin condition, it can reduce ⁸_____ and redness. Anyway, how's your asthma?

Carol It's starting to bother me again. ⁹_____ I'm seeing a specialist, there's not much he can do. I even have trouble with flowers if they are too overpowering.

Tina Really! Well, I don't think my mud will help to ¹⁰_____ your asthma, but you should try it anyway. It's really therapeutic.

2 Decide if the sentences are true or false. Correct the false sentences.

1 Tina went to the Dead Sea for her treatment.
2 Carol doesn't like raw sea food.
3 Carol suggests that Tina is quoting the product description.
4 Tina has a negative view of alternative therapies.
5 Carol doesn't feel that her doctor can help her.
6 Tina claims that mud is good for respiratory conditions.

3 Write sentences from the prompts, using preparatory *it* and a clause or infinitive expression.

1 strange / see / uncle / television
2 interesting / alternative medicine / have a better effect than conventional medicine
3 advisable / save money / when you want to buy a house or flat
4 a good idea / take an umbrella / the sky is dark grey
5 nice / visit sick people / hospital / cheer them up

Homophones

1 Check the meaning of the homophones in the box. Complete the sentences (1–6) with the correct form of the appropriate word.

> colonel / kernel complementary / complimentary council / counsel loot / lute pore / pour stationary / stationery

1 The lawyer gave excellent _____ to the government.
2 I must get more _____. I've run out of staples and post-its.
3 Remedies like acupuncture are considered to be _____ to traditional medicine.
4 She was fascinated by the illustrations and used to _____ over the book for hours.
5 My sister and I both play in the orchestra – I play the violin and she plays the _____.
6 At the last minute, the _____ decided to send in more troops.

Words with similar meanings

2 Look at the pairs of words that are often confused. Choose the correct word in sentences (1–4).

> imply / infer official / officious sensible / sensitive racial / racist

1 The TV programme **implied** / **inferred** that acupuncture was a waste of time.
2 Berta always comes out with nasty **official** / **officious** remarks. She's very unpopular.
3 This issue is delicate and requires **sensible** / **sensitive** treatment.
4 **Racial** / **Racist** equality is a key objective of the new government.

I CAN ...

Read the statements. Think about your progress and tick (✓) one of the boxes.

| ✳ | I need more practice. | ✳✳ | I sometimes find this difficult. | ✳✳✳ | No problem! |

	✳	✳✳	✳✳✳
I can understand a text about plant medicines.			
I can use preparatory *it* and end-weighting for emphasis.			
I can describe sensations and talk about medical treatments.			
I can use preparatory *it* as an object.			
I can write a blog, using metaphors and similes.			

(●●●●● Workbook: Self check pages 42–43)

Can birth order affect your personality?

BEFORE READING

1 How would you describe yourself? Which of the following groups of words (a–c) matches your personality best?

a	confident	determined	ambitious
b	quiet	easy-going	considerate
c	charming	creative	outgoing

2 Are you the eldest, middle or youngest child in your family? How do you think your personality may be affected by your position in the family?

3 Read the *Reading tip* and identify the experts in the article.

Reading tip

Expert opinions and studies are referred to in articles to validate or give authority to the facts and arguments presented. To identify an expert opinion, first of all scan the text and underline the names of experts referred to and any references to groups of specialists, for example, scientists or doctors. Next, look out for verbs that introduce opinions such as *claims*, *says*, *cites*, *believes*, *reports*, *states* or sentences that begin with *According to*, or *In the opinion of*. Sometimes expert opinions are quoted directly in the text, so look out for quotation marks.

Birth order and success

If asked, most parents would say that they love and treat all their children equally. However, according to several experts in psychology, a child's position in the birth order has an impact on his or her personality, behaviour, learning, and ultimately the child's career path. Conventional wisdom says that there are natural differences in the way that birth order affects people. For example, parents often keep tabs on first-born children, while children born later typically have fewer rules. Furthermore, many people believe that the youngest child seems to get away with murder because parents have experienced everything before.

But is there truth to this theory that birth order can affect our personalities? Ben Dattner, a psychologist based in New York, believes there is. He says, 'Depending on birth order, there are special roles within families, leading to different adaptation patterns and different personalities.' He believes that the stricter upbringing of first-born children leads to them being more extroverted and confident. They also tend to be more responsible because their parents rely on them to help with the younger children. As a result, first-born children usually have some power over younger siblings, who may even look up to them as substitute parents.

Second-born, and middle children, often feel overlooked by their parents, especially if another child is born before they are two years old. Second-born children are not given as much responsibility as first-born children. According to Dattner, they are more accommodating and they are also receptive to new experiences. Many second-born children are quiet, and they prefer to observe instead of participate in family dramas. The youngest child is usually the most creative. Dattner believes this is a result of the more relaxed attitude their parents often have towards them. They are given freedom to experiment in play and they often have fewer restrictions. However, youngest children tend to enjoy the attention they receive, and this can cause them to be manipulative to get what they want.

Clearly, birth order can affect personality, but what about career advancement and success? Michael Grose, author of *Why Firstborns Rule the World and Last Borns Want to Change It*, strongly believes that birth order affects career choices and, ultimately, earning potential. To support his opinion, Grose cites several studies which have shown that first-borns and only children usually reach higher educational goals, obtain greater status, and have greater financial

READ

1 🎧 (2.07) Read the text. Which birth order position (1–3) matches the personality descriptions (a–c)?

1 first-born child
2 second-born or middle child
3 youngest child

a They are often relaxed and want to fit in with what other people want.
b They love attention and like to get their own way.
c They make strict rules for themselves and want to do well at work.

2 Read the text again. Choose the best answers.

1 An example of the conventional wisdom stated in the article is that
   a the youngest child is the favourite.
   b first-born children have fewer rules than later-born children.
   c parents are more lenient with the youngest child.
   d the youngest child is most likely to commit murder.
2 Ben Dattner believes that
   a birth order has an effect on the way parents treat children.
   b parents try not to treat their children differently.
   c there isn't any truth in conventional wisdom.
   d children should be brought up strictly.
3 The youngest children often
   a have more responsibility.
   b like being the centre of attention.
   c have a relaxed attitude towards their parents.
   d look up to their older siblings.

4 According to Michael Grose, birth order explains
   a the relationship between siblings.
   b the relationship between children and their parents.
   c how higher education affects earning power.
   d what career choices we are likely to make.
5 In order to support the ideas in his book, Grose
   a reports his observations about birth order and career choices in his own family.
   b is planning to conduct studies about birth order and financial success.
   c has made his own theory about birth order.
   d relies on other people's studies on birth order and career choice.
6 Bill Gates is an example of somebody
   a whose birth order probably influenced his career choices.
   b whose birth order probably did not determine his career choices.
   c who is a youngest child who went into business.
   d who has a had less successful career than other middle children.

UNDERSTANDING IDEAS

Answer the questions. Look at the text, and use your own words and ideas.

1 Where are you in the birth order of your family? Is your personality similar to the description?
2 Do you think the theories on birth order are true for other people you know? Give examples to support your opinion.
3 What other careers do you think would be attractive to people with the personality of a first-born, a middle child, or a youngest child? Why?

VOCABULARY

Birth order and success

Match the highlighted words in the text with these definitions.

1 To do something bad without being punished.
2 Willing to listen to or to accept new ideas.
3 People who support or speak in favour of something.
4 The centre of attention.
5 Willing to help or cooperate.
6 Ignored or forgotten.
7 Explanations, information or beliefs generally accepted as true.
8 To be more important in determining something.
9 To move towards something that you are attracted to.
10 Mentions as a reason or example of something.
11 Controlling others to get what one wants.
12 To watch and supervise someone closely.
13 To admire or respect someone.
14 Brothers and sisters.
15 Only.

(●●○○○ Workbook: page 44)

success. They tend to be ambitious and disciplined compared with their younger siblings. They are usually determined to succeed, yet fearful of losing position and rank. They are more likely to have careers that require higher education, like medicine or engineering. If they choose a business-related career, they are more likely to reach the senior management level.

Second-born or middle children are good at negotiation, peacemaking and compromise, Grose says. They are easy-going and are usually closer to friends than to family. They tend to have excellent people skills, so they may enter fields such as law enforcement, counselling, or marketing. Youngest children love the limelight and are used to being in it. They are charming, creative and have a good sense of humour. According to Grose, they often gravitate toward artistic careers. Because of this, they may earn less money than their older siblings. However, not all youngest children are interested in the arts. They're also successful in journalism, advertising, and professional sports.

Although Grose and Dattner are strong advocates of birth order differences, it is important to acknowledge that birth order is not the sole determiner of an individual's career or earning power. For example, Bill Gates, founder of Microsoft and one of the richest men in the world, is a middle child, thus showing that other factors can override birth order in determining one's career and financial success.

Birth order and success

ACTIVATE

Complete these sentences with the correct form of the words in the box.

> accommodating advocate cite conventional wisdom
> get away with murder gravitate keep tabs on
> limelight look up to manipulative overlook override
> receptive siblings sole

1 I need to _____ my money as I've already spent too much.
2 The staff at the hotel were extremely _____ . They did everything we asked.
3 If you become a famous celebrity, you can expect to be in the _____ with everyone looking at you.
4 Health considerations _____ financial gain, so we're closing the factory.
5 Mrs Anderson is _____ to students' suggestions, so you should speak to her.
6 According to the _____ of 1400, the world was flat.
7 People in my family _____ toward scientific fields. My mum is a doctor and my dad is a chemist.
8 My teacher is a strong _____ of traditional grammar lessons.
9 Don't _____ the material at the bottom of the page. There will be an exam question on it.
10 My younger sister can _____ because she is the favourite child.
11 Many teens _____ famous athletes and want to play as well as them.
12 In his article on the origins of Sumerian architecture, Professor Hartley _____ three examples.
13 I don't like concerts very much. The _____ reason I came was to support your band.
14 Josh wasn't truthful with us. He was being very _____ .
15 Sometimes I wish I had _____ , but I enjoy having all of my parents' attention.

EXTEND

Personality synonyms

1 Replace the words in bold with a synonym from the box.

> aloof confident determined opinionated reliable
> stubborn unpredictable

1 Jen is quite **stand-offish**. She's never friendly. aloof
2 You can confide in Jake. He's very **trustworthy**.
3 It's not worth discussing anything with Helen – she's so **dogmatic**.
4 Simon studies a lot, so he is very **self-assured** when speaking out in class.
5 Mr Barr is **capricious**. He accepted Anna's excuse, but rejected the same one from Alan.

6 Betty is very **resolute**. She applied for the scholarship again after being rejected.
7 Oscar can be **uncompromising**. He refused to change his plan although there's an easier option.

Personality idioms

2 Check the meaning of the idioms in bold. Match them with their definitions (a–h).

1 Louise is a **shrinking violet**. She would rather watch a DVD alone than meet new people. d
2 Maya is such **a wet blanket**. She always stops me from playing innocent jokes on people.
3 Harry and Jim are **like chalk and cheese**. Harry is outgoing and athletic. Jim is aloof and studious.
4 Although we'd had a huge argument, Philip was **as nice as pie** when I saw him.
5 I'm glad we invited Thomas. He's **the life and soul of the party**.
6 Annabelle has **a good head on her shoulders**. I'd take her advice if I were you.
7 Students tend not to misbehave in Mr Bryson's classes because he has **a very short fuse**.
8 Social scientists have to be **thick-skinned**, their studies are frequently criticized.

a kind and friendly, especially when you are not expecting it
b completely different from each other
c someone who doesn't want others to have fun
d someone who is very shy
e becomes angry easily
f the most amusing person at a party
g able to take criticism or correction without becoming upset
h someone who is sensible

3 Describe the scenes in the pictures. Use the idioms from exercise 2.

●●○○○ Workbook: page 45

Ellipsis with *either / too*

EXPLORE

1 🎧 (2.08) **Read and listen to the dialogue. Why is Jade going to the career guidance office?**

Jade What did you think about the career and personality test we took last week?

Pam It was interesting, but I haven't spoken to the career guidance counsellor yet.

Jade I haven't, either. But I need to speak to her because I thought my results were confusing!

Pam Did you? Mine seemed to fit my personality perfectly.

Jade Really? Mine didn't. Perhaps I'm not reading them correctly.

Pam The explanations are on the yellow paper, but you'll need some time to read through them.

Jade Yellow paper? I didn't receive a yellow paper.

Pam That's strange. I did.

Jade Should I get one at the career guidance office before I meet with the guidance counsellor?

Pam I would. You won't be prepared without it.

Jade You're right. I won't.

Pam I think the office is open late today.

Jade Yes, it is. Thanks! I'd better go now.

2 Read the *Learn this!* box. Then read the dialogue again and find six more examples of ellipsis. Identify the main verb that has been omitted.

LEARN THIS!

Sometimes we omit words to avoid repetition. This is called ellipsis. A common form of ellipsis involves omitting the main verb and simply using the auxiliary verb. We frequently use *either* and *too* with ellipsis. We use *either* when the first statement is negative and the response is also negative.

I haven't spoken to the career guidance counsellor yet.
Paul hasn't, either. [= Paul hasn't spoken to the counsellor yet]

Use *too* when the first statement is positive and the response is also positive.

I think personality tests are useful.
I do, too.

We don't use *either* or *too* when the response contradicts the original statement.

I think personality tests are useful.
I don't. [= I don't think they are useful.]

●●●○○ Grammar Reference: page 104

EXPLOIT

1 Complete the sentences with *either*, *too*, or leave blank if nothing is needed.

1 Fiona has two sisters. I do, too.
2 Jason's brother is annoying. Fortunately, mine isn't _____.
3 Kelly doesn't have a large family, and James doesn't _____.
4 Deborah wanted to see a film last night, but I didn't _____.
5 Your class is studying in the library today, and ours is _____.
6 Cameron doesn't believe the studies on birth order are accurate, and I don't _____.

2 Complete the response to each statement, using ellipsis.

1 A I love psychology. It's my favourite subject.
  B I _____. I think it's boring.
2 A Sara and I haven't read the assignment for today's class.
  B I _____. There's some useful information in there.
3 A Should I bring a doctor's note for missing last week's exams?
  B I _____. Mr Cole is very strict about exam absences.
4 A Should I buy that new phone everyone is talking about?
  B I _____. I've heard it's got a lot of problems.
5 A My research paper was almost 20 pages long.
  B Mine _____. It was only 15.

3 Match the sentences halves.

1 She said that she would call, but
2 She said that she would lend me her car, and
3 He is angry with Samantha, but
4 Carly isn't happy with her test score, and
5 Dan has applied for university, and

a I have, too.
b I'm not, either.
c she did.
d she didn't.
e I'm not.

4 Write five statements about yourself, using different tenses. Compare your statements with a partner and report their situation, using ellipsis.

I prefer people that like going out.
Jane does, too. / Jane doesn't.

●●●○○ Grammar Builder: page 105

●●●○○ Workbook: page 46

All about me

VOCABULARY

1 Are the descriptions positive or negative? Write *P* (*positive*) or *N* (*negative*).

1 Jane is not very considerate of her friends' feelings. N
2 Kevin is very down to earth, so I'm sure he will give you good advice. __
3 Evan is an outstanding athlete, but he isn't conceited. __
4 Why is Amanda wearing those expensive sunglasses in class? She's very pretentious. __
5 Don't expect a quick-witted reply from Alan. He's very serious and dull! __
6 Everybody likes Alice because she is very charismatic. __
7 My brother is such a happy-go-lucky child. __
8 Daniel is well known for his spontaneous ideas, even though they get him into trouble. __

2 Complete the blog profiles with words from the box.

> charismatic conceited considerate down to earth
> happy-go-lucky pretentious quick-witted spontaneous

Karina George
I enjoy doing things without a lot of planning, so I think I'm a ¹_____ person. My friends also think I'm ²_____ because I don't worry about the future. I know things will be fine, even if they're not going well at the moment. I value friends who are ³_____ since it's important to be sensible and realistic in life. I don't have time for ⁴_____ people – I can tell if someone is trying to impress me by appearing important or by wearing expensive clothing or jewellery.

Desmond Fenty
If more people thought about others, there'd be fewer problems in the world, so I think being ⁵_____ is one of the most important things in life. My favourite quality about my character is that I'm ⁶_____ – I'm fairly intelligent, and I can see the funny side of things easily. At least my friends have told me as much, and that's a great compliment! I also think I'm quite ⁷_____ because people seem to like me and I make friends easily. Actually, I've been called ⁸_____ but I don't believe this is true because I've never thought I'm better than anyone else.

(●●●●● **Workbook: page 47**)

LISTEN

1 🎧 (2.09) Listen to the interview about blood type personality theory. Complete the chart with the characteristics associated with each of the four blood types.

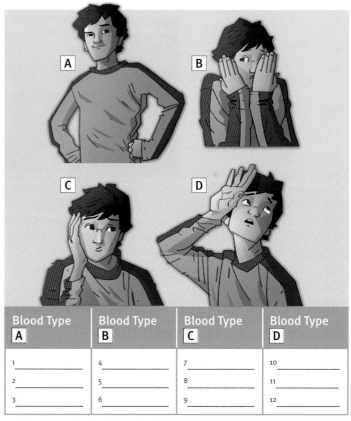

Blood Type A	Blood Type B	Blood Type C	Blood Type D
1 _____	4 _____	7 _____	10 _____
2 _____	5 _____	8 _____	11 _____
3 _____	6 _____	9 _____	12 _____

2 🎧 (2.09) Listen again. Answer the questions.

1 Where is blood type theory popular?
2 Why do some employers want to know a job candidate's blood type?
3 What is the interviewer's blood type? Does Dr Miller think that the theory is accurate for her? Why?
4 Why does the villain of a story often have blood type AB?

SPEAK

1 Choose three adjectives from Vocabulary exercise 2 to describe your personality. Support your description with examples.

> I'm not very spontaneous because I tend to plan activities carefully in advance.

> I think I'm quite a down to earth person because I think of solutions quickly.

2 Which blood type are you? Is the personality description true for you? If you don't know your blood type, which description best matches your personality?

3 How would you describe your parents' personalities? Which personality traits do you think you've inherited from them? Give examples to support your opinion.

GRAMMAR

Ellipsis in comparisons

EXPLORE

1 Read the text. Have you got a Type A or Type B personality?

No two people have the same personality, but some social scientists believe most people can be classified as a Type A or a Type B personality. Type A people are more comfortable with multi-tasking than Type B people are. For example, a Type A person can read a book while watching TV, but a Type B person would be satisfied doing just one activity. This means that Type A people often take on more work than is sensible, whereas Type B people tend to know their limits at work. They can do a good job, and although they don't work as fast, they don't spend more time than is necessary on a project.

Type A people need more control over their lives than Type B people do. This often leads to an increase in stress levels for Type A people since it is impossible to have control over many things in life. As a result, Type A people are believed to be at greater risk of developing heart disease than Type B people are.

Nowadays, some social scientists don't have as much confidence in the Type A and Type B personality distinction. After giving a large number of people personality tests, the results were more uncertain than scientists had expected. As a result, these scientists now believe that many people are actually Type AB, showing characteristics of both Type A and B personalities in different situations.

2 Read the text again and underline the comparisons.

> **LEARN THIS!**
>
> We can use ellipsis after *than* and *as* in comparative structures.
> *Some people are happier about being busy than other people are (happy about being busy).*
> *Students sometimes learn more grammar than (it) is necessary (to learn).*
>
> Verbs without an auxiliary verb are replaced with *do* or *did*.
> *Excellent students don't struggle as much with exams (as other students do).*
> *People living in cities spend more money on clothes than people living in the countryside do. [NOT people in the countryside spend]*

3 Read the *Learn this!* box. Which words have been omitted from the sentences that you underlined?

(●●●◎◎ Grammar Reference: page 104)

EXPLOIT

1 Cross out or replace the unnecessary words in each sentence.

1 Down to earth people are less likely to make mistakes than happy-go-lucky people are ~~to make mistakes~~.
2 Type A people often suffer from more stress than Type B people suffer from.
3 In the 19th century people paid less attention to personality than they pay attention to today.
4 Some languages have complicated grammar rules to learn, but studying English isn't as difficult as studying other languages.
5 There were higher numbers of Type AB than scientists originally thought there to be.
6 The essay on personality types was longer than it was necessary to be.

2 Reorder the words to make sentences.

1 there / as / applicants / weren't / last year / many / as
There weren't as many applicants as last year.
2 than / he / more / fails / is / assignments / allowed
3 necessary / collected / more / than / data / was / they
4 we / does / do / experiments / than / more / my sister's class
5 took / recommended / more / she / medicine / was / than
6 more / the results / than / to be / them / expected / were / significant / we

3 Write sentences comparing the following things. Use ellipsis where possible.

1 scientists / politicians
Scientists are more truthful than politicians.
2 chemistry / history
3 charismatic people / shy people
4 mobile phones / laptops
5 people in the 19th century / people today
6 my grandparents / my parents

(●●●◎◎ Grammar Builder: page 105)

(●●●◎◎ Workbook: page 48)

A comparison and contrast essay

READ

Read Josie's essay comparing herself with her sister Emma. Complete the chart with information from the text.

Sisters, but more different than similar

It stands to reason that most siblings share some basic personality characteristics. Siblings have the same parents, so they have a common biological heritage. They are raised in the same environment, so their living conditions are similar. Although my sister Emma and I have the same parents and shared a home for our entire childhood and teenage years, our personalities are more different than similar.

The first basic difference in our personalities is our comfort level with others. I am extremely outgoing. I enjoy meeting new people, and I find it easy to talk to them. Once my flight was delayed, and by the time we boarded the plane, I had become friends with many of the other passengers. In contrast, Emma is very timid. She is even shy around our family. At our cousin's wedding last year she didn't feel at ease because she hadn't seen the family in ages.

Another way in which our personalities are more different than similar is our sense of humour. I think that this is based on our intelligence. Emma is extremely intelligent, and when she is confident enough to speak to others, she is very quick-witted. She can immediately think of an intelligent response and she is good at playing with words. On the other hand, I am not as intelligent as Emma. I can never think of anything witty to say. While Emma enjoys humour in clever uses of language, I find physical gags and jokes funny.

Despite being siblings, Emma and I are more different than similar. This is demonstrated in our comfort level with others as well as our senses of humour. I am extroverted and enjoy physical humour, whereas Emma is shy but quick-witted with her humour. Nevertheless, we are still close.

Introduction:
Josie and Emma's personalities: _____
Difference 1: _____
Josie's personality: _____
Emma's personality: _____
Difference 2: _____
Josie's personality: _____
Emma's personality: _____

PREPARE

Writing tip: comparing and contrasting

Contrasting points can be presented using linking words such as *although, despite, on the other hand, while, whereas,* and *in contrast*. These expressions are used to balance two equally important facts or ideas that contrast but do not contradict each other. *While* and *whereas* show a contrast within one sentence.

On the other hand and *in contrast* typically use two sentences to show a contrast.

While Josie is comfortable in large groups, Emma is not.

Emma enjoys school whereas Josie is more interested in sport.

Josie always feels at ease talking to new people. On the other hand, Emma is nervous speaking to people she doesn't know.

Emma loves to read long historical novels. In contrast, Josie prefers magazines or short stories.

1 Read the *Writing tip*. Find the contrasting sentences in the text.

2 Rewrite the sentences, using the expressions in the brackets.

   1 Isabella's best subject is chemistry. Her brother's best subject is French. (while)

   2 Rob is the best basketball player at school. Joe, his brother, is hopeless at sport. (in contrast)

   3 Marissa can sing extremely well. She's no good at maths. (on the other hand)

   4 My parents read the newspaper daily. I only read the news online. (whereas)

   5 Learning languages requires a good memory. Learning maths requires problem-solving skills. (while)

WRITE

1 Think about the personality of a friend or family member and contrast it with your own. Organize your ideas, using the writing plan.

> **Introduction**
>   Personalities compared
> **Paragraph 2**
>   Similarity or difference 1
>   Your personality
>   Friend's / Family member's personality:
> **Paragraph 3**
>   Similarity or difference 2
>   Your personality
>   Friend's / Family member's personality
> **Conclusion**

2 Write 200–250 words contrasting the personality of a friend or family member with your own. Use your notes from exercise 1 to help you. Use comparing and contrasting phrases.

●●●●○ Workbook: page 49

What type are you?

LANGUAGE SKILLS

1 🎧 (2.10) Complete the dialogue with the words from the box. Then listen and check your answers.

> can   chalk and cheese   either   inviting   is
> reliable   pretentious   stand-offish   sure   too

Andy Have you met the new student in our chemistry class?

George You mean the guy that always wears a pair of silly sunglasses on top of his head?

Andy That's the one. His name's Juan. I just think he seems so [1]_____.

George Yes, I do [2]_____. But I also think that maybe deep down he's very nervous and shy.

Andy I'm not [3]_____. The other day I smiled and tried to speak to him, but he was very [4]_____ and he didn't even say hello.

George Well, maybe he can't speak English very well.

Andy Actually, he [5]_____! I heard him talking to Brendon the other day.

George Brendon? What do they have in common? They must be like [6]_____!

Andy I know. Brendon is much more down to earth than Juan [7]_____. And Brendon seems much more [8]_____ and trustworthy than he does.

George True. But anyway, we should do something to get to know Juan a bit better. How about [9]_____ him for coffee tomorrow? I haven't got any classes in the afternoon.

Andy No, I haven't, [10]_____. Let's speak to Juan tomorrow morning.

2 Answer the questions.

1 What class do Andy and George have together?
2 What doesn't Andy like about Juan?
3 How does George explain Juan's behaviour?
4 According to Andy, how are Brendon and Juan different?
5 How does George want to resolve the situation?
6 What adjectives would you use to describe the personalities of Andy and George?

3 Choose the correct answer.

1 Jane was more upset than _____.
   a John.   b John is.   c John was upset.
2 He's trying to do more exercise _____
   a than it is safe.   b than safe.   c than is safe.
3 I don't agree with the results of the survey.
   a I don't.   b Me, too.   c I don't, either.
4 The test was more difficult _____
   a than we expected.   b than we expected it.
   c than it was expected.
5 We had a better holiday this year _____ last year.
   a than we had   b than had we   c than we were

Words with multiple meanings

1 Some words have more than one meaning. Match each of the words with two definitions.

> pitch   platform   quack   school   scratch   shoot

1 scratch to make or remove a mark
2 _____ a group of fish
3 _____ the sound that a duck makes
4 _____ to teach or educate someone
5 _____ to make a film
6 _____ the part of a plant that grows from the ground
7 _____ how high or low a sound is
8 _____ to make a noise by rubbing
9 _____ a place to express your opinions in public
10 _____ a person who claims to have medical knowledge but doesn't
11 _____ the raised area beside a track at a train station
12 _____ an area of ground marked for playing games

2 Words can have different meanings when they are used in different fields, such as science, sport or music. What fields are these words used in? Circle two answers for each word.

1 **cap**: (sports,) farming, (clothing)
2 **club**: sport, farming, entertainment
3 **line**: manufacturing, communications, entertainment
4 **plug**: entertainment, medicine, electrical engineering
5 **stand**: banking, politics, music
6 **wing**: entertainment, buildings, transport

3 Choose two words from exercise 2. Write example sentences to show the words in different fields.

We had to wear a cap as part of our uniform.
He won his first cap in the match against Germany in the World Cup.

I CAN ...

Read the statements. Think about your progress and tick (✓) one of the boxes.

| ✷ | I need more practice. | ✷✷ | I sometimes find this difficult. | ✷✷✷ | No problem! |

	✷	✷✷	✷✷✷
I can understand a text about personality and birth order.			
I can use ellipsis with *either* and *too*.			
I can describe and talk about people's personalities.			
I can use ellipsis in comparisons.			
I can write a comparison and contrast essay.			

●●●○○ Workbook: Self check pages 50–51

The Lost World
by Arthur Conan Doyle

Biography

Arthur Conan Doyle is best known as the author of the *Sherlock Holmes* detective stories. He was born in Edinburgh in 1859, and trained and worked as a doctor before he started writing. He wrote historical fiction and science fiction, as well as his famous detective novels. *The Lost World* was published in 1912, twenty-four years after his first *Sherlock Holmes* story had appeared.

Early next morning we were again afoot, and found that the character of the country had changed once again. Behind us was the wall of bamboo, as definite as if it marked the course of a river. In front was an open plain, sloping slightly upwards and dotted with clumps of tree-ferns, the whole curving before us until it ended in a long, whale-backed ridge. This we reached about midday, only to find a shallow valley beyond, rising once again into a gentle incline which led to a low, rounded skyline. It was here, while we crossed the first of these hills, that an incident occurred which may or may not have been important.

Professor Challenger, who, with the two local Indians, was in the van of the party, stopped suddenly and pointed excitedly to the right. As he did so we saw, at the distance of a mile or so, something which appeared to be a huge grey bird flap slowly up from the ground and skim smoothly off, flying very low and straight, until it was lost among the tree-ferns.

'Did you see it?' cried Challenger, in exultation. 'Summerlee, did you see it?'

His colleague was staring at the spot where the creature had disappeared.

'What do you claim that it was?' he asked.

'To the best of my belief, a pterodactyl.'

Summerlee burst into derisive laughter. 'A ptero-fiddlestick!' said he. 'IT was a stork, if ever I saw one.'

Challenger was too furious to speak. He simply swung his pack upon his back and continued upon

his march. Lord John came abreast of me, however, and his face was more grave than was his wont. He had his Zeiss glass in his hand.

'I focused it before it got over the trees,' said he. 'I won't undertake to say what it was, but I'll risk my reputation as a sportsman that it wasn't any bird that ever I clapped eyes on in my life.'

So there the matter stands. Are we really just at the end of the unknown, encountering the outlying pickets of this lost world of which our leader speaks? I give you the incident as it occurred and you will know as much as I do. It stands alone, for we saw nothing more which could be called remarkable.

1 🎧 (2.14) **Read the text. Choose the correct answer.**

1 The story takes place **outdoors** / **indoors**.
2 The leader of the expedition is **Professor Challenger** / **the narrator**.
3 On the expedition, Professor Challenger hopes to find rare **birds** / **dinosaurs**.
4 Summerlee **supports** / **disagrees** with Challenger's opinion about what they have seen.
5 Lord John is inclined to agree with **Challenger** / **Summerlee** about the sighting.

2 Answer the questions. Look at the text, and use your own words and ideas to explain your answers.

1 What kind of place is the 'Lost World'?
2 Why does Professor Summerlee make fun of Professor Challenger's ideas?
3 What is the role of the narrator in the expedition?
4 How do you think the story ends?
5 In your opinion, does the topic of dinosaurs make a good adventure story? Why? Why not?

3 Imagine that you were participating in the expedition with Professor Challenger. Write a paragraph explaining why you have joined the expedition and what you hope to find. Describe what equipment and supplies you would need.

Cultural icons

READ

1 Look at the photo of a typical American diner. What type of food is on the menu? Read the text and find out.

Authentic diners are classic cultural icons of the US and Canada. They are often established in pre-fabricated buildings and offer a range of typical American food. The first diners were located in the north-east of the United States and they soon became popular with factory workers who wanted a quick meal or a cup of coffee before or after their night shifts. Newspaper employees who also worked late into the evening tended to gravitate to diners after sending their articles off to the printers. As a result, the diner was open for business 24 hours a day to accommodate these workers.

Diners today are still open for business around the clock, and have maintained their casual atmosphere. As a result, they serve a wide range of customers. Urban diners cater to businesspeople, students, and workers between shifts. Diners along main roads and highways are popular with travellers or lorry drivers, who haul goods thousands of kilometres across the US. And in rural areas, the diner is a good place for agricultural workers to gather and to discuss crop prices and other farming issues.

Regardless of the location, the interiors of diners have a distinct look. There is typically a glass case displaying pies or cakes. In addition, there is a long counter where customers sit side-by-side. The counter is preferred by people looking for a coffee or quick snack such as a slice of cake. Customers who are alone tend to sit at the counter so that they don't need to occupy a table intended for two or more people.

In addition to their distinctive interior look, diners also tend to offer similar menu items. Grilled or fried food such as burgers and chips are offered at nearly every diner. Similarly, nearly every diner serves breakfast on demand, so if you fancy a cheese omelette, waffles, and coffee at midnight, a diner will satisfy your cravings. Ice cream dishes and other desserts are also specialties of many diners. The ice cream float is a popular diner favourite; it consists of vanilla ice cream in a glass of cola or other carbonated soft drink.

2 Read the text again. Answer the questions.

1 Why were the first diners popular with newspaper employees and factory workers?
2 What types of customers are more typical these days?
3 What are two common features of diner interiors?

3 Answer the questions. Use your own words and ideas.

1 Are there any iconic places to eat in your country? What are they like?
2 Would you go to a diner to eat? Why or why not?
3 Does the ice cream float sound appetizing to you? Why or why not?

LISTEN

1 🎧 (2.15) Look at the photos of some of Britain's cultural icons. Do you know what they are? Listen and find out.

2 🎧 (2.15) Listen again. Simon is planning a trip for his American friend Brad. Tick the things that Brad wants to do in London.

1 Go on a double-decker bus. ☐
2 Visit the British Museum. ☐
3 See the changing of the guard. ☐
4 Eat British food. ☐
5 Visit the Tower of London. ☐
6 Take photos of the Beefeater guards. ☐

WRITE AND SPEAK

1 Imagine you are going to plan a tour of your city or country for a foreign visitor. With a partner, plan an itinerary for the visitor. Make sure you include some cultural icons. Use the list to help you:

- ancient wonders
- places of natural beauty
- museums
- historical places
- popular shopping districts
- popular restaurants

2 Prepare a travel guide describing the cultural icons you have chosen. Design the information as a poster or a web page. Explain the itinerary with maps, background information and travel recommendations.

Food, glorious food!

Food for thought

BEFORE READING

1 Look at the different types of food (A–B). How do you think they have been produced? Do you think the production methods have a positive or negative impact on the environment?

From farmland to the supermarket

In many countries in the latter half of the twentieth century, the general consensus in the agriculture community was that food should be easy to buy and as inexpensive as possible. In order to achieve this, farmland needed to produce more crops, and food shopping needed to be more convenient. This attitude did not focus on the well-being of people or the environment. Fortunately, a number of successful pioneering projects show us that it's possible to have a balance between food demands and caring for the environment.

FAF (Fazenda Ambiental Fortaleza) – Brazil
Since the 1900s, the Barretto family has owned a coffee farm in Brazil. In 2002 they began transforming it into a model farm that uses environmentally sustainable techniques.

FAF now uses two methods for growing coffee: organic and natural. Both methods differ significantly from the conventional method in which the coffee plants are spaced far apart so that a tractor can drive between them. The tractor spreads fertilizers to make the coffee plants grow and herbicides to kill unwanted plants around the coffee crop. In contrast, in the organic method, the only fertilizers used are natural. They are made from collecting the waste of the farm's cows. Furthermore, plants such as bananas, pumpkins, and salad greens are grown between the coffee plants to make the soil richer. They are

then sold throughout Brazil. In the natural method, nothing is done to the coffee plant. The plants are grown close together and the only intervention of the farmers is the harvesting of the beans.

All the coffee from FAF is recognized as organic by the International Foundation for Organic Agriculture. As a result, it can be sold throughout the world as an organic product.

Duchy Originals – UK
Back in the 1980s, the UK's Prince of Wales recognized that the long-term future of our environment and farmland was extremely important and should not be sacrificed. In 1986, he arranged for part of one of his country farms to be converted into organic farmland. Pleased with the results, he commissioned some research into whether there was a market for the organic food produced from all natural ingredients and sustainable farming techniques designed to preserve the health of the land.

The results of the market research were positive, and in 1992, a biscuit made from organic oats was marketed to the British public under the name Duchy Originals. In 1999, Duchy Originals began to make a profit, and The Prince donated all of it to various charities. Duchy Originals now markets over 200 products throughout the United Kingdom, ranging from bakery goods to meat; and over six million pounds has been donated to the Princes' Charities Foundation.

Sekem – Egypt
In the 1970s, an Egyptian, Dr Ibrahim Abouleish, bought some land in the desert bordered by farmland. His mission was to develop it and to improve crop harvests using biodynamic methods. Biodynamic farming is a sustainable farming method that uses natural fertilizers to maintain the balance between soil and plants. Abouleish named his agricultural venture *Sekem*. He gave the Bedouins from the area work and allowed them to build homes on the land.

In 1983, Sekem began marketing organic herbal teas such as mint and chamomile in Egypt. Sekem guaranteed organic herbs in pre-measured packets, making them more convenient.

Sekem expanded its organic food production, and in 1988 Libra Egypt was formed to export organic Egyptian fruits and vegetables to Europe. To serve the European demand, many farms throughout Egypt switched to biodynamic farming methods. Sekem began to advise many of these farms and leased more land of its own. In addition to this, some of the company's profits were invested in social projects, including schools for children and an adult education centre.

READ

Reading tip

When an unknown word prevents your understanding of a part of a text, first of all decide what type of word it is: a noun, a verb, an adjective, etc. What is the function of the word? Does it describe something, in a positive or negative way, or is it an action or a name that is associated with the topic? Then read around the word, using the context to help you guess its meaning.

1 Read the *Reading tip*. Find these words in the text and guess their meaning from their context.

1 organic 2 conventional 3 oats 4 biodynamic

2 🎧 (2.16) Read the text. Which food company or companies is each sentence about? Write *FAF* (Fazenda Ambiental Fortaleza), *D* (Duchy Originals), or *S* (Sekem).

1 It advises other farmers on organic farming methods.
2 It has been in business for over a hundred years.
3 It sells its food primarily to people in one country.
4 It gives company money to charities or other social programmes to help others.
5 It grows fruit and vegetables as a secondary crop.
6 It entered the organic food market by making biscuits.

3 Read the text again. Choose the best answers.

1 In the latter half of the twentieth century, most people believed
  a food needed to be healthier.
  b there should be more environmental protection.
  c the profit was more important than the environment.
  d price and easy availability of food were the most important things.
2 FAF (Fazenda Ambiental Fortaleza)
  a began growing coffee in 2002.
  b now only produces coffee.
  c was bought by the Barretto family in 2002.
  d did not use to use sustainable farming techniques.
3 Both farming techniques now used by FAF
  a rely on a tractor and other farm equipment.
  b only put natural fertilizers on the coffee plants.
  c produce coffee that is recognized as organic.
  d kill the unwanted plants between the coffee plants.
4 The Prince of Wales' main reason for starting Duchy Originals Food Company was
  a to produce food using farming techniques that protected the environment.
  b to earn a profit so that he could donate the money to different charities.
  c to grow and provide healthier food for British people.
  d to create a demand for all-natural foods in the UK.

5 Biodynamic farming
  a was developed by the Bedouins living near Dr Abouleish's farm.
  b keeps a balance between the soil and plants by using natural fertilizers.
  c is the origin of the name of Sekem, Dr Abouleish's company.
  d is the most common farming method used throughout Egypt.
6 Sekem's first business activity was
  a marketing herbal teas throughout Egypt.
  b selling fruits and vegetables throughout Europe.
  c advising other farms on how to change to organic farming.
  d introducing biodynamic farming to Europe.

UNDERSTANDING IDEAS

Answer the questions. Look at the text, and use your own words and ideas.

1 Is it important for you to know if your food is organic? Why?
2 Would you be willing to pay more for organic food? Why? Why not?
3 Are there any organic food companies based in your country? What do they produce? Are they popular?
4 Do you think it's important for companies to support charities or social projects? Why? Why not?

VOCABULARY

From farmland to the supermarket

Match the highlighted words in the text with these definitions.

1 Gave money to charitable organizations.
2 A farming method using natural products and energy to protect the environment.
3 A task, job or objective that you think is your duty to carry out.
4 Involving new ideas or methods.
5 The cutting and gathering of crops at a certain time of year.
6 An opinion that all members of a group agree with.
7 Chemicals that are poisonous to plants.
8 Changed or made something change from one thing to another.
9 To be different.
10 An action to improve something.
11 Substances added to soil to make plants grow better.
12 Rented out to other parties for a period of time.
13 The general health and happiness of a person or a thing.
14 A business project or activity.
15 Abandoned something that is important or valuable in order to do something that seems more important.

⬤⬤⬤◯◯ Workbook: page 52

From farmland to the supermarket

ACTIVATE

Complete the sentences with the correct form of the words from the box.

consensus differ donate fertilizer harvesting herbicide intervention lease mission pioneering sacrifice sustainable switch venture well-being

1 The family _____ everything to make sure they could afford to send their children to university.
2 Jack's new business _____ was very risky and it took a long time to secure financial investment.
3 We've decided to _____ to organic vegetables. It's much better for the environment.
4 His great _____ in life was to promote peace and prosperity throughout the world.
5 We organize some school events every year to raise money to _____ to charity.
6 The owners _____ the land to the university to use for agricultural research.
7 There is a general _____ among scientists that global warming is due to human activity.
8 _____ are necessary to control the growth of grass and other unwanted plants.
9 _____ the crops last year was difficult due to the rain.
10 Those plants don't look very healthy to me. They need more _____ to help them grow in these poor soil conditions.
11 Unfortunately, our opinions _____ considerably – I don't think we can come to an agreement.
12 As part of their assessed work, the students had to carry out some experiments without any _____ from teachers.
13 _____ farming methods are becoming essential as the need to protect the environment increases.
14 Teachers are responsible for the physical and mental _____ of their students as well as their education.
15 The _____ work of Henry Ford led to the mass production of affordable cars at the beginning of the 20th century.

EXTEND

Types of food

1 Match the words with the photos.

artichokes bay leaves cinnamon ginger okra pomegranates parsley tangerines

okra –1

2 Put the words from exercise 1 in the correct column.

Fruit	Vegetables	Herbs	Spices
_____	okra	_____	_____
_____	_____	_____	_____

Idioms: food

3 Read the sentences, looking at the idiomatic expression in bold. Match each idiomatic expression with a definition (a–f).

1 I said Bob wasn't good enough to play for the school football team, but he made it, so I had to **eat my words**. b
2 I got an email promising £1000 for a £100 pound investment in a foreign bank. Something was **fishy** about it.
3 Erika wants to use her mother's car all the time, but she expects her mother to buy all the petrol. She wants **to have her cake and eat it**.
4 Camilla said she didn't like your necklace because she couldn't afford one for herself. It's just **sour grapes**.
5 All my cousins have lived abroad and speak several languages. I feel like **a fish out of water** with them.
6 Jasper could have finished his report in an evening, but he **made a meal of it** and spent three days on it!

a to spend more time doing something than is necessary
b to admit that something one said was wrong
c to have the advantage of something without the disadvantage of it
d uncomfortable or out of place in one's surroundings
e involving dishonesty
f to respond negatively to something because one is angry that he or she can't have it

●●●●● Workbook: page 53

1

2

3

4

5

6

7

8

Cleft sentences (1): *it*

EXPLORE

1 🎧 (**2.17**) Read and listen to the dialogue. What did Alice think of Indian food?

Eliza How was your holiday? It looks like you've lost some weight.
Alice India was terrific, but I didn't eat much.
Eliza What a shame! Indian food is delicious.
Alice I know. India is a fabulous place, and it's Indian food that I adore more than anything.
Eliza So what happened? Were you ill?
Alice No, but it was incredibly hot, so I really didn't feel like eating.
Eliza It's the heat that decreases your appetite. That's why hotter parts of India have the spiciest food.
Alice Really? What's special about spicy food?
Eliza Spicy food makes you feel hungry. It's the spices that stimulate your appetite.
Alice And when I did eat, I sweated a lot. It was the spicy food that made me feel uncomfortable.
Eliza Well actually, it's the sweating that cools your body. That's another reason why spicy food is popular in hotter climates. As the sweat dries, you feel cool. Think about getting out of a hot bath or a pool...
Alice Mmm. I wish I'd known this before I travelled!

2 Read the *Learn this!* box. Read the dialogue again. Find the cleft sentences. In which sentences can *that* be omitted?

LEARN THIS!

We can emphasize certain concepts or ideas by using a cleft sentence. In a cleft sentence we use preparatory *it* as the subject, and the words and phrases we want to emphasize are made into a relative clause. As with relative clauses, the pronoun *that* may be omitted when constructing a cleft sentence about a direct object.
*I adore **Indian food** more than anything.* → *It's **Indian food** (that) I adore more than anything.* [direct object]
***The heat** decreases your appetite.* → *It's **the heat** that decreases your appetite.* [subject]

```
●●○○○ Grammar Reference: page 106
```

EXPLOIT

1 Read the cleft sentences. In which sentences can the pronoun *that* be omitted?

  1 It's food technology classes that make us feel hungry.
  2 It's the amount of waste that we want to eliminate with the new process.
  3 It's a new kitchen that we need in order to improve the food.
  4 It's the cold weather in winter that my parents can't stand!
  5 It's oat biscuits that are a good example of low-fat, high-energy food.
  6 It's learning English that we need to concentrate on for the exam.

2 Rewrite the sentences as two cleft sentences, one focusing on the subject and the other focusing on the object. Omit *that* where possible.

  1 City planners often overlook agricultural needs as cities expand.
    It's city planners that often overlook agricultural needs as cities expand.
    It's agricultural needs city planners often overlook as cities expand.
  2 Dieticians can deal with problems caused by poor diet.
  3 The green revolution focused on improvements in irrigation.
  4 The farming community wants to protect agricultural land from pollution damage.

3 Rewrite the sentences as cleft sentences to emphasize the words in bold. Use preparatory *it*.

  1 Tea has lots of **caffeine** that makes you feel alert.
    It's the caffeine in tea that makes you feel alert.
  2 **Eating sweet things** when you're hot makes you more thirsty.
  3 Mediterranean food is healthy because they use **olive oil**.
  4 Overeating is often caused by having **too much stress**.
  5 Students often forget that **sleep** is important when studying.
  6 **The introduction of refrigeration** allowed people to eat imported food.
  7 **The green revolution of the 1960s** improved the farming techniques of many developing countries.

```
●●○○○ Grammar Builder: page 107
```
```
●●○○○ Workbook: page 54
```

In the kitchen

VOCABULARY

1 Match the words in the box with the correct picture.

> casserole   colander   food processor   garlic press
> ladle   pestle and mortar   potato peeler   whisk   wok

2 Match the beginnings (1–9) with the ends (a–i) of the sentences.

1 A wok is used for
2 A casserole is used for
3 A food processor is used for
4 A whisk is used for
5 A colander is used for
6 A ladle is used for
7 A mortar and pestle is used for
8 A potato peeler is used for
9 A garlic press is used for

a peeling.
b serving liquid food.
c stewing or braising.
d crushing.
e stir-frying.
f chopping, slicing, and mixing.
g beating.
h draining.
i crushing.

3 What types of food would you need the following equipment for?

1 colander   pasta   6 food processor   _____
2 wok   _____   7 casserole   _____
3 whisk   _____   8 mortar and pestle _____
4 ladle   _____   9 garlic press   _____
5 potato peeler _____

> ●●●●● Workbook: page 55

LISTEN

1 🎧 (2.18) Look at the pictures. Listen to the dialogue. Which recipe is Bruce Taylor going to make? Which two pieces of kitchen equipment are needed for the recipe?

2 🎧 (2.18) Listen again. Answer the questions.

1 According to Bruce Taylor, what is the number one trend in food preparation?
2 What is the second trend in food preparation according to Bruce?
3 Why doesn't Olivia like her food processor?
4 According to Bruce, where should people buy their vegetables and meat?
5 What are two ingredients in Bruce's recipe?
6 Why doesn't Bruce like to cook his vegetables for a long time?

SPEAK

1 Which dish above looks most appetizing to you? Why?

2 Think of one of your favourite dishes. What ingredients do you need? How do you prepare it? Describe your dish to the rest of the class without mentioning what it's called. Can they guess what it is?

Cleft sentences (2): *what*

EXPLORE

1 Read the restaurant review. Would you like to eat in this restaurant? Why? Why not?

EATING AT KOUS KOUS

Authentic dishes are what every diner hopes for when visiting an ethnic restaurant. And Brookfield's new Moroccan restaurant Kous Kous does not disappoint! What diners expected at this new restaurant were delicious dishes to make them feel as if they had landed in the middle of Casablanca. And Chef Benjaloune has certainly delivered the best Moroccan cuisine this side of the Atlantic.

Chef Adil Benjaloune opened the restaurant last week after five months of intense preparation. He is not what you would consider a typical chef. Until five months ago, he was teaching Arabic and French at a local secondary school. However, what he has dreamed of for years is being a chef in his own restaurant. Last week, Benjaloune realized that dream, and he has certainly made a good decision.

The menu offers a variety of dishes, including tagines made with salmon, beef, or chicken. Another speciality of the restaurant is the traditional Moroccan soup called harira, which means *silk* in Arabic. Harira is made primarily from lentils and tomatoes, but what gives it a special flavour is the chopped coriander added just before serving.

Besides the menu, the service and the atmosphere are what you could expect from a restaurateur who is passionate about his food and his country.

2 Read the *Learn this!* box. Find six examples of cleft sentences with *what* in the text.

LEARN THIS!

> We can use *what* and other question words in cleft sentences to emphasize certain parts of the sentence. The words we want to emphasize are joined to the cleft clause by *is / was* (or *are / were* in informal styles) and *what*, *where*, *why*, or an expression such as *the man who* or *the day when*. Note that the word order of the question-word clause does not change.
> *What diners want are / is authentic dishes.*
> [NOT *What do diners want ...*].
> We can put the words that we want to emphasize at the beginning or at the end of the sentence. Compare:
> *What diners want are authentic dishes* with
> *Authentic dishes are what diners want.*

●●●◑◔ Grammar Reference: page 106

EXPLOIT

1 Match the sentence halves

1 What will impress your dinner guests is
2 What gives meat a special flavour is
3 What restaurateurs appreciate most is
4 What keeps you healthy is
5 What chefs must have is
6 What you need to remember is

a a full restaurant.
b good chopping knives.
c giving them a chance to try something new.
d to take your time when cooking.
e a balanced diet.
f marinating it well in advance.

2 Combine the questions and answers to make cleft sentences.

1 What do you like most about Italian food? — It is the olive oil.
   What I like most about Italian food is the olive oil.
2 What is the service like? — It is the most critical factor.
3 What makes this restaurant famous? — It is the authentic cuisine
4 What makes an Irish stew so tasty? — It is the lamb and onions.
5 What gives a good impression in a restaurant? — It is friendly staff.
6 What brings customers to a restaurant? — It is a lively atmosphere.

3 Rewrite the sentences from exercise 1, using your own ideas.

What will impress your dinner guests is a relaxed atmosphere.

●●●◑◔ Grammar Builder: page 107

●●●◑◔ Workbook: page 56

An informative article

READ

Read the magazine article about a traditional English dish. What is the main point of each paragraph? Complete the table.

	main point
paragraph 1	
paragraph 2	
paragraph 3	
paragraph 4	

A Ask most people what they think a typical British dish is, and they will probably say fish and chips. It consists of white fish, such as cod or haddock, which is deep fried, accompanied by chips, which are also fried. All this frying makes this dish delightful, but its health benefits are questionable. In other words, although fish and chips may be the best-known British dish, it may also be one of the unhealthiest. Fortunately, not all traditional British dishes are unhealthy.

B A good example of something healthy is Lancashire Hotpot. The traditional Lancashire Hotpot consists of lamb, onions, and potatoes. The ingredients are put in a large casserole and baked in the oven all day on a low temperature. No frying needed! In addition, people add seasonal vegetables like carrots or other root vegetables such as turnips. That is to say, there is no specific vegetable requirement for Lancashire Hotpot, which makes it an easy meal option.

C The dish takes its name from the English county of Lancashire, which is on the west coast of England. This area has a long history of agricultural production and heavy industry. The traditional dishes of Lancashire were based on local ingredients, for example, potatoes and lamb. To put it another way, fresh ingredients produced inexpensive and healthy dishes that would keep hard-working people well fed. The Lancashire Hotpot was created at a time when coal miners and industrial workers had to take their food with them if they wanted to eat at lunchtime. The name Hotpot comes from the fact that the dish was made at home and then the pot was wrapped in a blanket to keep it warm until lunchtime.

D Although food trends change and traditional dishes lose their popularity, the Lancashire Hotpot has certain characteristics that make it attractive to today's families. It can be prepared in one casserole dish, for instance. There is no need to use many pots, pans, bowls, or plates. Furthermore, it does not require additional steps beyond the initial preparation. To put it differently, it is quick to prepare. In addition, it's the seasonal ingredients that make it appealing to the modern day, food-conscious family. For these reasons, the Lancashire Hotpot is a great example of a traditional British dish that is both healthy and enjoyable.

PREPARE

When we write an informative article, we often give examples to give a better idea of what we mean. We call this exemplification. We use words and phrases such as *for example*, *for instance*, *such as*, and *like* when giving examples.
Fish and chips consist of white fish, such as cod or haddock.

Informative articles also require clarification. Clarification restates or gives additional information to explain things. We use phrases such as *in other words*, *to put it another way / differently*, and *that is to say* when clarifying examples or information.
In other words, although fish and chips may be the best-known British dish, it may also be one of the unhealthiest.

1 Read the *Writing tip*. Then read the text again and find two more sentences using exemplification and two more sentences using clarification.

2 Complete each sentence with a phrase from the *Writing tip*. Are these examples of exemplification or clarification?
  1 There are many famous food specialities from the UK, _____, marmalade, tea, roast beef and Yorkshire pudding.
  2 This dish tastes best with a thick sauce. _____, when you are preparing it, do not add a lot of water.
  3 Children need to have a balanced diet when they are growing up, _____, they shouldn't eat too many foods that contain a lot of sugar and artificial flavouring.
  4 Slow cooking is a method that has become more popular recently. It's great for cooking family dishes _____ casseroles, using cheaper cuts of meat.
  5 The snowstorm has created problems for buses, trains, and air travel across the UK. _____ all forms of transportation have been greatly affected.
  6 This university offers a lot of interesting courses, _____ Islamic architecture, Japanese literature, and Latin American politics of the 19th century.

WRITE

1 Choose a traditional dish from your country. Find information about it.

2 Develop a writing plan organized into paragraphs. What is the main point of each paragraph?

3 Review your article when you have finished writing. Have you included exemplification and clarification?

●●●●○ Workbook: page 57

Food, glorious food!

LANGUAGE SKILLS

1 🎧 (2.19) Complete the dialogue with the words from the box. Then listen and check your answers.

> casserole chop colander drain food processor
> is oven starving that what

Bob   Would you mind getting the ¹_____ out of the cupboard?

Diana Sure. Why do you need it?

Bob   I need it to slice these onions and ²_____ this aubergine into small pieces.

Diana What are you making?

Bob   I'm preparing a Turkish dish. What you need to do ³_____ put okra, onions, tomatoes, aubergine, and peppers in a ⁴_____ and bake them in the ⁵_____. It's really simple but very tasty!

Diana I'm sure. It's Turkish food you love more than anything, isn't it! Would you like me to get the ⁶_____? I'll wash and ⁷_____ the okra.

Bob   Yes, thanks. And, could you get some parsley from the fridge, too?

Diana What other herbs do we need?

Bob   Bay leaves. It's the bay leaves ⁸_____ give it a special flavour.

Diana Oh, wonderful! I'm ⁹_____ already.

Bob   Now, let's get busy. We need to think about ¹⁰_____ to serve with it …

2 Answer the questions.

1 What is Bob going to put in the food processor?
2 What kind of dish is Bob making?
3 What is Bob's favourite kind of food?
4 What is Diana going to do with the okra?
5 What herbs are needed for this dish?
6 What gives the dish a special flavour?

3 Correct the errors.

1 It's the fish makes this dish a more healthy option.
2 What do the chefs need for the fish is the chopping board.
3 The food is great, but it the service we can't stand at that restaurant.
4 It's baking is her hobby.
5 What was important for industrial workers' diets is to have food that was both nourishing and high in calories.

Weight and measurement

1 Use your dictionary to write the abbreviations for each weight or measurement.

1 centimetre	cm	7 milligram	—
2 foot	—	8 millilitre	—
3 gallon	—	9 ounce	—
4 kilogram	—	10 pint	—
5 litre	—	11 pound	—
6 metre	—	12 yard	—

2 Check the meaning of *metric* and *imperial*. Then complete the table with the words from exercise 1.

	metric	imperial
weight	1_____ 2_____	3_____ 4_____
length	5_____ 6_____	7_____ 8_____
liquid measurements	9_____ 10_____	11_____ 12_____

3 Circle the correct answer.

1 A kilometre is **longer / shorter** than a mile.
2 A litre is **larger / smaller** than a gallon.
3 There are 16 ounces in a **pound / pint**.
4 A kilogram is slightly **more / less** than two pounds.
5 There are **two / three** feet in a yard.
6 A milligram is **larger / smaller** than an ounce.

I CAN …

Read the statements. Think about your progress and tick (✓) one of the boxes.

✱ I need more practice.   ✱✱ I sometimes find this difficult.   ✱✱✱ No problem!

	✱	✱✱	✱✱✱
I can discuss sustainable farming methods.			
I can form cleft sentences with *it*.			
I can talk about cooking techniques and utensils.			
I can use cleft sentences with *what*.			
I can write an informative article.			

(●●●●● Workbook: Self check pages 58–59)

When in Rome

Intercultural communication

THIS UNIT INCLUDES ● ● ●

Vocabulary • sports terminology • verbal communication • idioms with *hit* • proverbs
Grammar • participle clauses • participle clauses after conjunctions and prepositions
Skills • discussing proverbs • listening to information about other cultures
Writing • giving travel advice • using more expressive language

BEFORE READING

Read the *Reading tip*. Look at the photos (A–C). Which of the games involve;

1 taking turns? 2 physical contact?
3 passing the ball? 4 working as a team?

> **Reading tip**
>
> If some concepts or ideas in a text are unfamiliar to you, it can be helpful to carry out some internet research before you begin reading.

Conversational styles – what sport are you?

A

Mustafa Alper from Ankara, Turkey was in his early 20s when he travelled to the United Kingdom to do a masters course. He soon made friends with other international students and he especially hit it off with a group of students from Argentina. Although their cultural backgrounds were quite different, they enjoyed sitting in cafés, drinking coffee and having lively discussions about football, food, and cars. Mustafa also met students from other countries, including Japan and Korea. Although they had some common interests, he found it more difficult to socialize with them. He felt that they were somewhat reticent, and his efforts to join conversations were often met with an uncomfortable silence.

After graduating, Mustafa returned home and began working for a pharmaceutical company. After a year he was promoted and his new position involved extensive travel. The company signed him up for a seminar on intercultural communication. Mustafa

wasn't convinced he needed it since he had studied in the UK and had friends from other countries. And in the first session, when the instructor wrote *Conversational Styles*: *rugby, basketball, and bowling* on the board, Mustafa thought there was little he could learn. But as the instructor started to explain, Mustafa suddenly realized why he had never felt as comfortable with his Asian friends.

Conversational styles differ throughout the world. It is possible to distinguish them in terms of pace, or speed, method of turn taking, pitch and volume changes, number of speakers participating simultaneously, and rapport between speakers. In order to illustrate these differences, Professor Susan Steinbach of the University of California created a sport metaphor.

Rugby

Conversational rugby is played in Latin America, Africa, Southern Europe, and the Middle East. As a conversation style, it is characterized by a great deal of energy. Ideas are brought up and dropped quickly. Speech is fast-paced and spontaneous. The speakers' turns overlap. In other words, it would be unusual for a speaker to pause and listen to another until he or she has finished. Conversations tend to be quite noisy, with very obvious changes in pitch and volume. Playing conversational rugby also involves more physical contact and gesturing, although the extent of this may depend on the gender of the speakers and cultural norms. Rapport between speakers is important, as is their camaraderie.

Basketball

Conversational basketball is played in the UK, the USA, Canada, and Australia. In this style, as in the game of basketball, speakers try to gain control of the conversation, which is symbolized by the ball. Speakers try to hold the floor by using phrases such as: *Let me see… I wanted to talk to you about… Just give me a minute to think…* This is like dribbling the ball. Speakers may interrupt each other, or 'steal the ball', in order to make a point. However, once a speaker has made his or her point, it is important to toss the conversational ball to others. This can be done by asking for an opinion. Without passing to other speakers, the conversational basketball can turn into conversational rugby, with speakers' turns overlapping as they tackle each other to gain control.

B

READ

1 Read the text. Which conversational style is described? Write B (bowling), BB (basketball), or R (rugby). There may be more than one answer.

1 It contains many changes in volume and pitch.
2 There is silence between speakers' turns.
3 Interruption is permitted.
4 Passing the conversation is expected.
5 It is the main style in North America.

2 🎧 (3.02) Read the text again. Then choose the best answers.

1 Mustafa went to the UK in order to
  a meet people from other countries.
  b pursue his studies.
  c study people's behaviour.
  d work for a pharmaceutical company.
2 Mustafa didn't think that he needed to learn about intercultural communication because
  a he had been promoted.
  b he had experience of living abroad.
  c he travelled a lot in his job.
  d he knew about conversational styles.

Bowling

Across East Asia, specifically in Japan, Korea, northern China, and parts of Thailand, the conversational style resembles bowling. Unlike basketball or rugby, there is no attempt to steal or take control of a conversation. In contrast, speakers watch and wait their turn. Speakers pause between turns to reflect on what has been said or done. Speakers follow clear guidelines of etiquette. To grab the ball from someone would be a mistake: it just isn't done. In addition to strict turn-taking, there are procedural rules based on the age or status of the speakers. The older the speaker, the more likely he or she is to speak first, and a more junior speaker would show deference by waiting. Similarly, in conversations with teachers or older family members, the older person would be expected to open the conversation.

Using a sporting metaphor can be a useful way of understanding cultural differences. However, we also have to be careful not to make overgeneralizations, and to remember that there are many variations and exceptions.

C

3 The characteristics of conversational rugby include
  a shouting a lot.
  b talking at the same time as others.
  c using hesitation devices.
  d waiting for other people to finish talking.
4 Passing the ball in basketball conversational style can be done by
  a asking someone what they think.
  b interrupting someone and change the subject.
  c talking at the same time as the other speakers.
  d using hesitation devices.
5 The bowling conversational style is characterized by
  a rules based on a person's age or status.
  b respect towards younger people.
  c taking the floor.
  d a lot of silence.
6 Using sport to describe conversational styles helps to
  a be successful speakers.
  b travel more widely.
  c get along with people of different cultures.
  d have more friends from other countries.

UNDERSTANDING IDEAS

Answer the questions. Look at the text, and use your own words and ideas.

1 According to the article, which conversational style is used in your country? Do you agree with the article's characterization of your country's conversational style? Why or why not?
2 Given the information in the article, what might you do differently in a conversation with people who use a different conversation style? Why?
3 Why would training on communication styles around the world be helpful? Which careers or professions would benefit most from such training?

VOCABULARY

Conversational styles – what sport are you?

Match the highlighted words in the text with these definitions.

1 Statements that are not accurate because they are too general.
2 Behaviour that shows that you respect someone.
3 The formal rules of polite behaviour.
4 To throw carelessly.
5 To have the right to speak during a discussion or debate.
6 An understanding between people.
7 To happen at the same time or to partly cover.
8 Got on very well with.
9 Unwilling to tell people about things.
10 Moving the ball along with several short bounces or kicks.
11 How high or low a sound is.
12 To take hold of something suddenly and firmly.
13 To try and take the ball from an opponent in a game.
14 Happening at the same time.
15 Loyalty and warm feeling between friends.

(●●○○○ Workbook: page 60)

Conversational styles – what sport are you?

ACTIVATE

Complete these sentences with the correct form of the words from the box.

> camaraderie deference dribble etiquette grab
> hit it off hold the floor overgeneralization overlap pitch
> rapport reticent simultaneously tackle toss

1 She was _____ about joining in the conversation because she wasn't familiar with the topic.
2 The best teachers develop a good _____ with students.
3 We were running late so we _____ a sandwich at the station before getting on the train.
4 Mobile phone _____ varies from country to country, but you should switch off your phone during a play.
5 Although Ellie and I hadn't met before, we _____ immediately and became friends.
6 When talking about human behaviour, it's important not to make _____ because everyone is different.
7 Elephants can hear sounds with a much lower _____ than humans can.
8 The player skillfully _____ the ball to the net without being _____, and scored.
9 He opened the letter but quickly _____ it in the bin when he realized it was junk mail.
10 I can't attend the last day of the course because it _____ with a school basketball tournament.
11 It's acceptable to _____ as long as your point is relevant to the discussion.
12 Speaking out of turn is rude and shows a lack of _____.
13 They used a split screen to broadcast two games _____.
14 The aim of the training course was to develop a sense of team spirit and _____ in the new group.

EXTEND

Verbal communication

1 Match the words with their definitions.

1	mutter	a	to speak in a very quiet voice
2	protest	b	to talk about people's private lives, usually in an unkind way
3	whisper	c	to talk in a friendly and informal way
4	discuss	d	to say something in a quiet voice that is hard to hear, especially because you are annoyed
5	gossip	e	to say or do something to show that you strongly disagree or disapprove of something
6	chat	f	to talk about something with one or more people, in order to agree on something or to make a decision

2 Complete the sentences with the correct form of a verb from exercise 1.

1 They spent all night _____ the details of the deal, and finally the contract was drawn up and signed.
2 Don't tell any of your secrets to Gail. She _____ a lot, so everyone will know if you tell her.
3 The students _____ loudly when they were told to come to school at the weekend.
4 It's bad manners to continue _____ with your classmates when the teacher comes into the room.
5 You can't talk in the library, but it's OK to _____ quietly.
6 She was angry, and _____ something as she left the room.

Idioms with *hit*

3 Match the idioms in bold (1–7) with the definitions (a–g).

1 My mum **hit the roof** when I told her I had broken her favourite antique vase. b
2 Gemma, who knows her brother very well, **hit the nail on the head** when she said that he likes to always be the centre of attention.
3 After two years of playing for small clubs, Harry **hit it big** when he was signed up to Manchester United.
4 Jane has had a lot of experience of living in foreign countries, so she'll **hit the ground running** when she begins working for the United Nations.
5 I'm not feeling very well, so I'm going to **hit the hay** and hope I feel better in the morning.
6 Although Sean had been a successful actor, his career **hit the buffers** when he appeared in a poorly-rated film.
7 We've got a long way to go tomorrow, so we're planning to **hit the road** quite early in the morning.

a to suddenly stop being successful, especially in a career
b to become very angry suddenly
c to start doing something successfully immediately
d to go to bed
e to start a trip or journey
f to become famous or very successful
g to say something that is exactly right

> ●●●●● Workbook: page 61

Participle clauses

EXPLORE

1 Read the text. What surprised Ethan? What is your mobile phone etiquette?

To ring or not to ring

Enjoying his Russian studies at university, Ethan decided to enrol in a Russian university for one semester before he finished his degree. He soon made many friends in Moscow. One of his new friends, Viktor, invited Ethan to a café to chat about Ireland. Feeling a little homesick, Ethan was looking forward to showing Viktor photos of his friends, family, university, and town.

Carrying his bag with his laptop, Ethan walked into the café and saw Viktor, who was sitting at a table in the corner. Ethan took a seat next to him. Ethan put his mobile phone on silent, not wanting to be disturbed during his conversation with Viktor.

Ethan and Viktor ordered some coffee, and then Ethan showed some of his favourite photos from home. Suddenly, Viktor's mobile phone rang. Answering in a loud voice, Viktor explained that he would ring back later. Ethan was a little surprised. He put his phone on silent, thinking that this was the polite thing to do. Looking around the café, Ethan noticed that everyone had put their mobile phones on the tables, and some people were even talking on their phones.

2 Read the *Learn this!* box. Complete the table above with participle clauses from the text.

LEARN THIS!

> Participle clauses can be used to express reasons and time relations. Participle clauses can only be used if the subject is the same as that of the main clause. None of the conjunctions that introduce the reason (e.g. *because*, *since*, *as*) or time relation (e.g. *while*, *as*, *after*) are required, because they are replaced by the participle.
> *Having written to her twice, I didn't want to write again.*
> [= Because I had written to her twice ...]
> [NOT *Because having written to her twice, ...*]
> *Enjoying his Russian studies at university, Ethan decided to ...* [= Because he (Ethan) was enjoying his Russian studies, Ethan decided to ...]
> Participle clauses can be used in the present, even if they are referring to a past event. Stative verbs that are not used often in the continuous form can be used as present participles.
> *... not wanting to be disturbed* [= because he didn't want to be disturbed]

Participle clauses to express reasons	Participle clauses to express time relations
Enjoying his Russian studies at university, Ethan decided to ... ... not wanting to be disturbed ... 1 _____ 2 _____	3 _____ 4 _____ 5 _____

●●●◌◌ Grammar Reference: page 108

EXPLOIT

1 Find the participle clause in each sentence. Does the participle clause express a reason or a time relation? Write *R* or *T*.

1 Having failed his exams, Shaun had to repeat them. *R*
2 Not being familiar with the queuing system in the UK, foreigners sometimes offend local people.
3 Using a mobile phone on the bus, you should speak quietly so that you don't disturb the other passengers.
4 Not wanting to hurt her feelings, we didn't tell Katie that she needed to improve her cooking skills.
5 Knowing about home life in the US, I was able to enjoy living there as a student.
6 Living away from home, Bruce kept in touch with his family using emails and skype.

2 Rewrite the sentences from exercise 1, using a conjunction.

1 Since / Because he had failed his exams, Shaun had to repeat them.

3 Rewrite the sentences with a participle clause.

1 I asked for directions because I didn't know where to go.
Not knowing where to go, I asked for directions.
2 Since I didn't want to become a doctor, I changed my programme of studies.
3 After he had finished writing his essay, he felt very knowledgeable about the topic.
4 As she looked around the room, she felt someone tap her shoulder.
5 Catherine waved to us because she was trying to catch our attention.
6 While he was living abroad, Ken realized that it was not always easy to make friends with foreigners.

●●●◌◌ Grammar Builder: page 109

●●●◌◌ Workbook: page 62

Proverbs

VOCABULARY

1 Read the sentences (1–5). Match each proverb in bold with its meaning (a–e).

1 Rodney always dresses well because he believes that **clothes make the man**. d
2 I don't believe that Karen is sorry because **actions speak louder than words**. If she were truly sorry, she would have written a letter to apologize.
3 Victor doesn't want to go on the school trip because he is worried that his team will replace him. He thinks that it will be a case of **out of sight, out of mind**.
4 If we all work together, we can finish this project quickly because **many hands make light work**!
5 You should buy the computer you want while it's on special offer. Remember, **he who hesitates is lost**.

a What a person does, not says, proves that what he or she says is genuine.
b If a person is not present, people forget about them.
c People who can't make quick decisions don't succeed or are not rewarded.
d A good appearance shows a serious attitude.
e A team of people working together can accomplish something more quickly.

2 Match the proverbs in exercise 1 with a proverb with the opposite meaning.

a Too many cooks spoil the broth. 4
b Look before you leap.
c Absence makes the heart grow fonder.
d The pen is mightier than the sword.
e Don't judge a book by its cover.

3 Complete the sentences with a proverb from exercise 1 or 2.

1 You shouldn't sign that contract before you have some advice from a lawyer. You should _____ .
2 Don't quit the team. Although the coach has been critical, he has arranged practice times to suit your schedule, so I think he wants you to stay. _____
3 Don't worry about being out of touch when you go abroad. Everything here will be the same, and your friends will really look forward to seeing you when you get back. _____
4 I don't think we need any more help with our project. We've already got each job covered. Remember, _____.
5 I think we should give the new player a chance. She doesn't look strong, but _____ . She's very serious at heart.
6 It's true that Ivan always looks smart for work, but I'm not sure how good he is at his job. Although some people believe _____ , I'd be more convinced if I'd heard him say something serious for once.

(●●●●● **Workbook: page 63**)

LISTEN

1 Look at the photos (A–D). Which empire would you associate with each picture: Roman, Umayyad, or British?

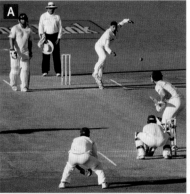
the game of cricket

the Great Mosque of Damascus

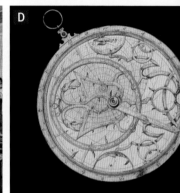
the senate

an astrolabe for navigation

2 🎧 (3.03) Listen to the class discussion and check your answers to exercise 1. What topics are discussed?

1 architecture   4 education   7 medicine
2 art   5 food / drink 8 sport
3 clothing   6 governance

3 🎧 (3.03) Listen again and answer the questions.

1 How long did the Roman Empire last?
2 Name three present-day countries which were part of the Roman Empire.
3 What aspects of Roman architecture did the Umayyad caliphs use?
4 What does the term 'the Dark Ages' refer to?
5 Why were navigational tools important in the 8th century?
6 In which countries is cricket popular? Why?
7 Which of the three empires was the most far-reaching in geographical terms?

SPEAK

Look at the proverbs in Vocabulary exercises 1 and 2. Ask and answer the questions with your partner.

1 Which proverbs do you think are true? Which do you think are not true?
2 Do you have similar proverbs in your language? What images do they create?

GRAMMAR

Participle clauses after conjunctions and prepositions

EXPLORE

1 Read the rules for taking taxis in New York and Tokyo. What are the similarities and differences between the two cities?

2 Read the *Learn this!* box. Then read the rules again and find more examples of present and past participle clauses after prepositions or conjunctions.

TOKYO

Taxis are available at taxi stands and on the street. If stopping a taxi in the street, do not whistle. Wave for the taxi, since whistling is not customary and may be considered discourteous. After stopping the taxi, the driver will open the door with an automatic remote. Once seated inside, allow the driver to close the door for you.

Taxis are expensive, but it may be worth the cost if you are not sure about an address. Instead of guessing incorrectly, taxi drivers typically ask for directions to be sure they can find the right address.

NEW YORK

Taxis are strictly controlled by the local authorities in all American cities. If offered a ride in a car other than a licensed taxi, do not accept. You may be overcharged, and more importantly, your safety depends on it.

There are special queues for taxis, or you may stop one in the street. Waving or whistling is the customary way of signalling that you would like the taxi to stop. Taxis have a light on the roof. If lit, the taxi is available for hire. Once hired, the driver turns off the light and starts the meter.

At the destination, the meter is turned off. If hired for a shorter journey, it is appropriate to tip the driver a small amount; many people simply tell the driver to keep the change. However, it is customary give a larger tip when using a taxi for a longer trip.

LEARN THIS!

Many conjunctions and prepositions can be followed by a present participle. Participle clauses are commonly used with *after*, *before*, *since*, *on*, *if*, *when*, *despite*, *while* and *without*.
If stopping a taxi in the street ...
*wave for the taxi, **since whistling** is not customary.*
Clauses with past participles can also be used with *if*, *when*, *while*, *until* and *once*.
If offered a ride in a car other than a licensed taxi, ...

●●●◉◉ Grammar Reference: page 108

EXPLOIT

1 Choose the correct conjunction or preposition.
1 (Once) / After closed, the door will lock automatically.
2 Please buy a ticket **before** / **since** proceeding to the ticket barrier.
3 You shouldn't use the London Underground for the first time **on** / **without** consulting a map.
4 **Despite** / **Since** appearing to be calm, most people using the Underground tend to be in a hurry.
5 Refuse to look after someone else's luggage **if** / **once** asked.
6 Remain seated **when** / **until** told to stand up.
7 **While** / **Despite** living in London, we learnt a lot about using the Underground.
8 It's advisable to have small change or the correct money **after** / **when** buying a ticket in rush hour.

2 Complete the text with the correct participle form of the words in the box.

> approach   be   enter   hold up   lose   reach   see
> sit   speak   ~~travel~~

When ¹travelling on the London Underground, there are some important rules to observe. You should walk at a comfortable pace without ²_____ the regular commuters. For example, on ³_____ the escalator, keep to the right if you want to stand. It's a good idea to consult a tube map before ⁴ _____ the platform to avoid confusion, as this may cause a delay for other passengers behind you. Not queuing in an orderly fashion is very much frowned upon. If ⁵_____ to be jumping the queue, other people will get annoyed with you. When the train arrives, be sure to let passengers get off before ⁶_____ the carriage. If ⁷_____ down in the carriage, it is polite to give your seat up for older people, who may need it more than you do. Despite ⁸_____ very crowded most of the time, people are not very friendly or talkative. Only speak when ⁹_____ to, and if possible avoid asking fellow passengers for help if you get lost. (If ¹⁰_____, get off the train and consult the nearest tube map.)

3 Write some etiquette rules for using taxis in your town or city, using participle clauses.

●●●◉◉ Grammar Builder: page 109

●●●◉◉ Workbook: page 64

Travel advice

READ

1 Read the travel advice. What three main pieces of advice does the writer give?

London Travel Etiquette

London is a ¹fun city for tourists. People are very ²friendly, too. However, there are a few ³things you should remember when travelling around London.

First of all, when taking a bus it is ⁴important to queue at the bus stop. People form a queue so they can get on the bus without pushing. It's not ⁵a good idea to jump the queue; in other words, don't go to the front of a long queue and expect to get on the bus first. This is extremely ⁶bad, and people will be ⁷angry with you. Waiting in a long queue is ⁸boring, but it is bad manners to try to avoid waiting.

Another thing to remember is that London is a city full of ⁹people who need to get to work on public transport. Many Londoners go to work on the underground, or the Tube, as it is also known. When riding the escalators to get to the trains, it is proper etiquette to stand to the right to let people who are in a hurry walk up or down the escalator on the left. If you block the escalator, people will easily get upset.

Finally, remember that personal space is very ¹⁰important to British people. For example, if you get a train and there is only one person in the carriage, do not sit next to this person. Choose a seat far away from him or her. Similarly, if the bus or the underground is very crowded, try not to touch the people around you. If you do touch someone ¹¹by accident, apologizing is a good idea.

If you remember these simple things, your trip to London will be a ¹²nice one!

2 Read the *Writing tip*. Read the travel advice entry again and replace the underlined words in the text with an alternative word from the box.

> action-packed advisable agreeable tips
> commuters discourteous furious imperative
> inadvertently pleasant precious tedious

Writing tip: using more expressive language

Try to use more expressive vocabulary, and try to avoid using the same word many times. Words that people tend to use too frequently are: *good, bad, fun, nice, big, things, get, go* and *say*. Use a dictionary or a thesaurus to help you find words that are more expressive and that help the reader to form a clear picture in his or her mind about what you are describing. For example, some alternatives to *good* are: *beneficial, deluxe, choice, exceptional, favourable, healthy, helpful, superior, delightful*.

PREPARE

Rewrite the sentences, using more expressive vocabulary.

1 There are nice things you can say to your host.
   There are several considerate remarks you might make to your host.

2 It's a good idea to go through London on the Tube.

3 We didn't get to meet a lot of nice people.

4 It's good to do the usual activities when visiting a place you know.

5 It's impolite to push to the front of the queue.

6 We are going on a big trip next month.

WRITE

1 Write some travel advice about etiquette on public transport in your town or city. Include three or more of the following points in your advice:

   1 Personal space on public transport
   2 Travelling by bus or underground
   3 Queuing for public transport
   4 Signalling to taxis and tipping taxi drivers
   5 Travelling alone
   6 Travelling at different times of the day
   7 Buying tickets for public transport
   8 Your own idea

2 Review your writing. Are there any words that you could replace with more expressive language?

(●●●●● Workbook: page 65)

When in Rome

LANGUAGE SKILLS

1 🎧 (3.04) Complete the dialogue with the words from the box. Then listen and check your answers.

> approving   finalized   followed   gossip
> hammer out   hit it off   hit the nail on the head
> not following   process   protests

Sandra   I hope Ms Woodson isn't angry with me. You know how we've never ¹_____ and I've just missed another of her extra maths classes.

Alice   What happened? Why weren't you in class?

Sandra   I had to attend a student council meeting. It took a long time because we were trying to ²_____ an easier procedure for student elections.

Alice   Can't student elections follow the usual procedure?

Sandra   If ³_____ correctly, the procedure works well, but ...

Alice   ⁴_____ the procedure correctly gives an unfair advantage to one or two candidates, and then everyone ⁵_____ about the election outcome.

Sandra   You've ⁶_____ ! So that's what we're trying to avoid.

Alice   I hope you're successful because it would make the ⁷_____ smoother for all the students.

Sandra   Exactly, but we haven't come to an agreement yet, so please don't talk about this with anyone. Students here love to ⁸_____ .

Alice   Will the changes be announced to everyone once ⁹_____ ?

Sandra   Definitely. After ¹⁰_____ the process, the administrator will email all students.

2 Answer the questions.

1 Why did Sandra not go to Ms Woodson's class?
2 Do students usually follow the correct procedures for student elections?
3 Who usually isn't happy with the outcomes of the student elections when procedures aren't followed correctly?
4 Have the new procedures been finalized yet?
5 Why doesn't Sandra want Alice to share this information with others right now?
6 Who will announce the new election procedures?

3 Choose the correct answer.

1 __, this ice cream dessert is ready to be served.
   a Freezing   b When freezing   c When frozen
2 __ shoes, please wear socks.
   a Trying on   b If trying on   c If tried on
3 __ her abilities, we encouraged her to go to university.
   a Knowing   b Because knowing   c Because known
4 __, this ticket cannot be refunded.
   a Purchased   b Once purchasing   c Once purchased

Register

> Register refers to whether language is more suitable for a formal or informal context. For example, we use informal language to speak to a close friend, but we would write a report or an essay using formal language.

1 Use your dictionary to complete the chart with the words and phrases from the box.

> attire   bash   butt in   endeavour   gear   have a shot at
> heap   interject   plethora   strike

Meaning	Formal word	Informal word
clothing	¹ attire	² gear
try hard	3	4
interrupt	5	6
to hit something	7	8
a large amount	9	10

2 Read the sentences and their contexts. Are the words in the appropriate register for the given context? Rewrite those that are not.

1 At a formal restaurant: 'Only diners wearing appropriate gear will be seated.'
2 In a newspaper: 'A train bashed a lorry on the tracks late last night.'
3 In a courtroom: The judge gave the solicitor permission to butt in.
4 To a friend: 'Do you fancy trying to solve this puzzle?' 'Yeah, I'll have a shot at it'.
5 In a report: 'There is a plethora of natural resources in the former Soviet republic.'
6 To a friend in conversation: 'I bought some new attire at the new store at the mall.'

I CAN ...

Read the statements. Think about your progress and tick (✓) one of the boxes.

✳ I need more practice.   ✳✳ I sometimes find this difficult.   ✳✳✳ No problem!

	✳	✳✳	✳✳✳
I can understand a text about conversational styles.			
I can use participle clauses correctly.			
I can discuss and use proverbs.			
I can use participle clauses after conjunctions and prepositions.			
I can give travel advice.			

●●○○○   Workbook: Self check pages 66–67

The Count of Monte Cristo

by Alexandre Dumas

Biography

Alexandre Dumas was born in 1802. He was the son of a nobleman who was one of Napoleon's generals. Dumas worked in Paris as a clerk before making a name for himself in French literary circles in 1829. His most famous novels include his works from the 1840s, *The Three Musketeers* and *The Count of Monte Cristo*, both of which are still widely read today. Dumas died in France in 1870.

Dantès ran down the rocks at the risk of being dashed to pieces; he listened, he strove to discover what was happening, but he heard and saw nothing, – all human cries had ceased; and the tempest alone continued to rage.

By degrees the wind abated; vast grey clouds rolled towards the west; and the blue firmament appeared studded with bright stars. Soon a red streak became visible on the horizon; the waves whitened, a light played over them, and gilded their foaming crests with gold. It was day.

Dantès stood silent and motionless before this vast spectacle; for since his captivity he had forgotten it. He turned towards the fortress, and looked both at the sea and the land.

The gloomy building rose from the bosom of the ocean with that imposing majesty of inanimate objects that seems at once to watch and to command.

It was about five o'clock; the sea continued to grow calmer.

'In two or three hours,' thought Dantès, 'the turnkey will enter my chamber and find the body of my poor friend, recognise it, seek for me in vain, and give the alarm. Then the passage will be discovered; the men who cast me into the sea and must have heard the cry I uttered will be questioned. Then boats filled with armed soldiers will pursue the wretched fugitive. The cannon will warn every one to refuse shelter to a man wandering about naked and famished. The police of Marseilles will be on the alert by land, whilst the governor pursues me by sea. I am cold, I am hungry. I have lost even the knife that saved me. Oh, my God! I have suffered enough surely. Have pity on me, and do for me what I am unable to do for myself.'

As Dantès, his eyes turned in the direction of the Chateau d'If, uttered the prayer, he saw appear at the extremity of the isle of Pomegue, like a bird skimming over the sea, a small bark, that the eye of a sailor alone could recognize as a Genoese tartan. She was coming out of Marseilles harbour, and was standing out to sea rapidly, her sharp prow cleaving through the waves.

'Oh!' cried Edmond, 'to think that in half an hour I could join her if I did not fear being questioned, detected, and conveyed back to Marseilles. What can I do? What story can I invent: under pretext of trading along the coast, these men, who are in reality smugglers, will prefer selling me to doing a good action. I must wait. But I cannot, I am starving. In a few hours my strength will be utterly exhausted; besides, perhaps I have not been missed at the fortress. I can pass as one of the sailors wrecked last night. This story will pass muster for there is no one left to contradict me.'

1 🎧 (3.08) Read the text and choose the correct answers.

1 The scene is set
   a on an island.   b in a fortress.   c on a ship.
2 In this scene Edmond Dantès is
   a a prisoner.   b a smuggler.   c a fugitive.
3 In the distance Edmond can see
   a Marseilles.   b a boat.   c the police.

2 Read the text again. Answer the questions.

1 What time of day is it? What is the weather like?
2 How do you think Edmond escaped from prison?
3 How does Edmond feel about his situation now?
4 What are the problems if Edmond is rescued by the smugglers?
5 How is Edmond planning to make his escape?

3 Answer the questions. Look at the text, and use your own words and ideas to explain your answers.

1 Edmond has been convicted of a crime. Do you get the impression that he is guilty? Why or why not?
2 Do you think Edmond is comfortable around the sea? Why or why not?
3 Why do you think Edmond is nervous about trying to be rescued? What would you do in his position?

4 Edmond is rescued by the smugglers. Write a short paragraph about how you think he attracts their attention, and how he convinces them to allow him to sail with them.

Celebration

READ

1 Read the text. Which New Year celebration would you most like to join in? Explain why.

Happy New Year!

New Year's traditions across the globe are diverse. For example, in Spain, people eat twelve grapes at midnight, one grape for luck in each of the coming months. In Denmark, people throw old dishes at the doors of their friends and family. Many broken dishes in front of a door indicate that the residents are quite popular! Here are some other New Year's traditions.

Scotland

In Scotland, the custom of first footing is still practised by some people. The 'first foot' is the first person to enter a home through the front door after midnight on New Year's Day. The first foot is traditionally a dark-haired male because in some parts of the UK, a female or fair-haired male is considered an unlucky first foot. The first foot traditionally brings gifts, including a coin, bread, salt, and a piece of coal. These gifts represent financial prosperity, food, flavour, and warmth.

The United States

Tens of thousands of people gather in Times Square in New York City for the dropping of the New Year's ball. Being the most famous tradition in the United States, it is also observed by millions of people on TV. This tradition began in 1907, with a ball made of iron and wood. The current ball is made of Waterford Crystal; weighing over 450 kilograms, and measuring almost two metres in diameter, it's a very impressive sight!

The idea of lowering a ball to signal passage of time dates back long before New Year's Eve was ever celebrated in Times Square. The first 'time-ball' was positioned on top of England's Royal Observatory at Greenwich, near London in 1833. This ball was dropped at one o'clock every afternoon, helping the captains of nearby ships to set their navigational instruments precisely.

Japan

It is in Japan that New Year is the most important holiday because here it signals renewal. Throughout the month of December, the Japanese hold 'forget-the-year' parties to say goodbye to the hardships and problems of the past year, while at the same time preparing for a new beginning. Houses are scrubbed clean to welcome the New Year. People expect to receive lots of greeting cards from family, friends and business associates. And gifts of money from relatives are what many children are eagerly waiting for. On New Year's Day people visit shrines to pray for prosperity in the coming year.

2 Read the text again. Which country is each custom from?

1 A ball made of crystal is lowered to welcome the New Year.
2 The first person to enter a home at the New Year brings a gift for warmth.
3 People clean their homes to prepare for the New Year.
4 Dishes are thrown at people's doors.
5 Children receive small gifts containing money and people send cards to each other.
6 Twelve grapes are eaten at midnight.

3 Answer the questions. Use your own words and ideas.

1 How do you think the grape-eating and plate-throwing in Spain and Denmark originated?
2 If you were a first foot in Scotland, what four gifts would you bring to the host? What would these gifts symbolize?
3 Do you think it's a good idea to forget the problems of the past and to have a positive outlook for the future? Explain your answer.

LISTEN

1 🎧 (3.09) Listen to a radio programme about the origin of New Year celebrations. How many different dates for New Year are mentioned?

2 🎧 (3.09) Listen again. Are the sentences true or false?

1 Only ancient civilizations used mid-March to begin a new year.
2 It was during the Roman Empire that 1 January was first used to begin a new year.
3 China used to use 1 January to begin a new year, but later adopted its own calendar.
4 The Chinese calendar is based on the moon.
5 The British accepted 1 January as New Year's Day in the 1600s.
6 1 January has begun the new year in the English-speaking world for over 300 years.

WRITE AND SPEAK

1 Write a description of how you and your family celebrate new year. When do you celebrate? Who do you celebrate with? Where do you go? What food do you prepare?

2 In pairs compare your family traditions. How are they similar? How are they different?

9 Being green

Small is beautiful

THIS UNIT INCLUDES ● ● ● ●

Vocabulary • housing and the environment • negative adjectives for impact • types of home • green issues
Grammar • inversion • emphatic use of *as...as*
Skills • discussing environmental issues • dealing with global problems
Writing • a report: cause and effect

BEFORE READING

Look at the photos. What do you think are the environmental benefits of living in a tiny house? Can you think of any disadvantages of living in such a small house?

A tiny step to save the environment

In 1997, American university professor Jay Shafer did something most people would find unimaginable. He moved into a home that was smaller than 9 square metres. 9 square metres is not much space. Many flats contain one room that is larger than 9 square metres, but Professor Shafer was undaunted by the thought of getting rid of many of his personal belongings so that he could live full-time in such a small home. He packed up the clothes that he never wore and the books that he never read and gave them to friends or donated them to charity. Once he had downsized, he moved into his first tiny home, which he called *Tumbleweed*.

1 What is a tiny home like?
A house is classified as a tiny home if its living space is less than 13 square metres. Some tiny homes are as small as 6 square metres. Although they are small, they are made of quality materials. They can withstand freezing temperatures and strong storms. In addition to this durable construction, another important characteristic of a tiny home is that it's portable. Constructed on wheels, they may be pulled behind a van or powerful car. Because of their portability, owners of tiny homes often move them to different locations. Professor Shafer has lived in the middle of an apple orchard, beside a lake in the mountains, and in the Redwood forest of California.

2 What is the incentive to live in a tiny house?
People choose to live in tiny houses for a variety of reasons, not least because they are much cheaper and more economical to run. Primarily the owners share certain beliefs, namely a concern for the environment and a desire to reduce consumption of material goods. Professor Shafer recalls growing up in his parents' huge home, annoyed by the exorbitant heating and cooling bills. A tiny home can be heated for an entire winter in a snowy climate for less than £70. This also includes the cost of heating water for showers and washing up. Tiny home residents also save money because they are unable to store much in their homes. Due to space limitations, they cannot buy something unless they truly need it. This decreased spending reduces the number of unnecessary purchases, leading to less waste.

3 Where are the appliances in a tiny house?
Although a tiny house has limited space, it still contains modern conveniences such as a fridge, a range or a toaster oven. A portable TV fits neatly in a cupboard next to a laptop computer. Electricity is supplied in a variety of ways. Some owners use solar panels while others' electricity needs are met by wind-powered generators. The tiny house can be connected to a public water source via a tube.

4 How can more than one person fit in a tiny house?
There are tiny houses which are home to married couples. The living room can hold two comfortable chairs, and the bedroom, located in a loft, is accessible only by a ladder. Although it's not possible to stand in the bedroom, two people can sleep comfortably in it. It is also possible to entertain in a tiny house. Professor Shafer has a fold-up table that holds place settings for four people, although the plates must be quite small. Some tiny homes have fold-out benches so that as many as six guests can be accommodated, although it is quite difficult to move around.

Reading tip

A text can be organized by starting each section with a question. The questions serve as headings and help to explain what each section is about. Reading through the questions can help us to understand what the text is about and what information is covered. They can also help us locate the right section to find particular information.

1 Read the *Reading tip*. Then read the headings in the text and predict what you are going to read about in each section.

2 In which section (1–4) would the following information be included if it were added to the text?

1 Clothes washing facilities inside a tiny house.
2 The materials used to make a tiny house.
3 Quotations from other residents of tiny houses about why they moved into one.
4 How grandparents can have their grandchildren sleep at their tiny house.
5 Satellite TV availability in a tiny house.
6 How much money people save on bills from living in a tiny house.

3 🎧 (3.10) Read the text again. Choose the best answers.

1 Before he moved into his tiny house, Professor Shafer
  a bought new clothing and books.
  b volunteered at a charity.
  c gave away many of his things.
  d bought some land near a lake in the mountains.
2 The living space of a tiny home is defined as
  a less than 9 square metres.
  b less than 13 square metres.
  c between 6 and 9 square metres.
  d no more than 6 square metres.

3 The disadvantage of living in a tiny home is
  a they are cheap to heat.
  b they are safe in storms.
  c they are portable.
  d there isn't much storage space.
4 Professor Shafer lives in a tiny house because he
  a grew up in one.
  b doesn't have a lot of money.
  c buys a lot of things that he doesn't need.
  d is concerned about his impact on the environment.
5 The electricity in tiny houses comes from
  a the wind or the sun.
  b a power appliance.
  c a variety of sources.
  d a power connection via a tube.
6 Up to six people can
  a live in a tiny house.
  b sleep in a tiny house.
  c attend a dinner in a tiny house.
  d move a tiny house.

UNDERSTANDING IDEAS

Answer the questions. Look at the text, and use your own words and ideas.

1 Would you want to live in a tiny house? Why or why not?
2 If you were going to live in a tiny house, which of your possessions would you definitely take with you? Why?
3 Would tiny houses be useful in your country? Why or why not?

VOCABULARY

A tiny step to save the environment

Match the highlighted words in the text with these definitions.

1 To be strong enough not to be damaged.
2 Very or too expensive.
3 Machines for producing electricity.
4 Impossible to believe.
5 Still enthusiastic despite difficulties.
6 Provided with enough space to live or to sit.
7 Can be made smaller by closing it so that it takes less space.
8 Throwing something away.
9 A space below the roof, often used for storage.
10 Reduced the number of belongings and costs.
11 Something that motivates you to do something.
12 Connected with money and possessions.
13 Easy to carry move.
14 Grouped according to features in common.
15 Likely to last for a long time without breaking.

(●●○○ Workbook: page 68)

A tiny step to save the environment

ACTIVATE

Complete these sentences with the correct form of the words from the box.

> accommodate classify downsize durable exorbitant
> fold-up generator get rid of incentive loft material
> portable unimaginable undaunted withstand

1 Most hospitals need to have a _____ in case there is a power cut.
2 The destruction after the hurricane was _____ . I'd never seen anything like it in my life.
3 The success of consumer goods such as mobile phones and MP3 players depends on the availability of _____ batteries.
4 The high price of petrol is a good _____ to encourage people to drive smaller cars.
5 The price of installing solar panels is _____ . Most people can't afford it.
6 We use the _____ to store our suitcases and other things we don't use often.
7 People's happiness doesn't depend only on the amount of _____ possessions they have.
8 Although many people advised against the venture, he remained _____ and succeeded in sailing across the ocean single-handed.
9 Buildings in Japan are built to _____ severe earthquakes.
10 Laptops are supposed to be _____ , so weight is a critical factor in the design.
11 The city-centre offices were too small to _____ the recent expansion in the company, so they moved to a new location.
12 Spanish and Italian are _____ as Latin-based languages.
13 Some people were made redundant when the company _____ in the recession.
14 We have a _____ bed for the living room, which we can use when guests stay overnight.
15 We had to _____ a lot of books when the library went digital.

EXTEND

Negative adjectives for impact

> Some adjectives are more common in their negative form because they are used for emphasis or to signal a strong feeling or emotion. These adjectives typically begin with *un-* or *in-*.
> *He did something most people would think unimaginable.*

1 Read the *Look out!* box. Match the words (1–7) and their definitions (a–g).

1	incapacitated	a	weird
2	intrepid	b	brave
3	inexplicable	c	clumsy or useless
4	uncanny	d	heavy or awkward
5	insignificant	e	not important
6	inept	f	injured or unable to act
7	unwieldy	g	not able to be explained

2 Complete the sentences with negative adjectives from exercise 1.

1 Nigel's recent behaviour is _____ . He has been ignoring his friends and nobody understands why.
2 After the statistical analysis, the results showed such an _____ difference that they were not reported.
3 Please don't ask me to be on your team. I am totally _____ at football.
4 She's an _____ leader. She's not afraid of anything.
5 Ivan is going to be _____ for several months because of his serious injuries.
6 My laptop is old and quite _____ . I only use it at home.
7 Alicia's resemblance to Nicole Kidman is _____ . She could be her twin! It's so strange!

Types of home

3 Match the words with the photos.

> bungalow caravan detached house ~~mansion~~
> semi-detached house terraced house

1	mansion	4	_____
2	_____	5	_____
3	_____	6	_____

●●●●○ Workbook: page 69

GRAMMAR

Inversion

EXPLORE

1 Read the email. What three reasons does the writer give to support her recommendation?

Dear Principal Stevenson,

On behalf of the school environment committee, I am writing to recommend that we change all the school light bulbs to energy-saving bulbs. Little do we realize how much energy we waste with traditional light bulbs. An ordinary light bulb uses 100 watts, whereas an energy-efficient one uses only 30 watts. Under no circumstances should we consider this a trivial detail. Our school has over 500 light bulbs.

The light from an energy-efficient bulb is as strong as that from a regular bulb. Seldom do people notice a difference in the quality of light between these bulbs, and some people even prefer the light from the energy-efficient bulb.

Not only can we make a small step to reducing energy consumption, but our school can also encourage other people in our community to change to energy-efficient bulbs. Never have we had such a good opportunity to be leaders in environmental action. Only after leading by example can we expect our students to care about the environment. The school should make these changes today.

Yours respectfully,

Ann Farnsley

Environment Committee

2 Look at the following sentence from the letter. Do you notice anything about the structure? Rewrite the sentence beginning; *We*...

Little do we realize how much energy we waste with traditional light bulbs.

3 Read the *Learn this!* box and find five other examples of inverted sentences in the email.

●●●●● Grammar Reference: page 110

EXPLOIT

1 Complete the sentences with the words and the tense in brackets.

1 Only after completing the exam should you leave the classroom. (you / leave – should)
2 At no time _____ an unfair advantage to her students. (she / give – present perfect)
3 Under no circumstances _____ the election. (we / repeat – future with *going to*)
4 Not until much later _____ the matter with the rest of the staff. (the principal / discuss – simple past)
5 Seldom _____ the importance of taking small steps. (we / recognize – present perfect)
6 Little _____ how easy it is for individuals to make a difference. (we / know – simple present)

2 Put the words in the correct order to make sentences.

1 should / under no circumstances / you / leave / unnecessarily / lights switched on
2 the damage to the environment/ they / did / realize / not until much later / the extent of
3 they / did / at no time / criticize / companies / for being wasteful
4 little / the danger to the environment / did / of using fertilizers / they / realize
5 have / seen / we / such successful business / seldom / downsizing
6 they / did / only after / the principal's speech / avoiding waste / appreciate / the benefit of

3 Read the *Look out!* box. Rewrite the sentences using inversion. Change the tense if necessary.

1 We didn't realize the benefits of downsizing our family car. (little)
2 We discovered that we were using less petrol, and we saved money on car tax and maintenance. (not only, but also)
3 We started using our new car and we noticed the savings in petrol. (no sooner)
4 When the price of hybrid cars using electricity and petrol went down, more people started buying them. (not until)

4 Look at the photo of the hybrid car. Using inversion, make sentences emphasizing the advantages and disadvantages of such a car.

Never have I seen such a ridiculous looking car.

●●●●● Grammar Builder: page 111

●●●●● Workbook: page 70

Green issues

VOCABULARY

1 Check the meaning of the words in the box and complete the text.

> break down   biodegradable   charge up   eco-friendly
> emissions   greenhouse gas   landfill   on standby   toxic

Think green

Protecting the environment is a global issue, so as individuals, how can we make a difference? The best place to start is in our own homes. Here's some ¹eco-friendly advice.

A carbon footprint is the amount of carbon dioxide a person contributes to the atmosphere. Carbon dioxide is a type of ²_____ which is believed to be damaging our environment by causing global warming. Here are two easy ways for us to reduce carbon ³_____ . Firstly, don't leave electrical appliances, such as your TV, ⁴_____. They are still consuming electricity despite not being switched on. Secondly, don't ⁵_____ your mobile phone unnecessarily. Use it until the battery is almost empty.

We should also be aware of what we put in the rubbish. Most rubbish is sent to ⁶_____ . If the rubbish isn't ⁷_____ , it won't ⁸_____ for years or even centuries. In addition, if rubbish is burned in your area, don't throw out plastics. When burned, plastics produce very ⁹_____ chemicals, which pollute the atmosphere and can cause long-term damage to the environment. Take your plastic rubbish to a recyclng centre.

2 Are the following actions good or bad for the environment? Explain why or why not, using words from exercise 1.

1 Throwing away things that are not biodegradable.
   Bad for the environment because it takes a long time for them to break down.
2 Keeping your computer on standby at all times.
3 Using eco-friendly shopping bags.
4 Sorting your rubbish and taking non-biodegradable rubbish to a recycling centre.
5 Charging up your MP3 player every day.
6 Reducing your carbon footprint by walking more.

(●●●●● Workbook: page 71)

LISTEN

1 Look at the photos (A–B) and explain how these environmental problems arise.

2 🎧 (3.11) Listen to an interview with scientist Stuart Brown about some major environmental problems facing the world today. Which of the following things are mentioned?

1 greenhouse gases   4 air travel
2 energy-saving light bulbs 5 biodegradable plastics
3 toxic chemicals   6 carbon footprint

3 🎧 (3.11) Listen again. Choose the correct answers.

1 Which issues are NOT being discussed at the conference?
   a Greenhouse gases and acid rain.
   b Deforestation and dioxins.
   c Landfills and electricity conservation.
2 Which parts of the world are affected by greenhouse gases emitted in China?
   a Only other Asian countries and the United States.
   b Every continent in the world.
   c Mainly North America and Europe.
3 Why is Dr Brown against deforestation?
   a Deforestation in one country spreads to another.
   b The removal of trees leads to more carbon dioxide in the atmosphere.
   c There are no economic benefits.
4 What is Dr Brown's opinion about dioxins?
   a It is an economic issue, not an environmental one.
   b It is not as serious a problem as deforestation.
   c It is the most serious environmental problem.
5 Why are dioxins dangerous?
   a They are a type of greenhouse gas.
   b They pollute the atmosphere.
   c They can enter the food chain.

SPEAK

Work in pairs and answer the questions. Present your ideas to the rest of the class.

1 What can people do as individuals to protect the environment that you live in?
2 Which environmental issue do you think is the biggest threat to your country? Why?
3 What environmental problems can be solved by international cooperation?

Emphatic use of *as...as*

EXPLORE

1 Look at the photo and read the text. How is this computer different from a modern computer?

The first computers were developed more than 60 years ago. They were huge and also very heavy, with some of them weighing as much as 500 kilograms. Despite their size, the first computers were not particularly useful. They could only do simple calculation and other limited functions. In the 1950s, nobody thought that computers would become such an integral part of daily life. Experts at the time predicted there would only ever be as few as 500 computers in the world.

In the early 1970s, government agencies, big corporations, and universities had computer systems, but these cost as much as £2 million each. Personal computers were not at all widespread. It was possible to buy a computer kit to assemble a personal computer. Although as many as 100,000 of these kits were sold, most people did not have the necessary skills to assemble their own computer.

In 1977 Steve Jobs and Steve Wozniak founded Apple Computers, and offered the first mass-market, pre-assembled computers. The Apple computer was extremely successful because it was small and very simple to use.

Since the 1970s, as many as one billion personal computers have been sold worldwide. The cost and size have also been reduced. It is now possible to buy a laptop or small computer for as little as £300!

2 Read the *Learn this!* box. Read the text again. Find six examples of *as...as* structures.

> **LEARN THIS!**
>
> We can use *as...as* to emphasize how big or small things are, by expressing the upper or lower limits of something. We use *as much as* with uncountable quantities (such as weight, cost, time) even when dealing with countable words such as *kilograms*, *pounds* or *hours*. We say *as little as £2* (NOT as few as £2) and *as many as* with countable quantities (such as the number of people or items) to emphasize how big something is, or to express an upper limit.
> *The first computers weighed as much as 500 kilograms.*
> [= The heaviest computers weighed 500 kilograms, but some weighed less than that.]
> We use *as little as* with uncountable quantities or *as few as* with countable quantities to emphasize how small something is, or to express a lower limit.
> *Now it is possible to find computers that weigh as little as 1 kilogram.* [= The lightest computers are 1 kilogram, but some laptop computers weigh more than that.]

(●●●○○ Grammar Reference: page 110)

EXPLOIT

1 Complete the sentences with *as...as* and *much*, *many*, *little*, or *few*.

1 I am concerned about the amount of domestic waste. Each household throws away *as much as* one full bag of rubbish per day.
2 Rhinos are an endangered species, and there may be _____ eight Northern White Rhinos living in captivity today.
3 Some species of deep ocean fish can weigh _____ 100 kilograms.
4 It is possible to fly from one European country to another for _____ 20 euro. That's a bargain!
5 The size of the average American home has grown by _____ 50 per cent in some states.
6 Some tiny homes can accommodate _____ four adults, though single occupancy is more common.

2 Rewrite the sentences with *as...as* to emphasize the quantities.

1 Some plastic can take 500 years to break down.
   Some plastic can take as much as 500 years to break down.
2 It takes 24 trees to make just 1 ton of newspaper.
3 Packaging accounts for 16 per cent of the price of an item.
4 60 per cent of the rubbish that is thrown out could be recycled.
5 Aluminium cans can be recycled and ready to use again in just 6 weeks.
6 Some small computers weigh only 0.6 kilograms.
7 Only two students in my class plan to study physics at university.

3 Correct the errors and explain what's wrong with them.

1 Some reports say as much as a million computers are put into landfill each year.
2 There are as little as two students who travel to school every day by bicycle.
3 We will need as much as 150 laptops to ensure that all students have access to the internet.
4 Some tiny houses don't weigh much as an elephant.
5 A tiny house can be built in as few as thirty days.

(●●●○○ Grammar Builder: page 111)

(●●●○○ Workbook: page 72)

A report: cause and effect

READ

1 Read the report. What possibility is the writer describing? Would it have a positive or negative effect?

The possible effects of climate change on Amman, Jordan

A Amman, the capital city of Jordan, is located on a plateau in the north-west of the country. Because of its elevated location, the city enjoys a pleasant climate with four seasons. In summer, the temperature ranges from 28 to 35 degrees centigrade, but humidity is low and there are cool breezes. In the winter, snow and rain are not uncommon, and they are welcome because they provide water to this very dry area. However, if the temperature of Amman increased by just three degrees, there would be several adverse effects, including an increase in demand for electricity, a decrease in available water, and a strain on medical facilities in the city.

B An increase of just three degrees would lead to an increase in air conditioning use. People using air conditioning in the summer would use it for longer periods during the day, since the temperature would remain hot for more hours of the day. They would use air conditioners for more days of the year, from April or May until October or November. As a result, there would be an increase in the demand for electricity.

C A temperature increase of three degrees would also lead to a decrease in the available water supply. Amman typically enjoys about 260 mm of rain per year. An increase in temperature would result in less rain because of the higher atmospheric temperatures. Less rain or snow would fall to the ground. Furthermore, the rain that did fall would evaporate more quickly in the warmer temperatures. This would lead to a decrease in the amount of water available.

D Finally, an increase in temperature would bring about a strain on medical facilities in the city. Higher temperatures would result in a larger number of elderly people and young children needing treatment in hospital. These groups of people are particularly affected by the heat. Amman currently has an adequate number of hospitals, but they are not equipped to handle a significant increase in patients.

Although Amman is a modern city with adequate resources, an increase in average temperature would undoubtedly have negative effects on the city and the lives of its people.

2 Read the *Writing tip*. Read the report again and complete the effects diagram below to show the consequences of the increase of temperature in Amman.

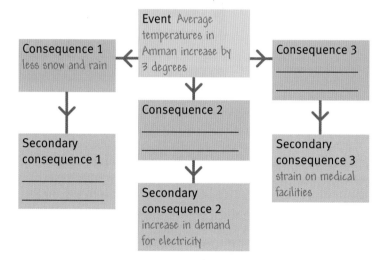

PREPARE

Read the following consequences. Which paragraph (B–D) should each consequence be added to?

1 The price of electricity would increase. B
2 There may not be enough water to maintain parks and gardens.
3 The high demand for electricity could cause more frequent power cuts.
4 It may not be possible to see a doctor on demand.
5 There may be an increase in deaths due to excessive heat.
6 Agriculture may suffer because of inadequate irrigation.

WRITE

1 Write a cause and effect report about one of the topics below. Organize your ideas with an effects diagram.

- An increase in population in my city would have negative consequences.
- One individual can have a positive effect on the environment.
- The effect of the car on modern society has been more positive than negative.
- A decrease in pollution would have positive effects on my city.
- Your own idea.

2 Write 200–250 words. Review your writing. Does it match your effects diagram?

●●●●● Workbook: page 73

Being green

LANGUAGE SKILLS

1 3.12 **Complete the dialogue with the words from the box. Then listen and check your answers.**

as many as · as much as · biodegradable · break down · eco-friendly · get rid of · landfill · mansion · should · you should

Trevor Hi, Mark. What have you got in that bag?
Mark Hi. Oh, it's my old printer. I got a new printer, so I'm going to [1]________ my old one.
Trevor I hope you aren't just going to put it in the rubbish, Mark! Under no circumstances [2]________ you put old electronic goods in the household rubbish. It'll be taken to [3]________, and printers are not [4]________, so it won't [5]________ for thousands of years.
Mark Well, what should I do with it? I don't live in a [6]________. I haven't got space for it.
Trevor Did you know that [7]________ half a million printers are thrown away every year, and that [8]________ 95 per cent of a printer is re-usable? I think [9]________ look for a more [10]________ way of disposing of it. Have you heard of 'Freecycle'?
Mark No. What is it?
Trevor It's a way of advertising unwanted goods on the internet. Anyone who is interested in taking the item can come and collect it from you for free.
Mark Great idea. Sounds like a good way to help the environment.

2 Answer the questions.

1 What is Mark going to put in the rubbish?
2 Why does Trevor think Mark shouldn't put this in the rubbish?
3 Is it common for people to throw away printers?
4 How does the 'freecycle' scheme work?
5 Why does Mark think that 'Freecycle' is a good idea?

3 Match (1–6) with (a–f) to make sentences.

1 Seldom do people realize
2 The world's population is likely to reach as
3 Not until we had bought the house
4 Freecycle has an international network and there are as
5 Little did he know that
6 Most of the world's species diversity is concentrated in as

a his idea would have such an important impact on the environment.
b many as 4,800 schemes around the world.
c how easy it is to recycle household goods.
d few as 25 regions covering just 1.4 per cent of the Earth's surface.
e did we find out that we had to assemble it ourselves.
f much as 9.15 billion in 2050.

DICTIONARY CORNER

Collocations: science and environment

1 Use the dictionary to match the collocations.

1 demographic — c
2 natural
3 solar
4 toxic
5 wildlife

a habitat
b waste
c trend
d resources
e heating

2 Complete the sentences with the correct forms of the collocations from exercise 1.

1 Recent *demographic trends* show significant decreases in the population of Eastern Europe.
2 Rapid economic growth can cause a severe strain on the ________ of a country.
3 The disposal of ________ is the main disadvantage of nuclear power.
4 The spread of urbanization means that more effort is needed to protect ________ .
5 Tiny homes are small enough to rely on ________ provided they are located in a sunny area.

3 Find a collocation with the following words. Write an example sentence for each one.

1 disposable
disposable income: An increase in tax will reduce our disposable income.
2 empirical
3 experimental
4 energy
5 laboratory

I CAN ...

Read the statements. Think about your progress and tick (✓) one of the boxes.

* I need more practice. ** I sometimes find this difficult. *** No problem!

	*	**	***
I can understand a text based on questions and answers.			
I can use inversions for emphasis.			
I can understand and discuss environmental issues.			
I can use emphatic *as...as* to describe limits of countable and uncountable quantities.			
I can organize and write a report using a cause and effect diagram.			

Workbook: Self check pages 74–75

THIS UNIT INCLUDES ● ● ● ●

Vocabulary • talent and ability • music • phrasal verbs and idioms with get • education
Grammar • phrasal verbs • phrasal verbs with objects
Skills • discussing educational needs
Writing • a summary

Gifted and talented
BEFORE READING

Read the *Reading tip*. Then preview the text and answer the questions.

1 What do the three people in the photos have in common?
2 A 'prodigy' is someone who is extremely intelligent or skilful at a young age. What is each person's skill?
3 In your opinion, what are some of the advantages and disadvantages of being very successful at a young age?

Reading tip

Preview a text before you start reading. Look at the photos, the title and the sub-headings. Scan the first and last sentence of each section and try to understand what the main theme of the text is. Think about the topic yourself – what are your views about it?

Rising stars
✴ ✴ ✴ ✴ ✴

Midori Goto

On New Year's Eve in 1982, the curtain opened on one of the world's most prestigious symphony orchestras, the New York Philharmonic. The audience was silent as the conductor took to the stage and announced that a special guest musician would perform that night. He spoke of a virtuoso who was a better violinist than any he had heard before. All eyes turned as Midori Goto walked onstage. Murmurs filled the concert hall as the surprised audience saw that Midori was only 11 years old. Midori earned a standing ovation for her performance, and her career was launched. Since then, she has travelled the world, playing with the finest orchestras and making several highly acclaimed recordings.

Midori's talent was discovered by her mother when Midori was just two years old. She found that Midori had a talent for humming classical songs. When Midori turned three, her grandmother bought her a violin. Midori was so small that her violin was one sixteenth the size of a regular violin. Midori progressed rapidly in her musical studies. She gave her first public performance in Japan at the age of seven. She then moved to New York to study in a preparatory programme for the Julliard School of Music.

Although Midori has a busy programme of concerts and recitals, she has always stayed level-headed by taking time off from practising and performing to give something back to others. She has founded several non-profit organizations that provide music education to children from underprivileged backgrounds.

Mahmoud Wael

To see Mahmoud Wael, you wouldn't think he is any different from other children his age. But Moody, as he is called, is different. At the age of three and a half, his father realized that Moody had a special aptitude for mathematics. As Moody explained, his dad was testing his sister's knowledge of mathematics. He asked her what seven times seven was, but she gave him the wrong answer and so Moody chipped in with the correct answer. By the age of four, Moody had got to grips with arithmetic and was performing two-digit multiplication with ease.

Despite his obvious intellectual gift, Moody's parents are adamant that he should remain a normal boy. His favourite sport is football, which he regularly plays with his friends. He also uses the internet to find information about his favourite football team, Brazil, and his favourite player, one of the stars of the team, Ronaldinho. His parents also refuse to allow him to go to a boarding school abroad. There have been several offers from wealthy sponsors to support Moody's studies in Canada, but his parents have made sure that he stays at home, with his family and friends.

Ricky Rubio

The clock ticks down to the final seconds in the 2006 Under-16 Championship between Russia and Spain. The Russian team leads by three points, an almost-certain victory – until Ricky Rubio grabs the ball at mid-court and hurls it toward the basket just as the buzzer sounds, making the game a three-point tie, and forcing overtime! At 1.91 metres tall, Ricky is not the tallest basketball player, but he is fast, and, as his impressive shot shows, he can successfully score under pressure.

Ricky caught the attention of basketball's top teams and coaches. On his sixteenth birthday, he was awarded a contract to play professional basketball in the Spanish League. This was unprecedented since most players are over 18 years old before receiving a contract for a professional team.

In 2008, Ricky was selected to play for the Spanish national basketball team in the Beijing Olympics. An honour for any athlete, it was even more so for Ricky because he was just 17 years old. He was called upon to play in the game for the gold medal against the United States. Despite being defeated 118–107, Ricky was proud of his team's performance. He said, 'Although we won silver, it felt like gold. The experience of hanging the medal around my neck was something I will always cherish.'

READ

1 Read the text. Decide if the sentences are true or false.

1 Midori's talent was discovered by her grandmother.
2 Midori wants other people to benefit from her talent.
3 Mahmoud's favourite footballer is from Canada.
4 Mahmoud's parents think being with his family is more important than going away to study.
5 Ricky was not the first 16-year-old player in the Spanish League.
6 Ricky was happy with the silver medal win in the Olympics.

2 🎧 3.16 Read the text again. Choose the best answers.

1 When Midori was three years old, she
   a played in New York.
   b began humming classical tunes.
   c received her first violin.
   d gave a performance in Japan.
2 In addition to performing, Midori also
   a plays music to children who can't afford to attend concerts.
   b donates money so that children from poor families can go to school.
   c helps children from poorer backgrounds get an education in music.
   d travels the world to find other children who are talented in music.
3 Mahmoud's gift for mathematics
   a was discovered by his sister.
   b has prevented him from having a normal childhood.
   c has earned him a chance to study in Brazil.
   d was discovered before he turned four.

4 Mahmoud Wael
   a looks different from other children his age.
   b doesn't have the same interests as other children his age.
   c loves to play football with his friends.
   d is going to study in Canada.
5 At the age of 16, Ricky Rubio
   a scored an important point in a game against Russia.
   b played for Spain in the Beijing Olympics.
   c began playing professional basketball.
   d was invited to join the Olympic team.
6 In the Beijing Olympics, the Spanish national basketball team
   a didn't win a gold medal.
   b was unhappy with their performance.
   c didn't have any players under the age of 28.
   d lost to Russia by 118 points.

UNDERSTANDING IDEAS

Answer the questions. Look at the text, and use your own words and ideas.

1 In your opinion, what are the difficulties of being a child prodigy?
2 If you were a child prodigy, what kind would you like to be? Why?
3 Do you think there are any problems with being cleverer than your brother or sister?
4 Do you have any special skills that you would like to develop?

VOCABULARY

Rising stars

Match the highlighted words in the text with these definitions.

1 An extremely skilled performer.
2 Sensible and able to make good decisions.
3 Joined a conversation or added to a discussion.
4 Of very high quality; esteemed.
5 Enthusiastic clapping by an audience as a sign of approval.
6 Success in a game, an election, or a war.
7 Began an activity.
8 Determined not to change your mind about something.
9 Natural ability or skill at doing something.
10 Praised by critics or experts.
11 Formally invited by somebody to take part.
12 A situation where both teams have the same number of points.
13 Never done or known before.
14 To keep an idea or pleasant feeling in your mind for a long time.
15 To be forced to do something quickly or successfully.

(●●○ Workbook: page 76)

Rising stars

ACTIVATE

Complete the sentences with the correct form of the words from the box.

> acclaimed adamant aptitude call upon cherish chip in
> launch level-headed prestigious standing ovation
> tie under pressure unprecedented victory virtuoso

1 I will always _____ the memory of childhood holidays spent with my grandparents.
2 Many believe Oxford and Cambridge are the most _____ universities in Britain.
3 It was a great honour when our team was _____ to play in the opening match of the tournament.
4 They were _____ that their invention would be a success, though many at the time were sceptical.
5 The amount of rain we received in the region last week was _____ . Many areas flooded because the drains were inadequate.
6 Her speech was so inspiring that the audience gave her a _____ .
7 'The game's almost over and the score's still 1–1. It looks like it's going to be a _____ !'
8 His first movie was highly _____ and it _____ his career as a film director.
9 As well as being a successful composer, he was also a violin _____ and performed with all the great orchestras.
10 Many graduates are _____ to find a job when they leave college, so they often end up job-hunting during their final exams.
11 In an emergency, you need someone who is _____ to take charge of the situation.
12 It was a long and difficult struggle, but in the end we claimed _____ and returned home with the trophy.
13 We were having an interesting discussion until Mark _____ with a personal comment which changed the discussion into a heated debate!
14 I have no _____ for maths or science so I want to focus on humanities for my university study.

EXTEND

Music

1 Put the words in the correct columns.

> anthem composer conductor flute opera pianist
> symphony synthesizer violin

Types of music / song	People	Instruments
anthem	_____	_____
_____	_____	_____
_____	_____	_____

2 Complete the sentences with words from exercise 1.
1 The national anthem of Spain hasn't got any words.
2 Beethoven's most famous _____ is probably his 5th.
3 Camilla will probably be a great _____ some day. Her scales are amazing and she has a great ear for music.
4 Stories are told through music and song in _____ .
5 A _____ has got four strings.
6 The _____ spent several days perfecting his new piece for a world premiere performance.
7 A lot of popular music is created with a _____ which can copy the sounds of lots of different instruments.
8 My _____ is made of metal, but my uncle has one made of wood.
9 The _____ motioned for all the musicians in the orchestra to stand up at the end of the performance.

Phrasal verbs and idioms with *get*

3 Match the phrasal verbs and idioms with *get* (1–9) with the definitions (a–i).

1 get across
2 get at sb
3 get by
4 get into
5 get over
6 get rid of sth
7 get to grips with sth
8 get to the bottom of sth
9 get up to

a to be busy doing something
b to throw away or dispose of something
c to communicate or explain something
d to begin to understand something difficult
e to criticize somebody
f to recover from something
g to investigate the real cause of the problem
h to become interested or involved in something
i to do something with limited resources

4 Complete the sentences, using the correct form of a phrasal verb or idiom from exercise 3.
1 It was a difficult concept to get across to the class.
2 We had to _____ a lot of excess furniture when we moved to a smaller house.
3 When we _____ it, we realized that there had been a misunderstanding.
4 My dad couldn't _____ his new mobile phone at first, but now he uses it all the time.
5 I don't know why everyone is _____ me – I haven't done anything wrong!
6 What did you _____ on holiday? I hope you had a good time.
7 It took me a while to _____ this new novel, but now I can't put it down.
8 My French is not great, but I know enough to _____ .
9 She _____ the disappointment of not getting the job and now she's looking for another one.

⬤⬤⬤⬤⚪⚪ **Workbook: page 77**

Phrasal verbs

EXPLORE

1 Read the text. What happened to Michael Scott's music contract?

Michael Scott was on his way to stardom. He had won the prestigious Young Musician of the Year competition by taking on the challenge of competing against other young and very accomplished musicians. Very quickly, his parents handed over his music career to a performance agent, Bob Edwards. He took over Michael's rise to the top with great enthusiasm, and turned down several good recording contracts before agreeing to a multi-million-dollar deal with Sunny Music Corporation. Sunny executives drew up a five-year contract for Michael, but suddenly, the deal was called off. Sunny executives came in for a huge shock when they tried to sign up the pianist. They discovered he was only 14 years old and below the legal age to have a contract! Edwards is now accusing the company of going back on the original agreement, and he says they had better come up with an alternative solution to resolve the situation.

2 Read the *Learn this!* box. Find ten examples of phrasal verbs in the text.

LEARN THIS!

Phrasal verbs are verbs that consist of a verb + a particle. Three-part phrasal verbs consist of a verb, an adverb, and a preposition e.g. *to go back on*.
Phrasal verbs are idiomatic. Their meaning can't always be understood from the separate parts of the verb.

3 Match the phrasal verbs from the text with the definitions.

1 to produce or find   *come up with*
2 to undertake to do something
3 to change an agreement
4 to contract with or employ someone
5 to take control of
6 to give responsibility to
7 to put together or prepare
8 to cancel
9 to reject
10 to receive something unexpectedly

(●●●●● Grammar Reference: page 112)

EXPLOIT

1 Check the meanings of the phrasal verbs in the box. Complete the sentences with the correct form of one of the phrasal verbs.

| bring up   figure out   get away with   live down   ~~pass up~~ |
| put up with   set off   water down |

1 You shouldn't pass up this opportunity. You may never have another like it.
2 I think you need to _____ the content of your speech for this audience or some people may be offended.
3 These maths problems are impossible to _____ without using a calculator.
4 I'm so embarrassed! I'll never _____ forgetting the headmaster's name during my speech.
5 It's not fair that some students can _____ not doing their homework, whereas other students receive severe punishment.
6 It's going to be quite noisy tonight because they are _____ fireworks as part of the celebration.
7 I wish you wouldn't _____ the topic again. It only makes us argue more.
8 He is a very patient teacher and can _____ a lot of bad behaviour before he really loses his temper.

2 Write your own sentences using six of the verbs in Exploit exercise 1.

She couldn't figure out why her computer wasn't working.

(●●●●● Grammar Builder: page 113)

(●●●●● Workbook: page 78)

Educational needs

VOCABULARY

1 Match words (1–8) with definitions (a–h).

1 accelerated
2 remedial
3 genius
4 special needs
5 augment
6 impediment
7 gifted
8 mediocre

a a disability or hindrance
b speeded up
c enhance or expand
d someone with unusual intelligence
e exceptional or talented
f educational requirements because of a physical or mental disability
g in the middle, average
h corrective or basic

2 Complete the sentences with a word from exercise 1.

1 I don't understand my physics lectures. I'm going to take a _____ course to cover the basics.
2 My younger brother has got _____, so it takes him longer to do his schoolwork.
3 Ruby is a real _____. She is a prodigy in music and mathematics.
4 The pace of our French lessons has really _____. We're covering a unit a week now!
5 Jeremy is a _____ student and athlete. He has won a scholarship to study at Oxford University.
6 Laura is a _____ student, but with a little more effort she could be top of the class.
7 My sister has a speech _____. It's difficult for her to pronounce certain sounds.
8 Our class is exceptionally fast, so our teacher _____ the lessons with additional material from other coursebooks.

3 Look at the photos of two classroom situations. Describe the students in each class. What factors do you think are important to create a good environment for teaching and learning?

●●●●● Workbook: page 79

LISTEN

1 🎧 (3.17) Listen to the conversation between a doctor and teachers of students with special needs. Complete the table with the phrases.

- able to express themselves easily in words
- good at learning in non-traditional ways
- afraid to leave their seat
- going to do well in a traditional school
- gifted at mathematics
- difficult to deal with in a traditional class

Many children with special needs are...	Many children with special needs are not...
1 _____	4 _____
2 _____	5 _____
3 _____	6 _____

2 🎧 (3.17) Listen to the conversation again. Choose the correct answers.

1 Experts on special needs **agree** / **don't agree** on the reasons why there are more children with special needs in schools these days.
2 Basic communication is something many children with special needs **do** / **don't do** well.
3 Behaving in unacceptable ways is something children with special needs **will stop** / **won't stop** on their own.
4 The teacher **reprimands** / **doesn't reprimand** the child with special needs in his class.
5 Kicking and shouting are common behaviour when children with special needs are **excited** / **frustrated**.
6 Many children with special needs **respond** / **don't respond** well to sensory stimulation and touch.

SPEAK

1 With a partner, choose one of the following statements. Discuss the statement and decide if you agree or disagree with it.

1 Students learn more in a traditional classroom environment.
2 Teachers shouldn't reprimand students for bad behaviour in class.
3 Children with special needs should be taught in separate classes.
4 Gifted students should be given more homework.

2 Prepare your arguments for or against the statement. Then present your arguments to the rest of the class.

3 After debating the statement as a class, take a vote and find out what the majority view is.

Phrasal verbs with objects

EXPLORE

1 Read the text. Why did journalists and cameramen want to meet Samantha Larson?

Samantha Larson is not one to back away from a big challenge – or even seven big challenges. She took them on and succeeded in becoming the youngest person to have climbed the world's seven highest mountains. She climbed to the top of Mount Everest in 2007. At times the weather was not good, but the group never thought about calling off the climb. They were prepared to wait out bad weather at their base camp. Finally, the weather cleared and the group made their way to the summit. Samantha blogged about her adventure, but she didn't realize that many newspapers around the world had picked up on her story. She thought the Los Angeles newspapers would pick up on it because LA is her hometown. However, when Samantha flew into Kathmandu on her way home, she was greeted by a mob of journalists and cameramen!

2 Read the *Learn this!* box. Find four more examples of phrasal verbs and their objects in the text.

LEARN THIS!

When a phrasal verb has an object, the phrasal verb can be separated. We can put the object between the main verb and the adverb.
The group never thought about calling off the climb.
The group never thought about calling the climb off.
The group never thought about calling it off.

We cannot place the object after the adverb if it is a pronoun.
What time shall we pick you up?
[NOT *What time shall we pick up you?*]

Three-part phrasal verbs cannot be separated.
[NOT *The newspapers would pick it up on.*]

(●●○○○ Grammar Reference: page 112)

EXPLOIT

1 Read the sentences. Find the phrasal verb and its object. Then rewrite the sentences, using pronouns.

1 We couldn't agree on what to do, but we managed to sort out the problem in the end.
  We couldn't agree on what to do, but we managed to sort it out in the end.
2 We had to get help from the computer shop because we couldn't set up the computers ourselves.
3 You need to find the letter before someone throws the letter away by mistake.
4 The storm is getting worse, so I think you should wait out the storm at home.
5 We asked for volunteers for the project but nobody wanted to take the project on.
6 If you want your legal papers to be accurate, you need a lawyer to draw up your papers.
7 We tried to solve the problem several ways but we just couldn't figure out the answer.
8 We had forgotten the news until Julie brought up the topic at dinner time.
9 The fireworks were very noisy last night. What time did they set off the fireworks?
10 He received an invitation to play with the national team. I told him not to pass up such a wonderful opportunity.

2 Correct the errors.

1 We're not going on the climbing expedition because the leaders called off it.
2 If we work together, I think we can come with some good ideas for our report.
3 I'm very upset about the mistake, but I'm trying to live them down.
4 I'm surprised the editor didn't pick it up on.
5 I don't trust him because he has gone back his promises so many times.
6 Our class can't do three projects because there aren't enough team leaders to take on it.
7 I forgot to finish my homework last night. I'm going to have to come up a good excuse with.
8 They tried to avoid paying the fine but they didn't get away it.

(●●●○○ Grammar Builder: page 113)
(●●●○○ Workbook: page 80)

A summary

READ

Read the article. What is the main idea that the author wants to convey?

A Rosie is misunderstood by her parents, so they need to talk to a psychologist.

B Most prodigies go through different stages of growth and may have difficult times at some point.

C Once some prodigies reach their teenage years, they lose interest in everything.

D Rosie is a very troubled girl whose parents need to support her.

It's tough being clever

When Rosie was three, she had already learnt to read. Psychologists, doctors, and teachers declared that Rosie was a prodigy. Rosie did incredibly well in primary school, earning top marks in all her subjects and in her spare time, she became a piano virtuoso. However, when Rosie entered her early teens, her marks in school dropped significantly and she no longer showed any interest in playing the piano. In fact, she essentially withdrew from the world, ignoring the TV, the computer, books, and her family. She seemed sad and lonely.

Because of this change in behaviour, Rosie's parents worried she was ill or had lost her intelligence. They took her to a psychologist, who concluded Rosie was like the twenty other prodigies he had seen in his career. Rosie felt that she was under tremendous pressure and stress to be perfect. The psychologist reported that this type of change in behaviour was extremely common among highly-gifted children. These children feel pressure to be perfect and become afraid of failing. At the same time, they want to be like other children their age. They don't want to feel different or strange, so they stop doing well in school, often turning into mediocre students. This process leads to sadness and behavioural changes.

The psychologist gave Rosie's family the same advice he had given the other families of troubled prodigies. He recommended that they be patient with her. He also recommended that they make a special effort to show they loved her, even if she wasn't doing well at school. He reminded them that prodigies go through the normal stages of childhood development, so they should expect Rosie to make mistakes and act like other teenagers who did not have her academic aptitude. Finally, he reassured them that Rosie was most likely going through a temporary condition, and that she would probably perform well in school again.

PREPARE

Writing tip: focusing on main ideas

A summary gives the main idea or important information from a text and shows that you have understood the main points. It is essential to write a summary using your own words. Don't include too many details, and don't include your opinions.

Effective summary content:
Many prodigies feel that they are under pressure to be perfect.

Ineffective summary content:
Rosie became a piano virtuoso as a child. [unnecessary detail]
I think Rosie will return to being her old self. [opinion]

1 Read the *Writing tip*. Which of the following information is suitable for inclusion in a summary of the text?

   1 Rosie wasn't interested in watching TV, reading, or studying, and she didn't want to socialize with her family.

   2 It is not uncommon for prodigies to show feelings of sadness and withdrawal when they enter their teens.

   3 Prodigies don't want to be different from others their age.

   4 The psychologist has worked with twenty other child prodigies who have had difficulties as they entered their teens.

   5 It is important for parents of teenage prodigies like Rosie to be patient and show their love under all conditions.

   6 Rosie will make mistakes, just like teenagers who aren't as academically gifted as she is.

2 Answer the questions about the text and use your answers to form your summary.

   1 What significant event happened in Rosie's childhood?

   2 What changed in her teens?

   3 What did her parents do?

   4 What did the psychologist conclude?

   5 What did the psychologist recommend?

WRITE

1 Choose one of the texts in this book or an article of your choice from a newspaper or magazine to summarize.

2 Find the main ideas and key pieces of information. Cross out any unnecessary details.

3 Write the main ideas in your own words.

4 Review your summary. Have you included only relevant information and used your own words?

●●●●● Workbook: page 81

Child's play

LANGUAGE SKILLS

1 🎧 (3.18) Complete the dialogue with the words from the box. Then listen and check your answers.

> aptitude   figure it out   get away with   get by
> get to grips with   level-headed   pass up   prestigious
> remedial   under pressure

Betty You look really fed up. What's the matter?

Mike It's this chemistry homework. I've been trying to do it for hours but I just can't ¹_____ it.

Betty Well, don't ask me to help! My exam marks were so bad that I'm taking ²_____ chemistry classes.

Mike Chemistry is not my best subject, but usually I can ³_____ . But today's homework is beyond me. I can't ⁴_____ at all.

Betty Actually I don't have much ⁵_____ for sciences. I do much better in humanities subjects.

Mike Yes, you must be good at literature. Didn't you get a ⁶_____ award for one of your poems?

Betty That's right. I won the Mary Turner Prize for poetry. I couldn't believe it. Unfortunately I wasn't able to attend the prize-giving ceremony.

Mike That's too bad. Why did you have to ⁷_____ the chance?

Betty I had an important exam the next day, so I couldn't ⁸_____ having the day off.

Mike You're just so ⁹_____! I'm sure I would have taken advantage of the chance to enjoy the limelight.

Betty Well, I decided that I wouldn't enjoy it if I was ¹⁰_____ to do well in an exam. Hopefully there will be another opportunity one day.

Mike I hope so. Anyway, I'd better get back to my homework!

2 Decide if the sentences are true or false. Correct the false ones.

1 Betty is in the advanced class for chemistry.
2 Mike usually finds chemistry easy.
3 Betty won an award for literature.
4 Betty didn't have time to go to the awards ceremony.
5 Mike wouldn't have gone to the ceremony either.
6 Mike and Betty are very serious about their studies.

3 Choose the correct words.

1 We were asked to **draw up** / **sign up** a contract for the recording deal.
2 The director had to apologize after making a silly mistake. It's going to take a while for him to live **it** / **them** down.
3 I **get into** / **get away** the football season every autumn.
4 We were all excited about the match but in the end they **called it off** / **called off it** because of bad weather.
5 What about question number two? Have you **got over** / **figured out** the answer yet?
6 They have found an unexpected fault with the new device. We need to **come up with** / **go back on** a solution as soon as possible.

DICTIONARY CORNER

Expressions with *dumb* and *smart*

1 Look at the entries for *dumb* and *smart* and complete the phrases. Match them with their definitions.

1 smart (from sth)
2 _____ move
3 struck _____
4 _____ down
5 _____ set
6 act _____

a connected with fashionable rich people
b an intelligent action
c to make something less educational or easier for people to understand
d to feel a sharp stinging pain in a part of your body
e to pretend that you don't know something
f temporarily not speaking or refusing to speak

2 Complete the sentences with the correct form of a phrase from exercise 1.

1 It was a smart move to sell that gold last year when the prices were high.
2 Don't _____. I know that you have my book.
3 I was _____ by her rude question. I couldn't believe she had asked it!
4 Since Denise got a job with a TV company, she spends all her time with the _____.
5 This course used to be very challenging, but the examiners _____ the syllabus, so more people pass now.
6 My eyes _____ from the smoke of the fire.

Example sentences

3 Look up these expressions related to intelligence, and write an example sentence to show their meaning.

> ~~brainwave~~   bright spark   clever clogs   dim-witted
> dumfounded   quick-witted

brainwave – We weren't sure what to do. Suddenly Matt had a brainwave.

I CAN ...

Read the statements. Think about your progress and tick (✓) one of the boxes.

| ✱ | I need more practice. | ✱✱ | I sometimes find this difficult. | ✱✱✱ | No problem! |

	✱	✱✱	✱✱✱
I can understand and discuss an article about child prodigies.			
I can use phrasal verbs correctly.			
I can form an opinion about educational needs.			
I can use phrasal verbs with objects and pronouns.			
I can summarize a long text.			

(●●○○○   Workbook: Self check pages 82–83)

Hamlet

by William Shakespeare

Biography

William Shakespeare was born in England in 1564. He wrote thirty-eight plays, which have been translated into almost every language. His plays include comedies (*The Merchant of Venice*, *A Midsummer Night's Dream*, and *As You Like It*), tragedies (*Hamlet*, *Macbeth*, and *Romeo and Juliette*), and historical plays (*King John*, *Richard II*, and *King Henry V*). Although he died in 1616, he is still considered by many to be the greatest writer in the English language.

Gertrude
Good Hamlet, cast thy nightly colour off,
And let thine eye look like a friend on Denmark.
Do not for ever with thy vailed lids
Seek for thy noble father in the dust.
Thou know'st 'tis common – all that lives must die,
Passing through nature to eternity.

Hamlet
Ay, madam, it is common.
Gertrude
If it be,
Why seems it so particular with thee?
Hamlet
Seems, madam? Nay, it is, I know not 'seems'.
'Tis not alone my inky cloak, good mother,
Nor customary suits of solemn black,
Nor windy suspiration of forced breath,
No, nor the fruitful river in the eye,
Nor the dejected haviour of the visage,
Together with all forms, moods, shows of grief,
That can denote me truly. These indeed seem,
For they are actions that a man might play;
But I have that within which passeth show –
These but the trappings and the suits of woe.

Claudius
'Tis sweet and commendable in your nature, Hamlet,
To give these mourning duties to your father;
But you must know your father lost a father;
That father lost, lost his; and the survivor bound
In filial obligation for some term
To do obsequious sorrow. But to persever
In obstinate condolement is a course
Of impious stubbornness, 'tis unmanly grief,
It shows a will most incorrect to heaven,
A heart unfortified, a mind impatient,
An understanding simple and unschooled;
For what we know must be, and is as common
As any the most vulgar thing to sense,
Why should we in our peevish opposition
Take it to heart? Fie, 'tis a fault to heaven,
A fault against the dead, a fault to nature,
To reason most absurd, whose common theme
Is death of father, and who still hath cried,
From the first corpse till he that died today,
'This must be so'. We pray you throw to earth
The unprevailing woe, and think of us
As of a father; for let the world take note
You are the most immediate to our throne,
And with no less nobility of love
Than that which dearest father bears his son
Do I impart towards you. For your intent
In going back to school in Wittenberg,
It is most retrograde to our desire,
And we beseech you bend you to remain
Here in the cheer and comfort of our eye,
Our chiefest courtier, cousin, and our son.

1 🎧 (3.21) **Read the text. Choose the correct answers.**

1 Gertrude is Hamlet's **wife / mother**.
2 Hamlet is mourning the death of his **father / grandfather**.
3 Hamlet is **a student / a king**.
4 Claudius **wants / doesn't want** Hamlet to go back to Wittenberg.

2 **Answer the questions. Look at the text, and use your own words and ideas to explain your answers.**

1 What is Gertrude's reaction to her husband's death? Do you think it's appropriate? Why or why not?
2 In your opinion, does Hamlet seem truly upset about the situation? Why or why not?

3 What is Claudius's opinion about showing grief? Do you agree with it? Why or why not?
4 What do you think is the relationship between Claudius and Hamlet?

3 **Look at some of the archaic language from the text. Match Shakespeare's language with its modern version.**

ask	no	your	you	it's	has	you know	sorrow

1 Nay _____   5 hath _____
2 'tis _____   6 thou know'st _____
3 thine _____   7 woe _____
4 thee _____   8 beseech _____

Types of home

READ

1 Look at the photos and read the text. In your opinion, which type of home is:

   a the most portable? **b** the cheapest? **c** the most convenient?

Home is where I hang my hat

Most people think of a typical home as a flat, a semi-detached house, or a detached house. However, in many parts of the world, people have chosen to opt for something more unusual.

Beyond Central Asia

Yurts are portable tent-like structures that originated with the nomadic people of Central Asia. Today, thousands of people in the UK and US live in yurts. Although some people live in yurts permanently, they are better suited to those who like to move around more frequently. Traditional yurts are supported by wooden poles and covered with heavy felt-like fabric. However, Western yurts often have metal poles and are covered with heavy cotton. It is possible to enjoy all the conveniences of modern life in a yurt, but this requires some effort since a yurt is essentially a portable home. Typically, those who choose to live in a yurt don't mind a less convenient life.

Cruising away

Houseboats are common in many cities and towns in the UK and US that have canals or rivers. Most houseboats are flat-bottom boats that can be motored to a different location, but more commonly, they are anchored permanently. Inside, the houseboat is similar to a small flat, complete with kitchen, living room, bedrooms, and bathroom. Space is very limited, so houseboats are not for people who have many possessions. However, this doesn't always lead to lower living expenses since houseboats must be properly maintained. It is important to keep the boat in good condition, which can be costly.

Park life

One kind of living that is more common in the US than anywhere else in the world is the trailer. A trailer is a long, narrow metal space that is typically covered with aluminium. Most people do not move their trailers, preferring to park them in small communities called trailer parks. Although trailer parks are viewed stereotypically as low-income housing, there are many hardworking families who live in them. Trailers are a good option for those who don't need a lot of space and don't want to spend a lot of money maintaining a house. They are also easy to equip with all the modern conveniences of life.

2 Read the text again. Are the sentences true or false?

  1 Traditional yurts use different materials from yurts in Western countries.

  2 It is impossible to equip a yurt with modern conveniences.

  3 Most houseboats are similar to flats on the inside.

  4 Living in a houseboat is less expensive than living in a traditional home.

  5 Houseboats and trailers are suitable homes for people who do not collect or keep many things.

  6 Most people who live in a trailer do not move the trailer to different locations.

3 Answer the questions. Use your own words and ideas.

  1 What are the advantages and disadvantages of living in each type of home?

  2 Which of the three types of home appeals to you most? Why?

  3 What other types of homes have you heard of? Where are they located?

LISTEN

1 🎧 (3.22) Listen to a conversation between Tony and a friend. Which of the following things do we learn about Tony?

  1 He has more than one sister. ☐

  2 He will be moving to a bigger house. ☐

  3 He is planning to go to university. ☐

  4 He is going to study environmental science. ☐

  5 His parents are interested in organic gardening. ☐

  6 He doesn't like his friend's suggestion. ☐

2 🎧 (3.22) Listen to the conversation again and answer the questions.

  1 Why do Tony's parents want to move?

  2 What is Sadie's opinion about Tony's current home?

  3 Why won't Tony's dad hire a gardener?

  4 What kind of home does Tony want his parents to think about moving to? Why?

  5 What kind of home does Sadie suggest for Tony's parents?

  6 Why is Tony enthusiastic about her idea?

WRITE AND SPEAK

Describe the home you live in. What do you like about it? What would you like to change? Describe your ideal home.

Stative verbs

- Stative verbs are verbs that describe states. These include verbs related to the senses (*feel*, *hear*, *see*, *smell*, *sound*, *taste*) and other verbs such as *believe*, *cost*, *hate*, *hear*, *like*, *know*, *matter*, *prefer*, *realize*, *understand*, *want*.

- The following are further examples of stative verbs:

  be, appear, astonish, concern, consist, deny, doubt, disagree, deserve, dislike, fit, impress, include, involve, lack, mean, need, owe, own, please, promise, realize, recognize, remember, suppose, surprise, wish

- Stative verbs are usually used in the simple, not the continuous form.

  Sports cars cost a lot of money.

  We don't understand the question.

  Did you hear me?

- Some stative verbs have a different, active meaning that can be used in the simple or continuous form. These include *feel*, *have*, *look*, *see*, *smell*, *taste*, *think*, *weigh*.

Verb	Stative meaning (simple only)	Active meaning (simple or continuous)
feel	This material feels soft. [sense]	Are you feeling OK? [emotion]
have	They have two houses. [own]	Jo's having a shower. [activity]
imagine	I imagine it's cold in Oslo. [suppose]	I'm imagining what I'd do with a million pounds. [think about]
look	You look lovely. [appearance]	I'm looking at some photos. [see]
see	Can you see anything? [sense]	You're seeing Mr Day at 3.00. [have a meeting]
smell	Your hair smells nice. [sense]	I'm smelling the milk to see if it's OK. [activity]
taste	This soup tastes watery. [sense]	I'm tasting the soup to check if I need to add salt. [activity]
think	I think this one is better. [opinion]	I'm thinking of dying my hair. [consider a plan]
weigh	How much do you weigh? [weight]	They're weighing the package to see how much it will cost to send. [activity]

Expressing trends with simple and continuous forms

- We do not use the present simple to describe trends, unless we are talking about situations that are generally true within a given context.

  Usually, people spend more money when the economy is doing well.

- We use the present continuous to talk about current developments and changes, whether these occur over a short period or are long-lasting. These changes may continue in the future.

  The universe is **expanding**.

  The number of people deciding to go to university is increasing.

- We use the past continuous to talk about temporary trends which were happening at a specific point in the past. These changes have finished.

  In the 1920s, electricity was becoming common in British homes.

- The past simple is not used to talk about trends.

- We use the present perfect simple to talk about trends that began in the past but which are still continuing, or trends that recently finished but which have results that are visible or relevant now.

  I think that exams **have got** easier over the past ten or fifteen years. There's no sign of this situation changing any time soon.

  Air travel **has become** more affordable. Even people on low incomes can fly to Europe for the weekend.

- We can also use the present perfect continuous to talk about trends. Its use is often similar to the present perfect simple.

  People say that exams **have been getting** easier over the past ten to fifteen years.

- The main difference is that the present perfect continuous places greater emphasis on the continuous nature of the change. This is often supported by expressions such as 'more and more' and 'over the past few months / weeks / years'.

  Air travel **has been becoming** more and more affordable for some time now.

1 Choose the correct option.

1 You **look** / **'re looking** a lot like Aunt Jean in this photo.
2 Who **do you write** / **are you writing** that letter to?
3 This perfume *is* **smelling** / **smells** of vanilla and orange.
4 Suddenly, a strange man **arrived** / **was arriving** from nowhere.
5 Who's that? **I'm not recognizing** / **don't recognize** her.
6 When I tried the dress on, it **didn't fit** / **wasn't fitting** me.
7 What music **is Jack listening** / **does Jack listen to**? It's really loud.
8 I called her name, but she **wasn't hearing** / **didn't hear** us.

2 Complete the dialogue with the present simple or present continuous form of the verbs in brackets. Sometimes more than one answer is possible.

Jon   What ¹_____ (you / think) about? You ²_____ (have) a really strange expression on your face.
Clare   What ³_____ (you / mean)?
Jon   You ⁴_____ (seem) a bit sad, that's all.
        ⁵_____ (You / feel) all right?
Clare   Yes, I'm fine. I ⁶_____ (think) about my sister, Chloe. She's in France for the summer and I really miss her.
Jon   Oh, I'm sorry. I hope she ⁷_____ (have) a good time, though.
Chloe   I ⁸_____ . She ⁹_____ (look) really happy in the photos she emailed me. It's just that I ¹⁰_____ (wish) I was with her!

3 Five of the sentences contain errors. Correct them.

1 Do you know what the time is?
2 I'm not understanding what this means.
3 My parents are thinking of buying a new house.
4 The milk wasn't smelling good.
5 He's very thin. How much is he weighing?
6 Jake and Sandra are having a fantastic time in France.
7 It's seeming unnecessary for all of us to go with you.
8 She is having a lovely cat called Rosie.

4 Put the following sentences into the correct category.

A	B	C
Current trends	Trends that have finished	Trends that began in the past but are still happening or relevant

1 The number of people booking holidays online has increased dramatically. ___
2 For several years, road traffic accidents were increasing. ___
3 People have been trying to reduce their carbon footprint. ___
4 We are all trying to economize. ___
5 The population was increasing for a long time. ___
6 The economy is continuing to grow. ___
7 Car ownership has gone up dramatically over the past forty years. ___
8 Many businesses weren't adapting quickly enough to changing tastes. ___

5 Write the sentences, using the present continuous, past continuous and present perfect simple. More than one answer is sometimes possible.

1 Recently, the evenings / start / to get darker earlier
2 The internet / change / the way we work and relax
3 people's lives / improve / over the past decades / ?
4 In the 1940s, the lack of food in Britain / start / to become a serious problem
5 Currently, we / experience / difficult economic conditions
6 So far this year, / the situation / not be / too bad
7 During the war, women / do / men's jobs
8 According to a report published today, / people / get / fatter.

6 Read the information and complete the sentences with a verb from the box. Use the present continuous, past continuous or present perfect simple form.

Packard biscuits started production in 1963. They didn't make a profit until 1965, but after that, they gradually made an impact on the biscuit market. Packard think that this steady growth is one of the main reasons for their present-day success. In 2007-2008, they introduced new technology, and this immediately improved their production methods. This process of modernization is still continuing. In 2007, Packard began a new marketing strategy, which increased their profits. As a result of this, Packard are in talks with a rival biscuit-maker, and it is likely that they will buy the other company. However, preparations have begun to discontinue some of the less popular types of biscuit.

speed up   stop   not make   aim
talk   improve   modernize   increase

1 Between 1963 and 1965, Packard biscuits _____ a profit.
2 During 2007 and 2008, they _____ their production processes.
3 The introduction of new technology _____ production considerably.
4 Packard _____ its technical operations very effectively.
5 Since 2008, Packard's profits _____ .
6 Packard _____ about buying another company.
7 One of the reasons for Packard's current success is the fact that, in the early days, they _____ to increase their impact on the biscuit market steadily rather than to make a quick profit.
8 Packard _____ the manufacture of the less popular types of biscuit.

Past tenses for distancing

- Past tenses are sometimes used instead of present tenses when we want to sound less direct, and therefore more polite. We use past tenses in this way when asking a question or making a request.

- The past simple is used instead of the present simple.

  Did you want to add anything to the discussion?
  (= 'Do you want to ...?')

  Did you have a particular present in mind?
  (= 'Do you have ... in mind?')

- The past continuous is used instead of the present continuous with verbs such as *hope*, *think* and *wonder*.

  Were you **hoping** to travel to Scotland on this visit?
  (= 'Are you hoping to ...?')

  What **were** you **thinking** of buying Jack for his birthday?
  (= 'What are you thinking of ...?')

- Sometimes a sentence beginning with a past tense for distancing purposes contains a second clause. If so, the verb in the second clause is usually in a present tense, because we are asking someone about a present or future situation.

  Were you hoping to travel to Scotland while you**'re visiting** the UK?

  NOT Were you hoping to travel to Scotland while you were visiting the UK?

- Another way to use distancing language is to introduce a question or request with the verb *wonder* in the past continuous. The question or request can be direct or indirect. Direct questions must follow a colon.

  I **was wondering**: is there a picnic area around here?

  We **were wondering** if you want to travel with us.

- In an indirect question following *was / were wondering*, we can use the past simple to add another layer of distancing.

  We **were wondering** if you **wanted** to travel with us.

- We can use *wonder* in the past simple also, but the verb in the indirect question is usually in the past simple.

  We **wondered** if you **wanted** to travel with us.

Modals for distancing

- The modal verbs *could*, *would* and *might* are sometimes used instead of present tenses when we want to make a question or request sound less direct.

  Questions with modals do not use an auxiliary. The word order is indirect.

  Could you tell me where the nearest bank is?

  NOT Could you tell me where is the nearest bank?

- A more tentative way of making a request is *could ... possibly*. We only use this when we think that our interruption may be unwelcome for a particular reason.

  Could you **possibly** tell me how to get to the station from here?

- We use *would* and *might* in requests and offers. *Might* is more tentative.

  Would you be interested in our latest promotion? [= offer]

  Would you like to see the wine list? [= offer]

  Might you prefer to sit near the window? [= offer]

  Might you take your feet off the seat, please? [= request / instruction]

- We can use *might* in the first person to introduce an indirect question, in expressions such as *Might I ask ...?*

  Might I ask who your meeting is with?

- *Would* can also be used before verbs of saying and thinking to make a statement sound more tentative and an instruction less direct.

  I **would think** we'll reach the hotel by five o'clock.

  We **would ask** that guests requiring breakfast in their rooms inform us by midnight.

- We can use *could*, *would* and *might* after the verb *wonder*.

  I **was wondering** if you **could** do something for me.

  We **wondered** if you **would / might** give a donation to charity.

1 Tick the correct sentence in each pair. Sometimes both are correct.

1 A I wondered if you had any change.
  B I was wondering: do you have any change?
2 A She was hoping to visit Bath while she's been here.
  B She was hoping to visit Bath while she's here.
3 A We were wondering if you want to accompany us?
  B We were wondering if you wanted to accompany us?
4 A What time were you hoping to have dinner this evening?
  B What time were you hoping to have dinner that evening?
5 A Jon and I were wanting to do some travelling.
  B Jon and I wanted to do some travelling.
6 A Did you think of staying another night?
  B Were you thinking of staying another night?
7 A I wondered: you could advise me?
  B I wondered if you could advise me.
8 A We were wondering if one of the sea-view rooms was still being available.
  B We were wondering if one of the sea-view rooms is still available.

2 Change the underlined verbs using distancing.

1 Do you want any help?   _____
2 Are you intending to dine here?   _____
3 I'm wondering if the café is still open.   _____
4 What time do you want to eat?   _____
5 We're hoping to see the sights.   _____
6 Have you got a reservation?   _____
7 Where do you want to sit?   _____
8 When are you thinking of going?   _____

3 Write sentences, using distancing techniques.

1 you / hope / to stay / in a hotel / while / you be / here / ?
2 you / want / to go / to bed immediately / when / you arrive / ?
3 I / wonder / what time / you / serve / breakfast / ?
4 what time / you / think / of / leaving / ?
5 we / hope / to stay / for another night
6 you / think / of / visit / the museum while you're here / ?
7 you / have / a particular excursion / in mind / ?
8 I / intend / to take a taxi

4 Say whether the following sentences are offers (O), requests (R) or instructions (I).

1 Would you like another piece of pie? ___
2 Would you pass the salt? ___
3 Could you take your feet off the seat? ___
4 Might you prefer the fish? ___
5 I would think you'd like a cup of tea after your journey. ___
6 Could you give me a bit more time? ___
7 Might I ask that you put your crisp packet in the bin? ___
8 Might I ask what you're doing in here? ___

5 Correct the modal verb, if necessary.

1 Could you possibly pass me those plates?
2 Could you be able to advise me?
3 I could ask you to keep your voice down in here.
4 Would I request that you eat your sandwiches outside?
5 It's going to snow? Yes, I would think you're right.
6 Might you possibly tell me how to get to the station?
7 We could ask that people using the library respect the rules.
8 Would you be interested in this, madam?

6 Complete the sentences with the phrases in the box.

I was wondering   Could I   Might you   Might you prefer Could you   I would think   I would ask   Would you like

1 _____ to go somewhere less noisy?
2 _____ that you finish your lunch and leave.
3 _____ to have another cup of tea?
4 _____ want to know more about our special offers?
5 _____ we'll reach Teresa's at about seven o'clock.
6 _____ if you'd like to go to the cinema some time?
7 _____ let me know if you're going to be late?
8 _____ possibly have a glass of water?

Conditionals without *if*

- There are several expressions that have a similar meaning to *if* in conditional sentences.

- The expressions *imagine (that)*, *suppose* and *supposing (that)* are used to talk about what might be the outcome of a hypothetical situation.

- These expressions are used with 2nd and 3rd conditional sentences, and always require two sentences. The first of these contains the condition, at the beginning of the sentence. The second expresses the outcome.

  Imagine (that) you won £1 million. You'd be very rich. [2nd conditional]

  Suppose I hadn't met you at the station. You wouldn't have been able to get home. [3rd conditional]

  Supposing (that) you didn't have to work. What would you do all day? [2nd conditional]

- The expressions *as / so long as*, *on condition that* and *provided (that) / providing* are used to make a condition.

- These expressions are used in all types of conditional structures, and link two clauses in a single sentence.

  I'll come to watch you play football **as / so long as** there's somewhere to sit. [1st conditional]

  I'd do anything to help **provided (that)** it wasn't illegal. [2nd conditional]

  I would have I lent him my new MP3 player **providing** he hadn't broken my old one. [3rd conditional]

- The expressions *as / so long as*, *on condition* and *provided (that) / providing* are generally not followed by *would*. These expressions occur frequently in mixed conditionals.

  She has agreed to sponsor me **on condition (that)** I **complete** the race. [mixed conditional]

  NOT She has agreed to sponsor me on condition (that) I would complete the race.

If only ...

- *If only* is a stronger form of *I wish*, and expresses a desire for a situation to be different. The tenses or structures that follow *if only* are determined by whether we are referring to the past, present or future.

- In a sentence with more than one clause, *if only* usually appears first, as a subordinate clause. The main clause uses a verb in the conditional form: either *would* + infinitive or *would* + *have* + past participle.

- *If only* + past simple refers to the present

  If only we **had** more time, we would stay to watch the match. (= but we don't have more time, so we won't stay to watch the match)

- When *if only* is followed by the past simple of *be*, it is common to use *were* rather than *was* in the first and third person singular.

  If only my brother weren't so stubborn, we **would** get on much better. (= but he is stubborn, so we don't get along very well)

- *If only* + *would* + infinitive refers to the future

  If only Chloe would wear nicer clothes, she **would** feel more confident. (= but she won't wear nicer clothes, so she won't feel confident)

- *If only* + past perfect refers to the past

  If only we had brought a map, we **wouldn't** have got lost. (= but we didn't bring a map, so we did get lost)

- We can use *might* or *could* in the main clause.

  If only we had more time, we **could visit the museum** today.

  If only we'd brought a map, we **mightn't** have got lost.

- *If only* can appear in a simple, one-clause sentence, without an expressed outcome.

  If only you would help more. (= in general or in future)

  If only you helped more. (= in general)

  If only you had helped more. (= in a specific past situation)

- Sometimes the outcome appears in a separate sentence.

  If only the world would use a vehicle that didn't need so much petrol! We could live on a cleaner planet.

1 Choose the correct sentence in each pair.

1 A Imagine that you lived to be 150, you'd have lots of memories! ___
  B Imagine that you lived to be 150. You'd have lots of memories! ___

2 A I'll meet Lee. Provided that you come with me. ___
  B I'll meet Lee provided that you come with me. ___

3 A My parents only let us go to the theatre on condition that we got a taxi home. ___
  B My parents only let us go to the theatre on condition that we would get a taxi home. ___

4 A Suppose you were asked to be in the school play. Would you do it? ___
  B Suppose that you were asked to be in the school play. Would you do it? ___

5 A We'll tell you the secret providing that you don't repeat it to anyone. ___
  B We'll tell you the secret providing you don't repeat it to anyone. ___

6 A Supposing that we hadn't found your jumper. It had been lost forever. ___
  B Supposing that we hadn't found your jumper. It would be lost forever. ___

2 Complete the sentences with the words in the box. More than one answer is possible.

> suppose   so   supposing   that   on condition   as   providing   imagine

1 _____ that we lived in a cold country. Life would be so much different.
2 You can watch the game so long _____ you don't interrupt.
3 I let him ride my bike _____ that he didn't go near a main road.
4 He was only allowed to have the key on condition _____ he didn't lose it.
5 _____ you were invisible. What would you do first?
6 She can have some sweets _____ she doesn't eat too many.
7 You can drive a car _____ long as you have a licence.
8 _____ what the world was like before electricity. We'd have been accustomed to living in much darker conditions.

3 Complete the sentences with *had* / *hadn't*, *would* / *wouldn't* or *doesn't* / *didn't*.

1 Imagine that you _____ won last week's competition. What _____ you have done with the prize money?
2 Supposing Dad _____ met Mum. I wonder who they _____ have married instead?
3 She only agreed to spend the summer in France on condition that her brother _____ go too.
4 He could have come on the picnic providing he _____ brought some food.
5 Imagine you _____ have to go to school. Do you think you _____ get bored?
6 I'll be able to buy Sarah's present as long as it _____

cost too much.

7 Suppose our team _____ win on Saturday. We'll be bottom of the league.
8 We told everyone that the barbecue _____ go ahead provided that it _____ rain.

4 Match the halves of the sentences.

1 If only you'd passed your test,
2 If only I hadn't forgotten to bring my boots,
3 If only whoever took my bike would return it,
4 If only we lived nearer to each other,
5 If only this weather were a bit warmer,
6 If only the rain had stopped earlier,

a we could have gone for a walk in the hills.
b we might meet up more often.
c we could have spent more time in the park.
d I would stop taking the train.
e we could all get outside and enjoy the countryside.
f you would have been able to take us down to Devon.

5 Complete the sentences with the correct form of the verb in brackets.

1 If only you _____ (help) your dad. You would both finish painting the living room in no time.
2 If only we _____ (not try) to carry that big vase, we wouldn't have dropped it.
3 If only your sister _____ (work) as hard as you. She'd get better marks.
4 If only everyone in the world would try to get on, it _____ (be) a happier place to live.
5 If only you looked after your goldfish more, I _____ (not have) to do it.
6 If only we _____ (not buy) the wrong ingredients, we'd have been able to make the cake.
7 If only people _____ (put) their rubbish in the bins, the streets wouldn't be so dirty.
8 If only your granddad hadn't read all his books by candlelight as a child, he _____ (not have) such poor eyesight.

6 Rewrite the sentences using *if only*, and making the necessary changes to the tenses.

1 We didn't phone her, so she didn't know we'd be late.
2 I'm allergic to seafood, so can't eat mussels or lobsters.
3 My brother doesn't tidy his room, so Mum has to do it.
4 Our team aren't very good, so they don't win a lot of matches.
5 Jake and I had an argument, so we aren't friends any more.
6 Lisa doesn't have any hobbies, so she is often bored.
7 I bought lots of CDs at the weekend, so I don't have any money now.
8 Caroline doesn't study, so she will get good marks in her exams.

The passive with preparatory *there*

- We can use *there* + a passive structure (form of *be* + past participle) to report information without specifying the source.

- Preparatory *there* + passive is followed by *to be* + noun phrase. This structure is often used with verbs of saying, thinking and knowing such as: *believe, consider, estimate, expect, feel, know, presume, report, say, suppose, think, understand*.

  There is believed to be a tunnel that leads from the house to the sea. (= people believe that there is a tunnel …)

- The passive verb form agrees in number with the noun phrase.

  There **is** said to be **a cask of gold** buried somewhere in that forest.

  There **are** thought to be to be **thousands of** undiscovered species of fish living in the oceans.

- Time expressions are often used to make it clear whether we are referring to the present or past.

  There is **thought** to be a very low number of people living in poverty in the UK **today**.

  Last year, there **were estimated** to be ten per cent fewer applications for university.

- We tend not to use the present perfect passive form, even with time expressions such as *so far* or *up to now*. Instead, we use the present passive or make the noun phrase the subject of a clause.

  So far this year, **there are reported to be** no violent crimes in the area.

  So far this year, no violent crimes have been reported in the area.

- Preparatory *there* + passive cannot be used with a *that*-clause. To report information beginning with a *that*-clause, we use the passive with preparatory *it*. Preparatory *it* is followed by a singular passive structure + *that* + clause.

  It is thought that there are thousands of undiscovered species of sea life in the oceans.

  NOT There is thought that there are thousands of undiscovered species of sea life in the oceans.

  It has been reported that the Prime Minister is going to make an announcement today.

  NOT There has been reported that the Prime Minister is going to make an announcement today.

Gerunds: perfect, passive, and negative

- The *-ing* form of a verb is called a gerund when it is used as a noun. Gerunds can be used as the subject or object of a sentence.

  Smoking is not permitted in any public building.

  I enjoy **cycling**.

- To form the negative, we put *not* before the gerund. The full form of the negative must always be used.

  Not understanding the rules was a major disadvantage.

  Not having given a speech in public before, she was terrified.

  Another problem was **not having** the right equipment.

  NOT Another problem wasn't having the right equipment.

- Gerunds can be used in the perfect and passive form. However, an *-ing* form is always included.

- Perfect gerund: *-ing* form + past participle

  Having written the story, she wanted to get it published.

- Passive gerund: *being* + past participle

  Oscar Wilde said that the only thing worse than **being talked about** was **not being talked about**.

- Gerunds can also be used after prepositions or prepositional phrases.

  I'm worried **about failing** the exam.

  They apologized **for having left** the restaurant without paying the bill.

  It was shocking that someone could break into our room **without being seen**.

- Gerunds are also used after certain verbs. However, it is not obvious which verbs are followed by a gerund, so these have to be learnt individually. They include *love, suggest, recall, remember, start, stop*.

  Most children **love being taken** for walks.

  He **remembered leaving** the building, but nothing else.

GRAMMAR BUILDER 4

1 Complete the sentences with the present or past passive of the verb in brackets.

1 There _____ (know) to be a decrease in vandalism and other minor crimes during major football tournaments. This is true in most countries.

2 In 2006, there _____ (estimated) to be 1.6 billion people without electricity across the world.

3 At the moment, there _____ (presume) to be no difficulties with the television reception in the valley.

4 Up to June this year, there _____ (think) to be no people in the village without access to the internet.

5 For many years, there _____ (say) to be a secret passage in the house, but none was ever found.

6 Currently, there _____ (understand) to be fewer than 4000 tigers living in India.

7 Until recently, there _____ (feel) to be too much emphasis on passing tests and exams in school.

8 There _____ (report) to be deer in the woods, but I've never seen them.

2 Write sentences using preparatory *there* and the present passive.

1 say / a tunnel that leads from here to the castle
_____

2 think / no tribes that remain undiscovered
_____

3 understand / a major problem with the underground cables
_____

4 feel / too many cameras watching our movements
_____

5 report / many occasions on which planes experience a near-miss
_____

6 rumour / a new teacher starting at our school tomorrow
_____

7 presume / many people in the UK with no desire to use a computer
_____

8 believe / a problem with the electricity
_____

3 Correct the errors.

1 So far this year, there have been known to have been three cars stolen from that car park.

2 There is thought that are too many problems with the new system.

3 There isn't expected to be many people at the event.

4 Last year, there is reported to be a decrease in the tiger population.

5 They are said to be one family on the estate who causes all the problems.

6 There are felt to be too little done to protect our environment.

7 Recently, there is rumoured to be a proposal to upgrade the transport system, but nothing came of it.

8 There are believed to being plans for a new supermarket.

4 Choose the correct alternative.

1 **Having** / **Being** bought the cake, she realized that she had nowhere to store it until Jo's birthday.

2 Not **giving** / **having given** a speech before, she was really nervous.

3 The best thing that ever happened to me was **being awarded** / **awarding** the prize, because I'd never won anything before.

4 **Having not** / **Not having** met her before, I didn't know what to expect.

5 I'm interested in **to learn** / **learning** about the kings and queens of England.

6 **Being** / **Having** from the USA, she was used to travelling long distances.

7 **Having** / **Having had** lunch, we went out for a walk.

8 **Feeling** / **Having felt** thirsty, she went into the kitchen for a glass of water.

5 Write the present, perfect or passive gerund form of the verb in brackets.

1 A lot of people that commit crimes don't worry about _____ (find out).

2 Who's in charge of _____ (recruit) staff here? I'd like to apply for a job.

3 After _____ (put) the phone down, she immediately left the house.

4 _____ (sign) his name on the document, he realized he couldn't deny what he'd said.

5 She couldn't stand _____ (ignore), and was always looking for attention.

6 _____ (put on) only a thin t-shirt earlier, she arrived feeling very cold.

7 I found _____ (not include) in the decision-making process unacceptable.

8 _____ (not smoke) at all during his life, he was shocked when he fell ill with a lung condition.

6 Correct the errors.

1 Many of the people at the match were intent on to cause as much trouble as possible.

2 We don't remember been told what to do.

3 Having spending ages writing the letter, she decided not to send it.

4 The worst thing was being not invited.

5 We were worried about having arrived late, so we set off early.

6 Having not flown before, my grandfather was very nervous.

7 I'm not very good at not speaking French.

8 Being having driven there was much nicer than driving myself.

Preparatory *it* as subject

- If the subject of a clause is an infinitive, it does not usually appear at the beginning of the clause.

  NOT To eat oily fish is very healthy.

- Instead, we use preparatory *it* to begin the clause. The structure is *it* + form of *be** + adjective (or adjective + noun) + infinitive.

  It is very healthy to eat oily fish.

  It's been a great pleasure to see you again.

  NOT To see you again has been a great pleasure.

- Preparatory *it* can be used in complex sentences. Note that preparatory *it* does not always come at the beginning of a sentence.

  I think it's rewarding to visit old people who don't have friends or family nearby.

  If you want to eat good food, it isn't a good idea to try the restaurants in town.

- If the subject of a clause is itself a clause, beginning with a pronoun such as *that*, *what*, *who* or *when*, we also use preparatory *it*. The structure is *it* + form of *be* + adjective + clause.

  It's unlikely that you've met Tom before.

  NOT That you've met Tom before is unlikely.

  It was irritating how much she depended on everyone's approval.

- We do not use preparatory *it* when the subject of a clause is a noun phrase.

  An exciting time was anticipated by all.

  NOT It was anticipated by all an exciting time.

Preparatory *it* as object

- If the object of a clause is an infinitive expression or a clause, we also use preparatory *it*.

  NOT To work with him I found difficult.

- The structure following the subject and verb is *it* + adjective (or adjective + noun) + infinitive / clause.

  I found it difficult to work with him.

  The instructions will make it clear where you're supposed to go.

  NOT Where you're supposed to go the instructions will make clear.

- We can't use a negative before the adjective.

  He didn't think it strange to get up at 5 o'clock every day.

  NOT He thought it not strange to get up at 5 o'clock every day.

- We can't use preparatory *it* if the main verb is not followed by an adjective or adjective + noun.

  She likes to see everyone having a good time.

  NOT She likes it to see everyone having a good time.

*other verbs are possible, such as *appear*, *become*, *feel*, *get*, *look*, *seem*, *sound*, *stay*

1 Choose the correct sentence in each pair.

1 A It was exciting see such a large crowd. ___
   B It was exciting to see such a large crowd. ___
2 A That you've seen the film yet is likely. ___
   B It's unlikely that you've seen the film yet. ___
3 A It was expected that we'd have a great time. ___
   B It was expected a great time. ___
4 A It seems odd how different he is from last year. ___
   B It seems odd that different he is from last year. ___
5 A To see Sam and Cathy again was wonderful. ___
   B It was wonderful to see Sam and Cathy again. ___
6 A It was very fortunate to be somebody at home. ___
   B It was very fortunate that somebody was at home. ___
7 A It was a huge relief that people laughed at my jokes. ___
   B That people laughed at my jokes was a huge relief. ___
8 A It wasn't clear that when they were planning to visit. ___
   B It wasn't clear when they were planning to visit us. ___

2 Put the words in the correct order to make sentences beginning with preparatory *it*.

1 annoying / how / he / good / at / is / it's / everything / !
   _____
2 come / clear / had / why / it / wasn't / he
   _____
3 think / seven / Tommy / it's / to / amazing / that / is / only
   _____
4 win / will / unlikely / team / it's / our / that
   _____
5 fantastic / getting / hear / they're / was / to / it / that / married
   _____
6 saying / to / what / it / always / understand / he / isn't / easy / is
   _____
7 it's / done / life / interesting / she / with / has / what / her
   _____
8 parents / to / your / know / everything / important / don't / it's / realize
   _____

3 Rewrite the sentences with preparatory it as subject and the adjective in brackets. Make any other changes that are necessary.

1 I was astonished to hear from her after so long. (astonishing)
   _____
2 We were worried when you didn't arrive. (worrying)
   _____
3 We were pleased to hear that Meg and Anna had won. (great)
   _____
4 I don't think the situation will improve. (unlikely)
   _____
5 I really enjoy working with older people. (rewarding)
   _____

6 She talked about herself non-stop, which irritated me. (irritating)
   _____
7 Nobody likes being picked last for school teams. (horrible)
   _____
8 I was surprised how much Paul had changed. (surprising)
   _____

4 Add preparatory *it* as object to each sentence.

1 My grandparents won't come because they find tiring to stand for so long.
2 I don't know anyone who considers normal to eat lunch at 11.00.
3 We didn't make clear that we'd only be there for the first half an hour.
4 You shouldn't find hard to do this puzzle.
5 I find odd that our aunt and uncle never visit us.
6 We consider unlikely that they'll tell us the full story.
7 They aren't hiring a car because they don't think necessary.
8 Do you find difficult to see in the dark?

5 Complete the sentences with an expression from the box.

throw away	difficult to	to see the children
strange that	have five	I'd already passed

1 They found it odd _____ looking so grown up.
2 She thought it amazing that _____ my driving test.
3 The shoes I was wearing made it _____ walk.
4 Don't you find it annoying how much we _____?
5 I consider it _____ many people are kinder to their pets than to other people.
6 We don't think it unusual to _____ meals a day.

6 Write sentences with preparatory *it* as object. Use the words in brackets to begin the sentence, and make other changes as necessary.

1 It was difficult to hear what he was saying. (we / found)
   _____
2 It's strange that she has so few friends. (I / think)
   _____
3 It was hard to concentrate. (my headache / made)
   _____
4 It was clear that he didn't want to come with us. (Peter / made)
   _____
5 It's not unusual to be nervous about an exam. (People / don't find)
   _____
6 It'll be important to economize this year. (My parents / consider)
   _____
7 It's been amazing to see how much Jo's improved. (Jo's teacher / has found)
   _____
8 It wasn't too difficult to stay awake all night. (None of us / thought)
   _____

GRAMMAR REFERENCE 6

Ellipsis with *either* / *too*

- Ellipsis is when we omit words in order to avoid repetition, or where the meaning is already clear.

  Who are you? ~ (I'm) Karen.

  He said he was French, but in fact he **wasn't** (French).

- A common form of ellipsis is to use the auxiliary verb on its own, without the main verb.

  You said that you'd tidy up, but you **haven't** (tidied up).

- We can use the auxiliary to replace an entire phrase. The whole of the phrase following the auxiliary verb is omitted.

  I wanted to try all the desserts on the menu, but I **couldn't** (try all the desserts on the menu).

- Where there is no auxiliary, we use a form of *do*.

  He was going to come round, but he **didn't** (come round).

- Ellipsis is used very frequently in this way with *either* and *too*. We use *either* and *too* at the end of a sentence to agree with what someone else has said.

- When agreeing with a negative first statement, we use *either* and a negative verb.

  I can't swim. ~ I can't, **either**.

  We haven't got any money. ~ We haven't, **either**.

- When agreeing with a positive first statement, we use *too* and a positive verb.

  He's tired after the race. ~ I am, **too**.

  I'm so thirsty. What I'd like now is a glass of lemonade. ~ I would, **too**.

- A form of *do* is used when there is no auxiliary.

  Our cat doesn't like getting wet. ~ Ours doesn't, **either**.

  My granddad loved his job. He didn't want to retire. ~ Mine didn't, **either**.

- If there is more than one auxiliary verb, we often only use the first one if the second one has already been used.

  Our bins haven't been emptied yet. ~ Ours **haven't**, either.

- We don't use *either* or *too* when the second statement contradicts the first one.

  I'm hungry. ~ **I'm not**.

  We haven't brought any money with me. ~ Don't worry. **We have**.

  A lot of people believe in UFOs. ~ **We don't**.

Ellipsis in comparisons

- We can use ellipsis in comparative structures such as *more*, *less* and *as ... as*, if the meaning is clear without them.

  We've got less homework to do than **they have** (got to do).

- If we decide to omit the verb following *than* or *as ... as*, we must use an object pronoun.

  We've got less homework to do than **them**.

  NOT We've got less homework to do than they.

  She likes the sun as much as us. / She likes the sun as much as we **do**.

- After *as* and *than*, we can omit the subject and verb if they are the same as in the first clause.

  We've raised more money **than** (we raised) last year. (OR ... than we did last year)

  They stayed at the same camp site **as** (they stayed at) before. (OR ... as they did before)

  He can speak much more fluent French **than** (he could speak) a few months ago. (OR ... than he could a few months ago)

- Rather than repeat a whole infinitive, we can simply use 'to' instead.

  The reason I'm not going is because I don't want **to** (go).

- This is also true in comparative sentences where the verb is the same in each clause.

  John bought more bread than he needed **to** (buy).

- *As* and *than* can replace subjects in a clause. This occurs very commonly when we might expect *it* to be the subject of that clause.

  You can use the car as much **as is necessary**. NOT ... as much as it is necessary.

  She does more exercise **than is considered advisable**. NOT ... than it is considered advisable.

  In the two examples above, we could omit 'is'.

- *As* and *than* also function as objects in a clause.

  The company made less money **than** they made last year.

  NOT The company made less money than they made it last year.

  People were happy to donate as many unwanted clothes **as** we needed.

  NOT People were happy to donate as many unwanted clothes as we needed them.

Ellipsis with *either* / *too*

1 Complete the sentences with *either*, *too* or nothing (-).

1 I can't leave now. John can't _____.
2 Why are you so sad? ~ I'm not _____.
3 I'm really happy. ~ I am, _____.
4 I haven't got a ticket for the concert. ~ I haven't, _____.
5 I've a ticket for the concert. ~ I haven't _____.
6 We both love The Zone's new album. ~ We do, _____.
7 Suzy can play the guitar. ~ John can't _____.
8 Joe went to the festival last year. ~ I did, _____.

2 Complete the dialogue with expressions from the box.

> am, too   would, too   'm not   can't, either
> didn't, either   don't   can   do, too

Megan I like our new school.
Cathy Yes, I ¹_____. I think the meals are great.
Megan I ²_____. I'd rather eat at home.
Cathy I ³_____, but there's nobody at home at lunchtime, so I can't.
Megan No, I ⁴_____. Anyway, I'm really pleased we've got nice teachers.
Cathy I ⁵_____. I didn't like all the teachers at our old school.
Megan I ⁶_____. Everyone seems really great. I'm not worried about making new friends here.
Cathy I ⁷_____, either. In fact, I can't wait for next week.
Megan I ⁸_____!

3 Complete the answers using ellipsis and *either* or *too* where necessary. Add one word per space.

1 I've got a headache. I _____.
2 Why are you both so nervous? We _____.
3 Paul didn't finish the exam. Sarah _____.
4 I've done all my revision. I _____.
5 I've been chosen for the football team. I _____.
6 The fire alarm went off yesterday. It _____. It was the day before.
7 We haven't lived in this town for very long. We _____.
8 I didn't have lunch at school yesterday. I _____.

4 Complete the sentences with expressions from the box.

> Dan can   you had   you would   yours are   you have
> others do   I did   you are

1 We'd enjoyed the party as much as _____.
2 I can jump higher than _____.
3 Some people take more interest in the environment than _____.
4 I'm as unhappy about the situation as _____.
5 My parents are a lot older than _____.
6 I'd like to go on the school trip as much as _____.
7 Tina studied harder for her exams than _____.
8 We've got as much right to be here as _____.

5 Use ellipsis to shorten the sentences as much as possible. Don't change any of the words.

1 Only take as much money as it is necessary to take.
2 She's trying a lot harder than she did last term.
3 We didn't buy as much ice cream as we were supposed to buy.
4 The guitar isn't as difficult to learn as the piano is.
5 You've given me the same birthday card as you gave me last year!
6 Don't pack more clothes than you need to pack.
7 He is a lot more mobile than he was after he left hospital.
8 You've got more time to spare than we've got time to spare.

6 There is one error in each sentence. Correct them.

1 She ate more fast food than it was considered advisable.
_____
2 The reason she isn't going to university is because she doesn't want.
_____
3 I like Lucy as much as they.
_____
4 Nobody likes camping more than John likes.
_____
5 We played more tennis this summer than we played it last year.
_____
6 Tom wouldn't need to lose as much weight as Chris would have.
_____
7 Everyone brought more food than they did need to.
_____
8 We don't go to the gym as often as him does.
_____

Cleft sentences (1): *it*

- *It* commonly appears as the subject at the beginning of an ordinary clause or sentence.

  Look at that dog. **It**'s trampling all over the flowers.

  It's a beautiful day and all the birds are singing.

- In a cleft sentence, however, preparatory *it* appears at the beginning of the sentence to highlight words and phrases (but not verbs) that would normally appear later in the sentence. The purpose of doing this is to emphasize specific facts or ideas.

- The words or phrases that we want to emphasize are made into a relative clause using *that*.

  Compare:

  I hate the cold weather in this country more than anything.

  and (more emphatic)

  It's the cold weather in this country **that** I hate more than anything.

- It is possible to use *who* instead of *that* when referring to a personal pronoun.

  It was Jane **who** phoned earlier, not Jim.

  It is also possible to omit *that* when *that* refers to the object of the relative clause.

  It's his high temperature (**that**) **we are** most concerned about.

  but

  It's his high temperature **that is concerning** us the most.

- Preparatory *it* can be followed by different tenses of *be*.

  It was Ryan who gave us the bad news.

- When there is a plural subject, preparatory *it* is still followed by a singular form of *be*, but the verb in the relative clause is plural.

  It's the **roadworks** that **are** causing all that noise.

Cleft sentences (2): *what*

- It is possible to use *what* instead of preparatory *it* in cleft sentences, as a means of emphasizing certain words or phrases.

- The structure is different from a cleft sentence with preparatory *it*, however. Compare the following.

  I need a long, hot, soak in the bath. (= ordinary sentence structure)

  It's a long, hot, soak in the bath that I need. (= cleft sentence with preparatory *it*)

  What I need is a long, hot, soak in the bath. (= cleft sentence with *what*)

- The part that we want to emphasize is linked to the relative clause by *is / was* and *what*.

  What I'd like to see is a massive improvement in the quality of your work.

- In the sentence above, *what = the thing which*. We can use other pronouns and expressions such as *the day when*, *the person who*, *the place where* and *the reason why*.

  The year when my parents met was 1989.

- The relative clause introduced by *what* or a similar expression can go at the beginning or at the end of the sentence.

  1989 was **the year when my parents met**.

- We can omit *which*, *when*, *who*, *where* and *why*.

  The reason I'm no good at sport is that my legs are different lengths.

GRAMMAR BUILDER 7

1 Choose the correct alternative. Note that (–) means a blank space.

1 It's / They're the people that I like most about Portugal.
2 It was / is the food I didn't like, not the location of the restaurant.
3 It was you what / who started the argument.
4 It was the atmosphere that / what made it such a special evening.
5 It were /was the boys that won the competition, not the girls.
6 It's the grammar that / (–) causes me problems, not the vocabulary.
7 Living in a foreign country, it was / 's the food and the humour I've missed most.
8 Of all the stories he wrote, it is the one about the prisoner that / who I like best.

2 Correct the sentences, if necessary.

1 It was his exam results we were most worried about.

2 It's our neighbours that is making all that noise.

3 It were my grandparents who brought me up.

4 It was Carla who won the prize for best sportsperson.

5 It's the last day of the festival interests us the most.

6 It was the child's breathing what caused most concern.

7 It's Mum that usually does the decorating in our house.

8 It was the garden made us want to buy the house.

3 Rewrite the sentences as cleft sentences with preparatory *it*.

1 People being mean with their money annoys me most.

2 I couldn't stand the heat.

3 We didn't like the way he spoke to us.

4 She was looking at the shoes, not the boots.

5 Cairo is his favourite holiday destination.

6 His worst characteristic is arrogance.

7 They go to the Scottish islands for the peace and solitude.

8 Greasy food, not spicy food, upsets my stomach.

4 Choose the correct sentence.

1 A What I'm looking for is a map of the town.
  B It I'm looking for is a map of the town.
2 A What is most important to us is choice.
  B What is most important to us choice.

3 A Place where we used to live has been demolished.
  B The place where we used to live has been demolished.
4 A The day which I got that letter was the best day of my life.
  B The day I got that letter was the best day of my life.
5 A The thing what interests me most is that it's a true story.
  B The thing that interests me most is that it's a true story.
6 A The people who has supported me the most is my family.
  B The people who have supported me the most are my family.
7 A What I like doing best is playing football with my friends on the beach.
  B What thing I like doing best is playing football with my friends on the beach.
8 A The reason why people like fruit is what fruit is sweet.
  B The reason people like fruit is that fruit is sweet.

5 Put the words in the correct order to make cleft sentences with *what* (or other question word). Put the relative clause is at the beginning of the sentence.

1 no / why / I've got / here / you're / idea

2 what / a / there / doing / they / is / were / mystery

3 reason / scared / unclear / felt / she / the / was / why

4 I / born / there / is / the / was / place / over / where

5 there / made / birthday / being / you / my / special / what

6 we / a Tuesday / when / the / met / day / was

7 me / grandfather / my / who / the person / most / was / influenced

8 can't / want / why / to eat / I / there / understand / would / anyone

6 Rewrite the sentences as cleft sentences beginning with preparatory *what* or other expressions. Make any other changes that are necessary.

1 Ice skaters need to have good balance.
2 Mr Thomson teaches us English.
3 I hid the photo because I look horrible in it.
4 David went to university in London.
5 I really like your honesty.
6 The worst day of my life was when I had the accident.
7 We live next door to an Italian family.
8 We're going to have a party after the exams.

Participle clauses

- The *-ing* form of a verb is often called a present participle. However, these can be used in such a way that they refer to the past, present or future. Participles are used with other words to make participle clauses.

  Driving as carefully as I could, I managed to make it home in one piece. (= past)

  Feeling as I do, I'm going to have a rest. (= present / future)

- Present participles can have a perfect or passive form, but always consist of an *-ing* element. They can be used in the negative.

  Having listened carefully, he made his decision.

  Not having been introduced, we faced each other awkwardly.

- We can only use participle clauses if the subject of the participle clause is the same as that of the main clause.

  Having stolen the car, **the man** then abandoned it.

  NOT Having stolen the car, it was then abandoned.

- Participle clauses are often used to talk about reasons and time relations. The participle replaces those words that introduce the reason (*because*, *since*, *as*, etc.) or time relations (*while*, *as*, *after*, etc.).

  Listening to the sound of the sea, I started to drift off to sleep. (= As / While I was listening ...)

  Working on a farm, I'm very tired at the end of the day. (= Because I'm working on a farm ...)

  NOT Because working on a farm ...

- A participle clause can be used to express condition and result.

  Taking one of her tablets every morning she slowly got better. (= If you take ...)

  She tripped on the rug and fell, **spilling** the contents of the tray everywhere. (= As a result of which the contents spilled ...)

- Participles can be formed from stative verbs, such as *be*, *know*, *want*, which are not usually be used in a continuous tense. These are generally used to talk about reason.

  Wanting something quick to eat, I went into the nearest burger restaurant.

Participle clauses after conjunctions and prepositions

- It is common to use clauses with present participles after certain conjunctions and prepositions. These include *after*, *as*, *before*, *despite*, *if*, *instead of*, *in spite of*, *on*, *since*, *when*, *while*, *without*.

  On reaching her pen friend's house, she phoned her parents, as agreed.

  He somehow managed to text his friend **while carrying** four bags of shopping.

  That old washing machine has lasted thirty years **without** once **being repaired**.

- As well as present participles (formed with *-ing*), there are past participles. Regular past participles end in *-ed*, but many are irregular. Like present participles, they can refer to the past, present or future; however, when used like adjectives, their meaning is usually passive.

  Opened on time, the new stadium was regarded as a triumph. (= past)

  The picture looks great, and, **mounted** on the wall, will look even better. (= future)

- We can use clauses with past participles after *if*, *once*, *until*, *when*, *while*. This is slightly formal, however, and is more often used when giving instructions.

  'Please contact the number below between 6 and 9, **if interested**.'

  Once opened, cream won't keep for very long.

  Put the bread mixture into the oven for forty minutes or so, **until risen**.

GRAMMAR BUILDER 8

1 Say whether the sentences express reason/result (R) or time (T). Sometimes more than one answer is possible.

1 Turning round quickly, he bumped into me. ___
2 Having finished his project, he turned the computer off. ___
3 Switching off the lights, he went up to bed. ___
4 Apologizing for his action, he opened the door and left. ___
5 Being a shy person, she wasn't looking forward to giving the speech. ___
6 Practising Arabic every day, she grew very confident in the language. ___
7 Having appeared on TV, he found that he was recognized everywhere. ___
8 Having fed the cat, she got up and went for a walk. ___

2 Replace the phrases in bold with a participle clause.

1 **Because we are** interested ancient history, we visit a lot of museums.
2 **After I bought** my bike, I immediately went out for a ride in the country.
3 **As we've lived** here all our lives, we feel we know the area very well.
4 **As he wrote** the letter, he started to feel sad.
5 **If you exercise and eat well, that** should keep your blood pressure down.
6 **As a result of walking** so far, her feet were aching.
7 **While she was talking to us,** she texted Nancy.
8 **Because we weren't** used to the heat, we suffered quite badly.

3 Rewrite the participle clauses in bold, using *because*, *after* or *while*.

1 **Not knowing** the answer to the question, I simply guessed it.
2 **Having walked** away from the man, I realized I'd given him the wrong directions.
3 **Having spent** so long working in a mine, he had coal dust In his lungs.
4 **Studying** all night, he eventually fell ill.
5 **Studying** ancient Egypt, she came across a document that had never been seen before.
6 **Not wanting** to interrupt, I waited until he had finished speaking.
7 **Holding** the phone, she felt it ring.
8 **Not having had my make-up done** before, I soon felt uncomfortable sitting in the same position.

4 Match the sentence halves.

1 Ed made the cake himself instead
2 I read the whole article without
3 We won't reveal the result until
4 He was unhappy with his performance in the race despite
5 The book is part-fiction, while also being
6 She failed all her exams, despite
7 The room is still being painted, but, once
8 It is a shy animal which, if

a of buying one.
b based on the author's own experiences.
c finished. It will look great.
d having won a medal.
e understanding any of it.
f seen in public, swiftly disappears.
g required to do so.
h being one of the best students.

5 Complete the sentences with *after, despite, if, once, until,* or *while.*

1 _____ offered a seat on a bus or train, I always accept it.
2 We missed the start of the concert, _____ having left home on time.
3 _____ giving someone some bad news, you should try to prepare them first.
4 _____ waiting for the bus for forty minutes, I decided to walk.
5 She realized that she'd been talking to her neighbour _____ covered in flour.
6 _____ taken apart, it was clear why the gadget wasn't working.
7 Nobody knows what's happening. I'm going to stay here _____ told differently.
8 _____ climbing up the ladder, she didn't once look down.

6 Complete the sentences with the correct participle form.

1 If _____ in an accident, you must report it immediately. (involve)
2 We love it here, in spite of _____ to put up with the weather. (have)
3 Until _____, nobody knew the identity of the mystery guest. (reveal)
4 While _____ away in a foreign prison, the author managed to write two books. (shut)
5 Despite _____ very good at science or geography, he announced that he wanted to be a pilot. (not be)
6 When _____ to a MP3 player on public transport, be careful to keep the volume down. (listen)
7 You should go out into the sunshine instead of _____ all your time upstairs. (spend)
8 This juice will keep for three days once _____. (open)

Inversion

- A way of changing the emphasis of a sentence is to use inversion. This involves putting a negative adverbial expression at the beginning of the sentence. These contain 'no' or 'not', e.g. *at no time, not only, not until, under no circumstances*. The structure is:

  negative adverbial expression + auxiliary verb (affirmative) + subject

  Compare:

  He caused the accident and tried to blame it on someone else.

  and

  Not only did he cause the accident, (but) he tried to blame it on someone else.

- We can use this structure after a much longer introductory clause, following *at no time* or *not until*.

  At no time during the two-hour ceremony were we invited to sit down.

  Not until everyone has put their pens down and is paying attention will you be allowed to go.

- We can also use inversion after restrictive expressions. These include: *hardly, little, never, only* (+ time expression), *rarely, scarcely, seldom*.

  Little did I realize how hard I was going to have to work.

  Never would we see that beautiful little cottage again.

  Only after she'd sent the letter **did she** realize her mistake.

- The adverbials *hardly* and *no sooner* follow a different pattern, as they introduce two events that almost happen simultaneously. The second event occurs only slightly after the first. We use the following structure:

  FIRST CLAUSE *No sooner / Hardly* + *had* + subject + past participle

  SECOND CLAUSE *than* + subject + verb

  No sooner had he reached the finishing line **than** he collapsed.

  Hardly had they started chatting than they started swapping their life stories.

Emphatic use of *as ... as*

- We can use *as* + adjective + *as* to emphasize an extreme quantity.

  The adjective generally agrees with the noun.

  Last year there were no **ducks** in the pond, but this summer there were **as many as** ten of them.

  As few as thirteen people attended the meeting.

- However, we can use *much* and *little* as well as *many* and *few* before a specific number. This is because we are referring to a surprisingly large or small amount rather than kilos, pounds, units of time, etc.

  In Britain, we eat **as much as three times** more chocolate per year than in Belgium.

  NOT as many as three times

  This car can travel all the way up on the motorway on **as little as three litres** of petrol.

  NOT as few as three litres

- The *as ... as* structure emphasizes the extreme nature of the quantity by suggesting that the upper or lower limit was achieved in a few cases, but not by the majority.

  Some of the jackets were on sale for **as little as** £20. (= £20 was the cheapest price for a jacket; some jackets cost this, but others were more expensive)

  There were **as many as** four times the expected number of people. (= four times the number of people expected is an upper estimate)

  As much as two metres of snow fell overnight. (= in some places, two metres of snow fell; in other parts, it was less than this)

  Some of us collected **as many as** four sacks of rubbish while walking along the beach. (some people collected four sacks; others collected less)

1 Choose the correct sentence.

1 A Not only we did have lunch in the cafe, we had dinner there, too.
B Not only did we have lunch in the cafe, we had dinner there, too.

2 A Seldom had I seen such a beautiful room.
B Seldom did I see such a beautiful room.

3 A We parted. Never would we meet again.
B We parted. Never had we met again.

4 A Only after I thought about our conversation I realized you were right.
B Only after I thought about our conversation did I realize you were right.

5 A Never do I have seen such a huge car.
B Never have I seen such a huge car.

6 A Not until we were leaving did we see Helen.
B Not until we were leaving were we seeing Helen.

7 A Hardly had we got in than the phone rang.
B Hardly had we got in that the phone rang.

8 A Under no circumstances wouldn't we go back.
B Under no circumstances would we go back.

2 Put the words in the correct order.

1 no / did / I / address / my / time / mention / at
_____

2 only / she / not / rich, / too / she's / is / but / pretty
_____

3 bought / the present / sooner / he / had / regretted / than / it / no / he
_____

4 circumstances / fish / I / would / no / eat / under
_____

5 I / know / little / they / that / listening / did / was
_____

6 texted / I / had / than / hardly / to him/ he / spoken / me
_____

7 will / we / this / in / never / room / again / sit
_____

8 she / forgive / apologized / until / I / did / me / not
_____

3 Rewrite the sentences, using inversion and an expression from the box. More than one answer may be possible.

> little   not until   not only   hardly   never   only after
> at no time   seldom

1 He was confident and he had lots of friends.
2 I'd been there for six weeks before anyone spoke to me.
3 You have to say the secret word before you can come in.
4 We'd just finished washing one pile of dishes when another one was brought in.
5 They never said we would have to wait two weeks for the results.
6 I was more embarrassed than I have ever been in my life.
7 She didn't realize that the conversation was being recorded.
8 At the very moment Ben arrived, most people left.

4 Choose the correct alternative.

1 I've got as **little** / **few** as ten pence in my purse.
2 I counted as **much** / **many** as eleven cats in our garden in one day.
3 I've got more money to spend, because this CD cost as **little** / **much** as £2.
4 As **few** / **little** as four people in this street had a car in the 1960s.
5 The show raised as **much** / **few** as £880 for charity. It was a great result.
6 She bought as **many** / **much** as ten bottles of water for the journey.
7 You've got as **few** / **little** as five minutes to finish what you're writing.
8 Although it's warm, this coat weighs as **much** / **little** as 100 grammes.

5 Three of the sentences contain errors. Find and correct them.

1 There were as few that twenty people at our school concert.
2 We'll need as much as forty pounds to buy him the present he wants.
3 The poor woman was carrying as many as six bags of shopping.
4 At her thinnest, she weighed as little as forty-five kilos.
5 We're going to need as many as fifteen people to help us organize the show.
6 Pocket calculators now cost as little as a couple of pounds.
7 At the end of some exams, you can have as much than ten minutes to finish off.
8 You can buy a laptop for as few as £150.

6 Rewrite the sentences in bold, using as ... as to emphasize how big or small the quantities are.

1 **Each person in the UK throws away** _____ 11.9 **million tons of food and packaging per year.** This figure needs to be reduced urgently.
2 The price of computers varies widely. **You can buy expensive makes, but you can also find models for** _____ **one or two hundred pounds.**
3 It was very disappointing. **We'd invited seventy people to the event, but** _____ **twenty turned up on the night.**
4 **There are** _____ 3700 **tigers left in India.** More needs to be done to protect them.
5 The number of birds migrating to the UK from Africa every spring has declined significantly, by _____ 75%.
6 When I was a child, I used to get hardly any pocket money. In fact, I got _____ fifteen pence a week.
7 Some animals are overweight. Some dogs weigh _____ 75 kilos and are put on a diet by the vet.
8 A lot of people competed in the road race. _____ 250 started the race, but less than 100 actually finished it.

Phrasal verbs (1)

- Phrasal verbs consist of a verb + particle. A particle is an adverb or preposition, such as *about, back, down, in, off, on, out, up*.

- Phrasal verbs are used very frequently in conversation. In more formal styles, we often prefer to use a one-word verb which has the same meaning, e.g. 'to put off (a meeting)' = to postpone, 'to take on' = to undertake, 'to water down' = to dilute.

- The meaning of some phrasal verbs is clear from the specific combination of verb + particle, such as 'to look up' = to direct your eyes upwards. The adverb 'up' often means 'completely', as in 'fill up', 'tear up'; 'on' can mean 'connected', e.g. 'turn on (the TV); 'off' can mean 'disconnected', e.g. 'cut off (a supply of water, etc.)'.

- However, with many phrasal verbs, the meaning can't be guessed, and in these cases the verb and meaning must be learned, e.g. 'look up (a word in a dictionary)' = 'consult (a dictionary)'. We refer to these meanings as 'idiomatic'. Examples of these are:

  cut back = spend or eat less   *give up* = stop doing something

  fall out = have an argument   *put on* = wear

  Other examples of phrasal verbs with idiomatic meanings are:

  bring up = mention   hand over = give responsibility to
  call off = cancel   live down = be allowed to forget
  carry on = continue   take over = take control of
  go back = retreat / return   turn down = reject

  Some phrasal verbs have more than one idiomatic meaning, e.g. *turn down* = refuse a request or offer / lower the volume (of a TV, etc.); *set off* = depart / explode fireworks.

- In statements or questions in which the object is at the beginning of a clause, we prefer not to separate the two parts of the phrasal verb.

  This is a situation which we need to **get over** as quickly as possible.

  NOT This is a situation over which we need to get ...

  Who are you **looking at**?

  NOT At who(m) are you looking?

- Some phrasal verbs are three-part verbs. This means that they consist of an adverb particle and a preposition. The meaning of most of these is idiomatic. Examples include:

  come up with = produce or find

  get away with = do something wrong without being punished

  get on with = be friendly with (a person); continue with (a task)

  go back on (a decision or promise) = do the opposite of what was agreed or promised

  look forward to = anticipate with pleasure

  put up with = tolerate

Phrasal verbs (2)

- Some phrasal verbs are followed by an object, e.g. *switch (the light) off*. Others, such as *get up*, do not have an object.

- Phrasal verbs that have an object can be separated.

  You need to **send back the package**.

  You need to **send the package back**.

  You need to **send it back**.

- A pronoun cannot be placed after the full phrasal verb.

  NOT You need to send back it.

- Some phrasal verbs change their meaning depending on whether they are followed by an object or not. Examples are *break down* and *work out*.

  During the fire, firefighters managed to **break down the door** and rescue the family.

  I'm late because my car **broke down**.

  We've been thinking about this all day, but we haven't **worked out a solution** yet.

  He looks so fit because he **works out** down the gym five times a week.

- Three-part verbs are never separated.

  I don't know how they **get away with it**.

  We're **looking forward to** the wedding immensely.

1 Choose the correct alternative.

1 I've got so much work to do; I can't take **up / on** any more.
2 You used to be such good friends. Why did you fall **off / out**?
3 You need to water **down / up** this juice. It's too strong.
4 If you've got too much to do, you should hand **in / over** some of the work to another person.
5 Carla's supposed to be in charge, but I'd prefer someone else to take **on / over**.
6 The path was blocked so we had to go **out / back**.
7 You eat too much chocolate. You really should cut **back / up**.
8 We've been working on this problem all day, but we still can't figure **out / over** a solution.

2 Replace the phrasal verb in bold with a correct alternative. Use the correct form.

1 They had to **call off** the picnic at the last minute. _____
2 He **turned down** the chance to be in a film. _____
3 After many delays, we finally **set off** at one o'clock. _____
4 Why don't you **put on** your new dress? _____
5 We're all spending too much, so we need to find ways to **cut back**. _____
6 My dad **gave up** tennis ten years ago. _____
7 The librarian told the boy to stop talking but he **carried on**. _____
8 James keeps **bringing up** the argument he and I had. _____

3 Six of the sentences contain three-word phrasal verbs. Choose words from the box to complete the phrasal verbs, if necessary.

on with	away with	up with	forward to	up with
back on				

1 I was really looking _____ seeing everyone again.
2 It's strange to think that Pete turned down _____ the opportunity to play for the Manchester United youth team.
3 We don't like her much, but we put _____ her.
4 She's a very friendly person. She gets _____ everyone.
5 He seems to get _____ with his behaviour. He's never punished.
6 He never lived down _____ the practical joke they played on him.
7 She promised that she would help us, but she went _____ her word.
8 The team came _____ a great idea for the class project.

4 Choose the correct sentence.

1 A They had to call off in the end the event. ___
  B They had to call off the event in the end. ___
2 A It's a day which we've been looking forward to for a long time. ___
  B It's a day to which we've been looking forward for a long time. ___

3 A This is a big project, and we need people that are prepared to take on it. ___
  B This is a big project, and we need people that are prepared to take it on. ___
4 A I was so tired I could hardly get me up this morning.
  B I was so tired I could hardly get up this morning.
5 A When you've done the dishes, could you put them away, please?
  B When you've done the dishes, could you put away them, please?
6 A You should never go back your promises on.
  B You should never go back on your promises.
7 A Please switch off all the lights.
  B Please switch them off all the lights.
8 A We were late for school because the bus broke it down.
  B We were late for school because the bus broke down.

5 Put the words in the correct order.

1 back / give / he / after / my / didn't / borrowing / it / book
_____
2 newspapers / up / on / story / several / her / picked / exciting
_____
3 it / think / he'd / away / get / didn't / we / with
_____
4 picked up / and / on / she / them / earrings / the / put
_____
5 off / about / two o'clock / with / at / they / friends / set / their
_____
6 could / later / up / pick / you / me / ?
_____
7 need / take / more / to / project / on / the / we / people / for
_____
8 with / it / situation / I / put / couldn't / a / was / up
_____

6 Correct the sentences.

1 I don't understand, but I'm sure I'll figure out it.
2 This kind of behaviour is something with which he shouldn't get away.
3 She's come up a great idea with for a present.
4 You should take a spare jumper; you might want to put it on later.
5 I was worried that they were going to go on back what we'd agreed.
6 We'd all forget about the incident if you didn't keep bringing up.
7 Everyone's really looking forward the holidays.
8 He couldn't open the door, but he managed to break it up.

Nouns

atmosphere ⚿ /'ætməsfɪə(r)/
baggage ⚿ /'bægɪdʒ/
bank holiday /ˌbæŋk 'hɒlədeɪ/
bargain ⚿ /'bɑːgɪn/
boardwalk /'bɔːdwɔːk/
breeze /briːz/
budget ⚿ /'bʌdʒɪt/
business class /'bɪznəs ˌklɑːs/
business traveller ⚿ /'bɪznəs ˌtrævələ(r)/
canal /kə'næl/
chalet /'ʃæleɪ/
cheetah /'tʃiːtə/
clatter /'klætə(r)/
comedian /kə'miːdiən/
creak /kriːk/
cuisine /kwɪ'ziːn/
custom ⚿ /'kʌstəm/
decade ⚿ /'dekeɪd/
destination /destɪ'neɪʃn/
elevator ⚿ /'elɪveɪtə(r)/
facility ⚿ /fə'sɪləti/
fondue /'fɒndjuː/
gag /gæg/
gazelle /gə'zel/
giraffe ⚿ /dʒə'rɑːf/
guide ⚿ /gaɪd/
gurgle /'gɜːgl/
habitat /'hæbɪtæt/
health concerns ⚿ /'helθ kənˌsɜːnz/
hippo /'hɪpəʊ/
hiss /hɪs/
holiday ⚿ /'hɒlədeɪ/
holidaymaker /'hɒlədeɪmeɪkə(r)/
jeep /dʒiːp/
landscape ⚿ /'lændskeɪp/
lift ⚿ /lɪft/
lion /'laɪən/
luggage ⚿ /'lʌgɪdʒ/
luxury hotel /ˌlʌkʃəri həʊ'tel/
market segment /ˌmɑːkɪt 'segmənt/
marvel /'mɑːvl/
meteorology /miːtiə'rɒlədʒi/
metro /'metrəʊ/
multitude /'mʌltɪtjuːd/
ocean ⚿ /'əʊʃn/
opportunity ⚿ /ɒpə'tjuːnəti/
pace ⚿ /peɪs/
participant /pɑː'tɪsɪpənt/
ping /pɪŋ/
predator /'predətə(r)/
process ⚿ /'prəʊses/
relaxation /riːlæk'seɪʃn/
resort ⚿ /rɪ'zɔːt/
rollerblading /'rəʊləbleɪdɪŋ/
rustle /'rʌsl/
rustling /'rʌslɪŋ/
safari /sə'fɑːri/
scenery /'siːnəri/

screech /skriːtʃ/
sea ⚿ /siː/
sea view ⚿ /ˌsiː 'vjuː/
ski run /'skiː ˌrʌn/
snow pass ⚿ /'snəʊ ˌpɑːs/
stand-up comedy /ˌstænd ˌʌp 'kɒmədi/
subway /'sʌbweɪ/
taxi rank ⚿ /'tæksi ˌræŋk/
taxi stand ⚿ /'tæksi ˌstænd/
travel industry ⚿ /'trævl ˌɪndəstri/
trend ⚿ /trend/
tube ⚿ /tjuːb/
underground ⚿ /'ʌndəgraʊnd/
vacation ⚿ /və'keɪʃn/
vacationer /və'keɪʃnə(r)/
vantage point /'vɑːntɪdʒ ˌpɔɪnt/
watering hole /'wɔːtərɪŋ ˌhəʊl/
whoosh /wʊʃ/
workshop /'wɜːkʃɒp/

Verbs

appeal (to) ⚿ /ə'piːl/
clatter /'klætə(r)/
crave /kreɪv/
creak /kriːk/
dine /daɪn/
dominate ⚿ /'dɒmɪneɪt/
dot /dɒt/
exclude ⚿ /ɪk'skluːd/
flock /flɒk/
glide /glaɪd/
gurgle /'gɜːgl/
hiss /hɪs/
overcome ⚿ /əʊvə'kʌm/
ping /pɪŋ/
portray /pɔː'treɪ/
purchase ⚿ /'pɜːtʃəs/
rustle /'rʌsl/
screech /skriːtʃ/
shimmer /'ʃɪmə(r)/
sport /spɔːt/
surpass /sə'pɑːs/
suspend /sə'spend/
view ⚿ /vjuː/
whoosh /wʊʃ/

Adjectives

adventurous /əd'ventʃərəs/
all-inclusive /ˌɔːl ɪn'kluːsɪv/
atrocious /ə'trəʊʃəs/
budget /'bʌdʒɪt/
charming /'tʃɑːmɪŋ/
cosy /'kəʊzi/
deserted ⚿ /dɪ'zɜːtɪd/
disposable /dɪ'spəʊzəbl/
downmarket /daʊn'mɑːkɪt/
downscale /daʊn'skeɪl/
dreadful /'dredfl/
enchanting /ɪn'tʃɑːntɪŋ/

extravagant /ɪk'strævəgənt/
fabulous /'fæbjələs/
five-star /'faɪv ˌstɑː(r)/
frosty /'frɒsti/
homely /'həʊmli/
hospitable /hɒ'spɪtəbl/
humorous ⚿ /'hjuːmərəs/
incompatible /ɪnkəm'pætəbl/
lavish /'lævɪʃ/
low-cost /'ləʊ ˌkɒst/
luxuriant /lʌg'ʒʊəriənt/
opulent /'ɒpjələnt/
sparse /spɑːs/
stark /stɑːk/
unassuming /ʌnə'sjuːmɪŋ/
uninviting /ʌnɪn'vaɪtɪŋ/
unpolluted /ʌnpə'luːtɪd/
upmarket /ʌp'mɑːkɪt/
upscale /ʌp'skeɪl/

Adverbs

dramatically ⚿ /drə'mætɪkli/
frighteningly /'fraɪtnɪŋli/
routinely /ruː'tiːnli/
significantly ⚿ /sɪg'nɪfɪkəntli/

Expressions and idioms

bargain hunting /'bɑːgɪn ˌhʌntɪŋ/
be intent on sth /ˌbiː ɪn'tent ˌɒn/
fulfil (your) ambition /fʊlˌfɪl (jɔːr) æm'bɪʃn/
off the cuff /ˌɒf ðə 'kʌf/
off the record ⚿ /ˌɒf ðə 'rekɔːd/
off the wall ⚿ /ˌɒf ðə 'wɔːl/
on tenterhooks /ˌɒn 'tentəhʊks/
on the boil ⚿ /ˌɒn ðə 'bɔɪl/
on the go ⚿ /ˌɒn ðə 'gəʊ/
on the hoof /ˌɒn ðə 'huːf/
on the off chance /ˌɒn ði 'ɒf ˌtʃɑːns/
on the one hand ⚿ /ˌɒn ðə 'wʌn ˌhænd/
on the other hand ⚿ /ˌɒn ði 'ʌðə ˌhænd/
per night ⚿ /pə 'naɪt/
per person ⚿ /pə 'pɜːsn/

⚿ a keyword of the **Oxford 3000 list**, denoting words which should receive priority in vocabulary study because of their importance and usefulness.

/i/ happy	/æ/ flag	/ɜː/ her	/ʊ/ look	/ʌ/ mum	/ɔɪ/ noisy	/ɪə/ here
/ɪ/ it	/ɑː/ art	/ɒ/ not	/uː/ you	/eɪ/ day	/aʊ/ how	/eə/ wear
/iː/ he	/e/ egg	/ɔː/ four	/ə/ sugar	/aɪ/ why	/əʊ/ go	/ʊə/ tourist

Nouns

acronym /ˈækrənɪm/
alliteration /əlɪtəˈreɪʃn/
anagram /ˈænəɡræm/
brainstorm /ˈbreɪnstɔːm/
calculator /ˈkælkjəleɪtə(r)/
cliché /ˈkliːʃeɪ/
collapse 🔑 /kəˈlæps/
computer science 🔑 /kəmˌpjuːtə ˈsaɪəns/
computer software
  /kəmˌpjuːtə ˈsɒftweə(r)/
couple 🔑 /ˈkʌpl/
creation /kriˈeɪʃn/
data mining /ˈdeɪtə ˌmaɪnɪŋ/
decade 🔑 /ˈdekeɪd/
deed /diːd/
denim /ˈdenɪm/
electronic mail 🔑 /ɪlekˌtrɒnɪk ˈmeɪl/
element 🔑 /ˈelɪmənt/
emoticon /ɪˈməʊtɪkɒn/
entry 🔑 /ˈentri/
epic poem /ˌepɪk ˈpəʊɪm/
equals sign /ˈiːkwəlz ˌsaɪn/
executive suite /ɪɡˈzekjutɪv ˌswiːt/
extinction /ɪkˈstɪŋkʃn/
fax machine /ˈfæks məˌʃiːn/
finite number /ˈfaɪnaɪt ˌnʌmbə(r)/
folklore /ˈfəʊklɔː(r)/
following /ˈfɒləʊɪŋ/
function 🔑 /ˈfʌŋkʃn/
graduate student /ˈɡrædʒuət ˌstjuːdnt/
hundred and one 🔑 /ˌhʌndrəd ən ˈwʌn/
ingenuity /ɪndʒəˈnjuːəti/
inspiration /ɪnspəˈreɪʃn/
internet age 🔑 /ˈɪntənet ˌeɪdʒ/
legend /ˈledʒənd/
lexicon /ˈleksɪkən/
malware /ˈmælweə(r)/
mass 🔑 /mæs/
mathematician /mæθəməˈtɪʃn/
mother tongue /ˈmʌðə ˌtʌŋ/
national identity 🔑 /ˌnæʃnəl aɪˈdentəti/
native land /ˌneɪtɪv ˈlænd/
officemate /ˈɒfɪsmeɪt/
phishing /ˈfɪʃɪŋ/
pinch /pɪntʃ/
podcast /ˈpɒdkɑːst/
publication 🔑 /pʌblɪˈkeɪʃn/
replacement part /rɪˈpleɪsmənt ˌpɑːt/
reservation /rezəˈveɪʃn/
search engine /ˈsɜːtʃ ˌendʒɪn/
simile /ˈsɪməli/
social networking /ˌsəʊʃl ˈnetwɜːkɪŋ/
tangerine /tændʒəˈriːn/
telecommunication system
  /telikəmjuːnɪˈkeɪʃn ˌsɪstəm/
telex machine /ˈteleks məˌʃiːn/
term 🔑 /tɜːm/
ton 🔑 /tʌn/

touch 🔑 /tʌtʃ/
trace 🔑 /treɪs/
transition /trænˈzɪʃn/
tribe /traɪb/
web address /ˈweb əˌdres/
webinar /ˈwebɪnɑː(r)/
wiki /ˈwɪki/
word processor /ˈwɜːd ˌprəʊsesə(r)/
zero 🔑 /ˈzɪərəʊ/
zillion /ˈzɪljən/

Verbs

appreciate 🔑 /əˈpriːʃieɪt/
brainstorm /ˈbreɪnstɔːm/
calculate 🔑 /ˈkælkjuleɪt/
care for (some tea) 🔑 /ˈkeə fə (səm ˈtiː)/
coin (a word) 🔑 /ˌkɔɪn (ə ˈwɜːd)/
collect (data) 🔑 /kəˌlekt (ˈdeɪtə)/
define 🔑 /dɪˈfaɪn/
delete /dɪˈliːt/
document 🔑 /ˈdɒkjument/
evoke 🔑 /ɪˈvəʊk/
explore (the internet) 🔑
  /ɪkˌsplɔː (ðɪ ˈɪntənet)/
extend 🔑 /ɪkˈstend/
feature 🔑 /ˈfiːtʃə(r)/
get (an idea) 🔑 /ˌɡet (ən aɪˈdɪə)/
get (data) 🔑 /ˌɡet (ˈdeɪtə)/
have (a holiday) 🔑 /ˌhæv (ə ˈhɒlədeɪ)/
have (an idea) 🔑 /ˌhæv (ən aɪˈdɪə)/
index 🔑 /ˈɪndeks/
invent (a word) 🔑 /ɪnˌvent (ə ˈwɜːd)/
like (some tea) 🔑 /ˌlaɪk (səm ˈtiː)/
locate 🔑 /ləʊˈkeɪt/
originate /əˈrɪdʒɪneɪt/
perfect 🔑 /pəˈfekt/
phish /fɪʃ/
preserve 🔑 /prɪˈzɜːv/
search (the internet) 🔑
  /ˌsɜːtʃ (ðiː ˈɪntənet)/
shut down (the computer) 🔑
  /ˌʃʌt ˌdaʊn (ðə kəmˈpjuːtə)/
switch on (a light) 🔑 /ˌswɪtʃ ˌɒn (ə ˈlaɪt)/
take (a holiday) 🔑 /ˌteɪk (ə ˈhɒlədeɪ)/
tire 🔑 /ˈtaɪə(r)/
turn off (the computer) 🔑
  /ˌtɜːn ˌɒf ðə kəmˈpjuːtə(r)/
turn on (a light) 🔑 /ˌtɜːn ˌɒn ə ˈlaɪt/
unite 🔑 /juˈnaɪt/

Adjectives

abundant /əˈbʌndənt/
apparent 🔑 /əˈpærənt/
colossal /kəˈlɒsl/
contemporary 🔑 /kənˈtempərəri/
eponymous /ɪˈpɒnɪməs/
extinct /ɪkˈstɪŋkt/
finite /ˈfaɪnaɪt/
heroic /həˈrəʊɪk/
immortal /ɪˈmɔːtl/
incredible /ɪnˈkredəbl/
innovative /ˈɪnəvətɪv/
intriguing /ɪnˈtriːɡɪŋ/
limited 🔑 /ˈlɪmɪtɪd/
mountainous /ˈmaʊntənəs/
obsolete /ˈɒbsəliːt/
obvious /ˈɒbviəs/
radioactive /reɪdiəʊˈæktɪv/
savoury /ˈseɪvəri/
toponymous /tɒˈpɒnɪməs/
unconquerable /ʌnˈkɒŋkərəbl/
unconventional /ʌnkənˈvenʃnl/
widespread /ˈwaɪdspred/

Adverbs

hence 🔑 /hens/
nevertheless 🔑 /nevəðəˈles/
precisely 🔑 /prɪˈsaɪsli/
rarely 🔑 /ˈreəli/
unimaginably /ʌnɪˈmædʒɪnəbli/
widely 🔑 /ˈwaɪdli/

Expressions and idioms

digitally enhance /ˌdɪdʒɪtəli ɪnˈhɑːns/
highly unlikely 🔑 /ˌhaɪli ʌnˈlaɪkli/
in a way 🔑 /ˌɪn ə ˈweɪ/
keep sth to a minimum 🔑
  /ˌkiːp ... tu ə ˈmɪnɪməm/
pardon me /ˌpɑːdn ˈmiː/
with regard to /ˌwɪð rɪˈɡɑːd tə/

Phrasal verbs

pass away /ˌpɑːs əˈweɪ/
point out /ˌpɔɪnt ˈaʊt/
refer to /rɪˈfɜː ˌtuː, tə/

Conjunction

albeit /ɔːlˈbiːɪt/
considering (that) 🔑 /kənˈsɪdərɪŋ (ðət)/

Literature Corner

bough (n) /baʊ/
in broad daylight (idm) /ˌɪn ˌbrɔːd ˈdeɪlaɪt/

/p/ pen	/d/ dog	/tʃ/ beach	/v/ very	/s/ speak	/ʒ/ television	/n/ now	/r/ radio
/b/ big	/k/ can	/dʒ/ job	/θ/ think	/z/ zoo	/h/ house	/ŋ/ sing	/j/ yes
/t/ two	/g/ good	/f/ food	/ð/ then	/ʃ/ she	/m/ meat	/l/ late	/w/ we

Nouns

ability 🔑 /ə'bɪləti/
academic 🔑 /ˌækə'demɪk/
account /ə'kaʊnt/
alphabet 🔑 /'ælfəbet/
asset /'æset/
automobile /'ɔ:təməbi:l/
bathtub /'bɑ:θtʌb/
breakthrough /'breɪkθru:/
car ownership /'kɑ:r ˌəʊnəʃɪp/
common sense /ˌkɒmən 'sens/
daily life 🔑 /ˌdeɪli 'laɪf/
definition 🔑 /defɪ'nɪʃn/
density /'densəti/
engineer 🔑 /endʒɪ'nɪə(r)/
expertise /ekspə'ti:z/
factor /'fæktə(r)/
fastener /'fɑ:snə(r)/
frustration /frʌ'streɪʃn/
genius /'dʒi:niəs/
goldsmith /'gəʊldsmɪθ/
hook 🔑 /hʊk/
inability 🔑 /'ɪnəbɪləti/
incident 🔑 /'ɪnsɪdənt/
insight 🔑 /'ɪnsaɪt/
inspiration /ˌɪnspə'reɪʃn/
intelligence 🔑 /ɪn'telɪdʒəns/
invention 🔑 /ɪn'venʃn/
inventor /ɪn'ventə(r)/
light bulb /'laɪt ˌbʌlb/
loop /lu:p/
manufacturing process 🔑 /mænju'fæktʃə rɪŋ ˌprəʊses/
microscope /'maɪkrəskəʊp/
microwave oven /ˌmaɪkrəweɪv 'ʌvn/
mobile phone /ˌməʊbaɪl 'fəʊn/
origin 🔑 /'ɒrɪdʒɪn/
patent /'pætnt, 'peɪtnt/
performance 🔑 /pə'fɔ:məns/
perseverance /pɜ:sɪ'vɪərəns/
perspiration /pɜ:spə'reɪʃn/
petrol 🔑 /'petrəl/
potential 🔑 /pə'tenʃl/
pre-packaged food /ˌpri: ˌpækɪdʒd 'fu:d/
printing press /'prɪntɪŋ ˌpres/
purity /'pjʊərəti/
quantity /'kwɒntəti/
satellite navigation device /ˌsætəlaɪt nævɪ'geɪʃn dɪ'vaɪs/
satellite technology /ˌsætəlaɪt tek'nɒlədʒi/
setback /'setbæk/
suspicion 🔑 /sə'spɪʃn/
text messaging /'tekst ˌmesɪdʒɪŋ/
tub /tʌb/
vehicle 🔑 /'vi:əkl/
volume 🔑 /'vɒlju:m/
wire 🔑 /'waɪə(r)/

Verbs

aggravate /'ægrəveɪt/
assist /ə'sɪst/
associate sth with sth /ə'səʊʃieɪt, -'sieɪt/
calculate /'kælkjuleɪt/
commission 🔑 /kə'mɪʃn/
confirm 🔑 /kən'fɜ:m/
craft 🔑 /krɑ:ft/
displace /dɪs'pleɪs/
divide /dɪ'vaɪd/
emerge 🔑 /ɪ'mɜ:dʒ/
enable 🔑 /ɪ'neɪbl/
exacerbate /ɪg'zæsəbeɪt/
frustrate /frʌ'streɪt/
hike /haɪk/
overcome 🔑 /ˌəʊvə'kʌm/
overlook /ˌəʊvə'lʊk/
persevere /pɜ:sɪ'vɪə(r)/
possess 🔑 /pə'zes/
prove (a case) 🔑 /ˌpru:v (ə 'keɪs)/
provide /prə'vaɪd/
speculate /'spekjuleɪt/
struggle 🔑 /'strʌgl/
submerge /sʌb'mɜ:dʒ/
underestimate /ʌndər'estɪmeɪt/

Adjectives

academic 🔑 /ˌækə'demɪk/
accidental 🔑 /ˌæksɪ'dentl/
affordable /ə'fɔ:dəbl/
bullet-proof /'bʊlɪt ˌpru:f/
childproof /'tʃaɪldpru:f/
duty-free /'dju:ti ˌfri:/
elaborate /ɪ'læbərət/
essential 🔑 /ɪ'senʃl/
fat-free /'fæt ˌfri:/
foolproof /'fu:lpru:f/
gifted /'gɪftɪd/
hands-free /'hændz ˌfri:/
interest-free /'ɪntrəst ˌfri:/
irrelevant /ɪ'reləvənt/
limited (to sth) 🔑 /'lɪmɪtɪd (tə ...)/
monumental /mɒnju'mentl/
ovenproof /'ʌvnpru:f/
significant 🔑 /sɪg'nɪfɪkənt/
smoke-free /'sməʊk ˌfri:/
soundproof /'saʊndpru:f/
suspicious 🔑 /sə'spɪʃəs/
tax-free /'tæks ˌfri:/
trouble-free /'trʌbl ˌfri:/
waterproof /'wɔ:təpru:f/

Adverbs

considerably 🔑 /kən'sɪdərəbli/
conversely /'kɒnvɜ:sli/
dramatically 🔑 /drə'mætɪkli/
indeed 🔑 /ɪn'di:d/
specifically 🔑 /spə'sɪfɪkli/
undoubtedly /ʌn'daʊtɪdli/

Expressions and idioms

as the story goes 🔑 /əz ðə ˌstɔ:ri 'gəʊz/
by nature 🔑 /ˌbaɪ 'neɪtʃə(r)/
come to a conclusion 🔑 /ˌkʌm tu ə kən'klu:ʒn/
equal to 🔑 /'i:kwəl tə/
go hand in hand 🔑 /ˌgəʊ ˌhænd ɪn 'hænd/
if only 🔑 /ˌɪf 'əʊnli/
in an instant 🔑 /ˌɪn ən 'ɪnstənt/
more importantly 🔑 /ˌmɔ:r ɪm'pɔ:tntli/
out of the question 🔑 /ˌaʊt əv ðə 'kwestʃən/
realize the significance /ˌri:əlaɪz ðə sɪg'nɪfɪkəns/
take a break 🔑 /ˌteɪk ə 'breɪk/
the vast majority (of) 🔑 /ðə 'vɑ:st mə'dʒɒrəti/

Phrasal verbs

break away 🔑 /ˌbreɪk ə'weɪ/
break down 🔑 /ˌbreɪk 'daʊn/
break into 🔑 /'breɪk ˌɪntə/
break off 🔑 /ˌbreɪk 'ɒf/
break out 🔑 /ˌbreɪk 'aʊt/
break up 🔑 /ˌbreɪk 'ʌp/
latch on (to sth) /ˌlætʃ 'ɒn (tə ...)/

Conjunction

provided 🔑 /prə'vaɪdɪd/

Prefixes

anti /'ænti/
auto /'ɔ:təʊ, 'ɔ:tə/
mal /mæl/
semi /'semi/
ultra /'ʌltrə/

/i/ happy	/æ/ flag	/ɜ:/ her	/ʊ/ look	/ʌ/ mum	/ɔɪ/ noisy	/ɪə/ here
/ɪ/ it	/ɑ:/ art	/ɒ/ not	/u:/ you	/eɪ/ day	/aʊ/ how	/eə/ wear
/i:/ he	/e/ egg	/ɔ:/ four	/ə/ sugar	/aɪ/ why	/əʊ/ go	/ʊə/ tourist

Nouns

advert 🔑 /'ædvɜːt/
advertisement 🔑 /əd'vɜːtɪsmənt/
advertiser /'ædvətaɪzə(r)/
advertising campaign 🔑 /'ædvətaɪzɪŋ kæm,peɪn/
appeal 🔑 /ə'piːl/
bargain hunter /'bɑːgɪn ,hʌntə(r)/
big business 🔑 /,bɪg 'bɪznəs/
billboard /'bɪlbɔːd/
brand /brænd/
cheap offer 🔑 /,tʃiːp 'ɒfə(r)/
conduct 🔑 /'kɒndʌkt/
consumer 🔑 /kən'sjuːmə(r)/
contribution 🔑 /kɒntrɪ'bjuːʃn/
customer 🔑 /'kʌstəmə(r)/
device 🔑 /dɪ'vaɪs/
disposable income /dɪ,spəʊzəbl 'ɪnkʌm/
earning power /'ɜːnɪŋ ,paʊə(r)/
economy 🔑 /ɪ'kɒnəmi/
endorsement /ɪn'dɔːsmənt/
fast-food restaurant /,fɑːst 'fuːd ,restrɒnt/
generation 🔑 /ʤenə'reɪʃn/
good buy 🔑 /,gʊd 'baɪ/
hype /haɪp/
impact 🔑 /'ɪmpækt/
increase 🔑 /'ɪŋkriːs/
individual 🔑 /ɪndɪ'vɪʤuəl/
influence 🔑 /'ɪnfluəns/
impulse buyer /'ɪmpʌls ,baɪə(r)/
issue 🔑 /'ɪʃuː/
jingle /'ʤɪŋgl/
key 🔑 /kiː/
logo /'ləʊgəʊ/
marketing department 🔑 /'mɑːkətɪŋ dɪ,pɑːtmənt/
multi-tasking /,mʌlti 'tɑːskɪŋ/
must-have item /,mʌst 'hæv ,aɪtəm/
option 🔑 /'ɒpʃn/
permit 🔑 /'pɜːmɪt/
potential 🔑 /pə'tenʃl/
preference 🔑 /'prefrəns/
price tag /'praɪs ,tæg/
product placement /,prɒdʌkt 'pleɪsmənt/
purchase 🔑 /'pɜːtʃəs/
purchasing decision 🔑 /'pɜːtʃəsɪŋ dɪ,sɪʒn/
record 🔑 /'rekɔːd/
refuse 🔑 /'refjuːs/
screen 🔑 /skriːn/
serious shopper /,sɪəriəs 'ʃɒpə(r)/
shopping centre 🔑 /'ʃɒpɪŋ ,sentə(r)/
shopping list 🔑 /'ʃɒpɪŋ ,lɪst/
shopping spree /'ʃɒpɪŋ ,spriː/
site 🔑 /saɪt/
slogan /'sləʊgən/
smart phone /'smɑːt ,fəʊn/
spending 🔑 /'spendɪŋ/
statistic /stə'tɪstɪk/
strategy 🔑 /'strætəʤi/

subject 🔑 /'sʌbʤɪkt/
survey 🔑 /'sɜːveɪ/
target 🔑 /'tɑːgɪt/
target market 🔑 /,tɑːgɪt 'mɑːkɪt/
technique 🔑 /tek'niːk/
teenager /'tiːneɪʤə(r)/
terrific deal /tə,rɪfɪk 'diːl/
usage /'juːsɪʤ/
wireless device /'waɪələs dɪ,vaɪs/

Verbs

attribute /ə'trɪbjuːt/
consult 🔑 /kən'sʌlt/
convince 🔑 /kən'vɪns/
direct 🔑 /də'rekt, dɪ-, daɪ-/
enable 🔑 /ɪ'neɪbl/
estimate 🔑 /'estɪmeɪt/
focus 🔑 /'fəʊkəs/
impact 🔑 /ɪm'pækt/
indicate 🔑 /'ɪndɪkeɪt/
influence 🔑 /'ɪnfluəns/
market 🔑 /'mɑːkɪt/
name 🔑 /neɪm/
object 🔑 /əb'ʤekt/
overcome 🔑 /əʊvə'kʌm/
participate /pɑː'tɪsɪpeɪt/
permit 🔑 /pə'mɪt/
present 🔑 /prɪ'zent/
promote 🔑 /prə'məʊt/
rebel /rɪ'bel/
recall 🔑 /rɪ'kɔːl/
represent 🔑 /reprɪ'zent/
respond 🔑 /rɪ'spɒnd/
survey 🔑 /sə'veɪ/
switch 🔑 /swɪtʃ/
target 🔑 /'tɑːgɪt/
text 🔑 /tekst/

Adjectives

associated (with) 🔑 /ə'səʊʃieɪtɪd, -sieɪt-/
awkward 🔑 /'ɔːkwəd/
digital /'dɪʤɪtl/
flexible /'fleksəbl/
hip /hɪp/
lightweight /'laɪtweɪt/
mobile 🔑 /'məʊbaɪl/
obsessed /əb'sest/
online /ɒn'laɪn/
ordinary 🔑 /'ɔːdnri/
part-time /,pɑːt 'taɪm/
persistent 🔑 /pə'sɪstənt/
personal 🔑 /'pɜːsənl/
previous 🔑 /'priːviəs/
quarrelling /'kwɒrəlɪŋ/
significant 🔑 /sɪg'nɪfɪkənt/
steady 🔑 /'stedi/
trendy /'trendi/
unprecedented /ʌn'presɪdentɪd/
wearable /'weərəbl/
well-off /,wel 'ɒf/

Adverbs

amazingly /ə'meɪzɪŋli/
critically /'krɪtɪkli/
eventually 🔑 /ɪ'ventʃuəli/
negatively /'negətɪvli/
recently 🔑 /'riːsntli/

Expressions and idioms

be intent on sth /,biː ɪn'tent ,ɒn/
come to an agreement 🔑 /,kʌm ,tu ən ə'griːmənt/
compared with 🔑 /kəm'peəd ,wɪð/
corner the market 🔑 /,kɔːnə ðə 'mɑːkɪt/
drum up business /,drʌm ,ʌp 'bɪznəs/
every waking moment /,evri ,weɪkɪŋ 'məʊmənt/
have a say 🔑 /,hæv ə 'seɪ/
in some instances /,ɪn 'sʌm ,ɪnstənsɪz/
in the pipeline /,ɪn ðə 'paɪplaɪn/
not up to scratch /,nɒt ,ʌp tə 'skrætʃ/
on a regular basis 🔑 /,ɒn ə ,regjələ 'beɪsɪs/
on the other hand 🔑 /,ɒn ði 'ʌðə ,hænd/
put sth on the line 🔑 /,pʊt ... ,ɒn ðə 'laɪn/
relatively little 🔑 /,relətɪvli 'lɪtl/
think outside the box /,θɪŋk aʊt,saɪd ðə 'bɒks/
wasteful with money /,weɪstfl wɪð 'mʌni/

Phrasal verbs

account for sth 🔑 /ə'kaʊnt fə/
leave out 🔑 /,liːv 'aʊt/
set aside 🔑 /,set ə'saɪd/

Literature corner

angle (n) 🔑 /'æŋgl/
arrest (v) 🔑 /ə'rest/
broom (n) /bruːm/
closet (n) 🔑 /'klɒzɪt/
constitute (v) /'kɒnstɪtjuːt/
fiercely (adv) /'fɪəsli/
peril (n) /'perəl/
perplexed (adj) /pə'plekst/
pride (n) 🔑 /praɪd/
punctuate (v) /'pʌŋktʃueɪt/
resurrect (v) /rezə'rekt/
seize (v) /siːz/
seldom (adv) /'seldəm/
slack (n) /slæk/
slight (adj) 🔑 /slaɪt/
spectacles (n) /'spektəklz/
stove lid (n) /'stəʊv ,lɪd/
switch (n) 🔑 /swɪtʃ/

/p/ pen	/d/ dog	/tʃ/ beach	/v/ very	/s/ speak	/ʒ/ television	/n/ now	/r/ radio
/b/ big	/k/ can	/dʒ/ job	/θ/ think	/z/ zoo	/h/ house	/ŋ/ sing	/j/ yes
/t/ two	/g/ good	/f/ food	/ð/ then	/ʃ/ she	/m/ meat	/l/ late	/w/ we

Nouns

acid 🔊 /ˈæsɪd/
amnesia /æmˈniːziə/
appendix /əˈpendɪks/
arthritis /ɑːˈθraɪtɪs/
aspirin /ˈæsprɪn/
asthma /ˈæsmə/
attitude 🔊 /ˈætɪtjuːd/
balanced approach 🔊 /ˈbælənst əˌprəʊtʃ/
bark /bɑːk/
blood vessel /ˈblʌd ˌvesl/
brain 🔊 /breɪn/
cancer 🔊 /ˈkænsə(r)/
colonel /ˈkɜːnl/
contamination /kəntæmɪˈneɪʃn/
council 🔊 /ˈkaʊnsl/
counsel /ˈkaʊnsl/
cramps /kræmps/
creature 🔊 /ˈkriːtʃə(r)/
cure 🔊 /kjʊə(r)/
diabetes /daɪəˈbiːtiːz/
disease 🔊 /dɪˈziːz/
dose /dəʊs/
experience 🔊 /ɪkˈspɪəriəns/
extract /ˈekstrækt/
extraction /ɪkˈstrækʃn/
face mask /ˈfeɪs ˌmɑːsk/
fever 🔊 /ˈfiːvə(r)/
foxglove /ˈfɒksglʌv/
headache 🔊 /ˈhedeɪk/
healing power 🔊 /ˈhiːlɪŋ ˌpaʊə(r)/
heart 🔊 /hɑːt/
herbal medicine /ˌhɜːbl ˈmedsn/
hose /həʊz/
intestine 🔊 /ɪnˈtestɪn/
irritation /ɪrɪˈteɪʃn/
jungle /ˈdʒʌŋgl/
kernel /ˈkɜːnl/
kidney /ˈkɪdni/
laughter /ˈlɑːftə(r)/
legend /ˈledʒənd/
liver /ˈlɪvə(r)/
loot /luːt/
lungs 🔊 /lʌŋz/
lute /luːt/
malaria /məˈleəriə/
medical school /ˈmedɪkl ˌskuːl/
medication /medɪˈkeɪʃn/
mosquito /məˈskiːtəʊ/
natural remedy /ˌnætʃrəl ˈremədi/
neutralization /njuːtrəlaɪˈzeɪʃn/
noblewoman /ˈnəʊblwʊmən/
orchard /ˈɔːtʃəd/
oxygen bar /ˈɒksɪdʒən ˌbɑː(r)/
pancreas /ˈpæŋkriəs/
patent /ˈpætnt, ˈpeɪtnt/
patient 🔊 /ˈpeɪʃnt/
peasant woman /ˈpeznt ˌwʊmən/
quinine /kwɪˈniːn, ˈkwɪ-/

recovery /rɪˈkʌvəri/
relief 🔊 /rɪˈliːf/
remedy /ˈremədi/
roadside /ˈrəʊdsaɪd/
science fiction /ˌsaɪəns ˈfɪkʃn/
situation 🔊 /ˌsɪtʃuˈeɪʃn/
sophistication /səfɪstɪˈkeɪʃn/
spleen /spliːn/
sponge /spʌndʒ/
stationery /ˈsteɪʃnri/
stomach 🔊 /ˈstʌmək/
stroke 🔊 /strəʊk/
substance 🔊 /ˈsʌbstəns/
swelling 🔊 /ˈswelɪŋ/
tank 🔊 /tæŋk/
tension 🔊 /ˈtenʃn/
tolerance /ˈtɒlərəns/
treatment 🔊 /ˈtriːtmənt/
treatment plan 🔊 /ˈtriːtmənt ˌplæn/
tropical rain forest 🔊 /ˌtrɒpɪkl ˈreɪn ˌfɒrɪst/
tuberculosis /tjuːbɜːkjuˈləʊsɪs/
ulcer /ˈʌlsə(r)/
variety 🔊 /vəˈraɪəti/
warning 🔊 /ˈwɔːnɪŋ/
well-being /ˌwel ˈbiːɪŋ/

Verbs

abate /əˈbeɪt/
absorb 🔊 /əbˈzɔːb/
contaminate /kənˈtæmɪneɪt/
contribute 🔊 /kənˈtrɪbjuːt/
crush 🔊 /krʌʃ/
cure 🔊 /kjʊə(r)/
diminish /dɪˈmɪnɪʃ/
extract /ˈekstrækt/
identify 🔊 /aɪˈdentɪfaɪ/
imply 🔊 /ɪmˈplaɪ/
infer /ɪnˈfɜː(r)/
involve 🔊 /ɪnˈvɒlv/
market 🔊 /ˈmɑːkɪt/
neutralize /ˈnjuːtrəlaɪz/
patent /ˈpætnt, ˈpeɪtnt/
poison 🔊 /ˈpɔɪzn/
pore /pɔː(r)/
pour 🔊 /pɔː(r)/
produce 🔊 /prəˈdjuːs/
record 🔊 /rɪˈkɔːd/
reduce 🔊 /rɪˈdjuːs/
relieve 🔊 /rɪˈliːv/
research 🔊 /rɪˈsɜːtʃ, ˈriː-/
suffer (from) 🔊 /ˈsʌfə (frəm)/
tolerate /ˈtɒləreɪt/
treat 🔊 /triːt/
upset /ʌpˈset/

Adjectives

accurate 🔊 /ˈækjərət/
anxious 🔊 /ˈæŋkʃəs/
aromatic /ærəˈmætɪk/
associated (with) /əˈsəʊʃieɪtɪd, -sieɪt-/
bitter 🔊 /ˈbɪtə(r)/
clammy /ˈklæmi/
complementary /kɒmplɪˈmentri/
complimentary /kɒmplɪˈmentri/
deadly /ˈdedli/
deafening /ˈdefnɪŋ/
effective 🔊 /ɪˈfektɪv/
humorous 🔊 /ˈhjuːmərəs/
lethal /ˈliːθl/
mouth-watering /ˈmaʊθ ˌwɔːtərɪŋ/
official 🔊 /əˈfɪʃl/
officious /əˈfɪʃəs/
pain-relieving /ˈpeɪn rɪˌliːvɪŋ/
racial /ˈreɪʃl/
racist /ˈreɪsɪst/
sceptical /ˈskeptɪkl/
scorching /ˈskɔːtʃɪŋ/
sensible 🔊 /ˈsensəbl/
sensitive 🔊 /ˈsensətɪv/
slimy /ˈslaɪmi/
stationary /ˈsteɪʃnri/
surrounding 🔊 /səˈraʊndɪŋ/

Adverbs

allegedly /əˈledʒɪdli/
otherwise 🔊 /ˈʌðəwaɪz/
particularly 🔊 /pəˈtɪkjələli/
potentially 🔊 /pəˈtenʃəli/
thereby /ðeəˈbaɪ/

Expressions and idioms

be under the weather 🔊 /bi ˌʌndə ðə ˈweðə(r)/
feel lightheaded /ˌfiːl laɪtˈhedɪd/
feel queasy /ˌfiːl ˈkwiːzi/
food for thought 🔊 /ˌfuːd fə ˈθɔːt/
get butterflies in (your) stomach /ˌget ˌbʌtəflaɪz ˌɪn (jɔː) ˈstʌmək/
give it a try /ˌgɪv ˌɪt ə ˈtraɪ/
have the sniffles /ˌhæv ðə ˈsnɪflz/
high blood pressure 🔊 /ˌhaɪ ˈblʌd ˌpreʃə(r)/
in order to 🔊 /ˌɪn ˈɔːdə tə/
lose track of time 🔊 /ˌluːz ˌtræk əv ˈtaɪm/
no exception 🔊 /ˌnəʊ ɪkˈsepʃn/
recharge your batteries /riːˌtʃɑːdʒ jɔː ˈbætəriz/
run out of steam 🔊 /ˌrʌn ˌaʊt əv ˈstiːm/
trial and error 🔊 /ˌtraɪəl ən ˈerə(r)/
worth every penny /ˌwɜːθ ˌevri ˈpeni/

/i/ happy	/æ/ flag	/ɜː/ her	/ʊ/ look	/ʌ/ mum	/ɔɪ/ noisy	/ɪə/ here
/ɪ/ it	/ɑː/ art	/ɒ/ not	/uː/ you	/eɪ/ day	/aʊ/ how	/eə/ wear
/iː/ he	/e/ egg	/ɔː/ four	/ə/ sugar	/aɪ/ why	/əʊ/ go	/ʊə/ tourist

Nouns

adaptation /ˌædæp'teɪʃn/
advocate /ˈædvəkət/
birth order 🔑 /ˈbɜːθ ˌɔːdə(r)/
cap 🔑 /kæp/
career advancement /kəˈrɪər ədˌvɑːnsmənt/
career choice 🔑 /kəˈrɪə ˌtʃɔɪs/
career guidance counsellor
  /kəˌrɪə ˈgaɪdəns ˌkaʊnsələ(r)/
career path 🔑 /kəˈrɪə ˌpɑːθ/
characteristic 🔑 /ˌkærəktəˈrɪstɪk/
club 🔑 /klʌb/
comfort level 🔑 /ˈkʌmfət ˌlevl/
compromise /ˈkɒmprəmaɪz/
conventional wisdom
  /kənˌvenʃənl ˈwɪzdəm/
counselling /ˈkaʊnsəlɪŋ/
crop 🔑 /krɒp/
cultural icon /ˌkʌltʃərəl ˈaɪkɒn/
determiner /dɪˈtɜːmɪnə(r)/
distinction /dɪˈstɪŋkʃn/
earning potential 🔑 /ˈɜːnɪŋ pəˌtenʃl/
earning power 🔑 /ˈɜːnɪŋ ˌpaʊə(r)/
financial success 🔑 /faɪˌnænʃl səkˈses/
founder /ˈfaʊndə(r)/
heart disease 🔑 /ˈhɑːt dɪˌziːz/
law enforcement /ˈlɔːr ɪnˌfɔːsmənt/
limelight /ˈlaɪmlaɪt/
line 🔑 /ˈlaɪn/
living conditions 🔑 /ˈlɪvɪŋ kənˌdɪʃnz/
multi-tasking /ˌmʌlti ˈtɑːskɪŋ/
night shift 🔑 /ˈnaɪt ˌʃɪft/
negotiation /nɪgəʊʃiˈeɪʃn/
people skills 🔑 /ˈpiːpl ˌskɪlz/
pitch 🔑 /pɪtʃ/
platform 🔑 /ˈplætfɔːm/
plug 🔑 /plʌg/
quack /kwæk/
rank 🔑 /ræŋk/
restriction 🔑 /rɪˈstrɪkʃn/
role 🔑 /rəʊl/
school 🔑 /skuːl/
scratch 🔑 /skrætʃ/
senior management 🔑
  /ˌsiːniə ˈmænɪdʒmənt/
shoot 🔑 /ʃuːt/
sibling /ˈsɪblɪŋ/
social scientist 🔑 /ˌsəʊʃl ˈsaɪəntɪst/
specialty /speʃiˈæləti/
stand 🔑 /stænd/
status 🔑 /ˈsteɪtəs/
substitute 🔑 /ˈsʌbstɪtjuːt/
upbringing /ˈʌpbrɪŋɪŋ/
wing 🔑 /wɪŋ/

Verbs

accommodate /əˈkɒmədeɪt/
acknowledge 🔑 /əkˈnɒlɪdʒ/
cite /saɪt/
classify /ˈklæsɪfaɪ/
determine 🔑 /dɪˈtɜːmɪn/
establish 🔑 /ɪˈstæblɪʃ/
experiment 🔑 /ɪkˈsperɪmənt/
gravitate /ˈgrævɪteɪt/
haul /hɔːl/
locate 🔑 /ləʊˈkeɪt/
overlook /əʊvəˈlʊk/
override /əʊvəˈraɪd/
plug 🔑 /plʌg/
quack /kwæk/
school /skuːl/
scratch 🔑 /skrætʃ/
shoot 🔑 /ʃuːt/
stand 🔑 /stænd/

Adjectives

accommodating /əˈkɒmədeɪtɪŋ/
aloof /əˈluːf/
authentic /ɔːˈθentɪk/
capricious /kəˈprɪʃəs/
carbonated /ˈkɑːbəneɪtɪd/
charismatic /ˌkærɪzˈmætɪk/
classic 🔑 /ˈklæsɪk/
close 🔑 /kləʊs/
conceited /kənˈsiːtɪd/
confident 🔑 /ˈkɒnfɪdənt/
considerate /kənˈsɪdərət/
determined 🔑 /dɪˈtɜːmɪnd/
disciplined 🔑 /ˈdɪsəplɪnd/
distinctive /dɪˈstɪŋktɪv/
dogmatic /dɒgˈmætɪk/
down-to-earth /ˌdaʊn tu ˈɜːθ/
easy-going /ˌiːzi ˈgəʊɪŋ/
entire 🔑 /ɪnˈtaɪə(r)/
extroverted /ˈekstrəvɜːtɪd/
fearful (of) /ˈfɪəfl/
first-born /ˈfɜːst ˌbɔːn/
happy-go-lucky /ˌhæpi ˌgəʊ ˈlʌki/
manipulative /məˈnɪpjulətɪv/
opinionated /əˈpɪnjəneɪtɪd/
outgoing /aʊtˈgəʊɪŋ/
pre-fabricated /ˌpriː ˈfæbrɪkeɪtɪd/
pretentious /prɪˈtenʃəs/
quick-witted /ˌkwɪk ˈwɪtɪd/
receptive /rɪˈseptɪv/
reliable /rɪˈlaɪəbl/
resolute /ˈrezəluːt/
self-assured /ˌself əˈʃʊəd/
sole /səʊl/
spontaneous /spɒnˈteɪniəs/
stand-offish /ˌstænd ˈɒfɪʃ/
stubborn /ˈstʌbən/
thick-skinned /ˌθɪk ˈskɪnd/
trustworthy /ˈtrʌstwɜːði/
uncompromising /ʌnˈkɒmprəmaɪzɪŋ/
unpredictable /ʌnprɪˈdɪktəbl/
witty /ˈwɪti/

Adverbs

equally 🔑 /ˈiːkwəli/
nowadays /ˈnaʊədeɪz/
typically 🔑 /ˈtɪpɪkli/
ultimately 🔑 /ˈʌltɪmətli/

Expressions and idioms

around the clock 🔑 /əˌraʊnd ðə ˈklɒk/
as nice as pie /əz ˌnaɪs əz ˈpaɪ/
at greater risk 🔑 /ət ˌgreɪtə ˈrɪsk/
be a shrinking violet
  /ˌbiː ə ˌʃrɪŋkɪŋ ˈvaɪələt/
be a wet blanket /ˌbiː ə ˌwet ˈblæŋkɪt/
conventional wisdom
  /kənˌvenʃənl ˈwɪzdəm/
feel at ease 🔑 /ˌfiːl ət ˈiːz/
get away with murder
  /ˌget əˌweɪ ˌwɪð ˈmɜːdə(r)/
have a good head on (your) shoulders
  /ˌhæv ə ˌgʊd ˌhed ˌɒn (jɔː) ˈʃəʊldəz/
have a very short fuse
  /ˌhæv ə ˌveri ˌʃɔːt ˈfjuːz/
have an impact on 🔑
  /ˌhæv ən ˈɪmpækt ˌɒn/
it stands to reason (that) 🔑
  /ɪt ˌstændz tə ˈriːzn/
keep tabs on /ˌkiːp ˈtæbz ˌɒn/
life and soul of the party 🔑
  /ˌlaɪf ən ˌsəʊl əv ðə ˈpɑːti/
like chalk and cheese /ˌlaɪk ˌtʃɔːk ən ˈtʃiːz/
on demand 🔑 /ˌɒn dɪˈmɑːnd/
open for business 🔑 /ˈəʊpən fə ˌbɪznəs/
playing with words 🔑 /ˌpleɪɪŋ wɪð ˈwɜːdz/
satisfy your cravings 🔑
  /ˌsætɪsfaɪ jɔː ˈkreɪvɪŋz/
side by side 🔑 /ˌsaɪd ˌbaɪ ˈsaɪd/

Phrasal verbs

look up to 🔑 /ˌlʊk ˈʌp ˌtuː, tə/

Literature Corner

abreast (of sth) (adv) /əˈbrest/
afoot (adj) /əˈfʊt/
bamboo (n) /bæmˈbuː/
derisive (adj) /dɪˈraɪsɪv/
exultation (n) /ˌegzʌlˈteɪʃn/
grave (adj) 🔑 /greɪv/
incline (n) /ˈɪnklaɪn/
outlying (adj) /ˈaʊtlaɪɪŋ/
picket (n) /ˈpɪkɪt/
pterodactyl (n) /terəˈdæktɪl/
skyline (n) /ˈskaɪlaɪn/
stork (n) /stɔːk/
whale backed (adj) /ˈweɪl ˌbækt/
wont (n) /wəʊnt/
van (n) 🔑 /væn/

/p/	pen	/d/	dog	/tʃ/	beach	/v/	very	/s/	speak	/ʒ/	television	/n/	now	/r/	radio
/b/	big	/k/	can	/dʒ/	job	/θ/	think	/z/	zoo	/h/	house	/ŋ/	sing	/j/	yes
/t/	two	/g/	good	/f/	food	/ð/	then	/ʃ/	she	/m/	meat	/l/	late	/w/	we

Nouns

agriculture /ˈægrɪkʌltʃə(r)/
appetite /ˈæpɪtaɪt/
artichoke /ˈɑːtɪtʃəʊk/
atmosphere ⚷ /ˈætməsfɪə(r)/
bakery goods /ˈbeɪkəri ˌɡʊdz/
bay leaf /ˈbeɪ ˌliːf/
blanket /ˈblæŋkɪt/
casserole /ˈkæsərəʊl/
centimetre ⚷ /ˈsentɪmiːtə(r)/
chamomile /ˈkæməmaɪl/
characteristic ⚷ /ˌkærəktəˈrɪstɪk/
charity ⚷ /ˈtʃærəti/
chef /ʃef/
cinnamon /ˈsɪnəmən/
coal miner /ˈkəʊl ˌmaɪnə(r)/
cod /kɒd/
colander /ˈkʌləndə(r)/
community ⚷ /kəˈmjuːnəti/
consensus /kənˈsensəs/
cooking utensils /ˈkʊkɪŋ juːˌtenslz/
coriander /ˌkɒriˈændə(r)/
crop ⚷ /krɒp/
cuisine /kwɪˈziːn/
diner /ˈdaɪnə(r)/
easy option ⚷ /ˌiːzi ˈɒpʃn/
farmland /ˈfɑːmlænd/
fertilizer /ˈfɜːtɪlaɪzə(r)/
flavour ⚷ /ˈfleɪvə(r)/
food processor /ˈfuːd ˌprəʊsesə(r)/
foot ⚷ /fʊt/
gallon ⚷ /ˈɡælən/
ginger /ˈdʒɪndʒə(r)/
harvesting /ˈhɑːvɪstɪŋ/
health benefit ⚷ /ˈhelθ ˌbenəfɪt/
heavy industry ⚷ /ˌhevi ˈɪndəstri/
herb /hɜːb/
herbal tea /ˌhɜːbl ˈtiː/
herbicide /ˈhɜːbɪsaɪd/
industrial worker ⚷ /ɪnˈdʌstriəl ˈwɜːkə(r)/
intervention ⚷ /ˌɪntəˈvenʃn/
kilogram ⚷ /ˈkɪləɡræm/
ladle /ˈleɪdl/
lentil /ˈlentl/
litre ⚷ /ˈliːtə(r)/
long-term future /ˌlɒŋ ˌtɜːm ˈfjuːtʃə(r)/
market research ⚷ /ˌmɑːkɪt rɪˈsɜːtʃ, ˈriː-/
menu ⚷ /ˈmenjuː/
method ⚷ /ˈmeθəd/
metre ⚷ /ˈmiːtə(r)/
milligram ⚷ /ˈmɪliɡræm/
millilitre /ˈmɪliliːtə(r)/
mint /mɪnt/
mission /ˈmɪʃn/
oat /əʊt/
okra /ˈəʊkrə, ˈɒkrə/
ounce /aʊns/
packet ⚷ /ˈpækɪt/
parsley /ˈpɑːsli/

pestle and mortar /ˌpesl ən ˈmɔːtə(r)/
pint ⚷ /paɪnt/
pomegranate /ˈpɒmɪɡrænɪt/
potato peeler /pəˈteɪtəʊ ˌpiːlə(r)/
pound ⚷ /paʊnd/
preparation ⚷ /ˌprepəˈreɪʃn/
product ⚷ /ˈprɒdʌkt/
profit ⚷ /ˈprɒfɪt/
pumpkin /ˈpʌmpkɪn/
restaurateur /ˌrestərəˈtɜː(r)/
root vegetable ⚷ /ˈruːt ˌvedʒtəbl/
salad greens ⚷ /ˈsæləd ˌɡriːnz/
service ⚷ /ˈsɜːvɪs/
silk ⚷ /sɪlk/
soil ⚷ /sɔɪl/
speciality /ˌspeʃiˈæləti/
specific requirement ⚷ /spəˌsɪfɪk rɪˈkwaɪəmənt/
tagine /tæˈʒiːn/
tangerine ⚷ /ˌtændʒəˈriːn/
technique ⚷ /tekˈniːk/
temperature ⚷ /ˈtemprətʃə(r)/
tractor /ˈtræktə(r)/
trend ⚷ /trend/
turnip /ˈtɜːnɪp/
variety ⚷ /vəˈraɪəti/
venture ⚷ /ˈventʃə(r)/
well-being /ˌwel ˈbiːɪŋ/
whisk /wɪsk/
wok /wɒk/
yard ⚷ /jɑːd/

Verbs

beat ⚷ /biːt/
braise /breɪz/
chop ⚷ /tʃɒp/
commission /kəˈmɪʃn/
convert ⚷ /kənˈvɜːt/
crush ⚷ /krʌʃ/
decrease ⚷ /dɪˈkriːs/
deep-fry /ˈdiːp ˌfraɪ/
differ ⚷ /ˈdɪfə(r)/
donate /dəʊˈneɪt/
drain /dreɪn/
expand ⚷ /ɪkˈspænd/
export ⚷ /ɪkˈspɔːt/
focus (on) ⚷ /ˈfəʊkəs/
guarantee ⚷ /ˌɡærənˈtiː/
invest ⚷ /ɪnˈvest/
lease /liːs/
mix ⚷ /mɪks/
peel /piːl/
sacrifice /ˈsækrɪfaɪs/
serve ⚷ /sɜːv/
slice ⚷ /slaɪs/
stew /stjuː/
stimulate /ˈstɪmjuleɪt/
stir-fry /ˈstɜː ˌfraɪ/
switch to ⚷ /ˈswɪtʃ tə/

transform ⚷ /trænsˈfɔːm/
wrap ⚷ /ræp/

Adjectives

additional ⚷ /əˈdɪʃənl/
authentic /ɔːˈθentɪk/
biodynamic /baɪəʊdaɪˈnæmɪk/
conventional ⚷ /kənˈvenʃənl/
ethnic /ˈeθnɪk/
food-conscious /ˈfuːd ˌkɒnʃəs/
imperial /ɪmˈpɪəriəl/
inexpensive /ˌɪnɪkˈspensɪv/
initial ⚷ /ɪˈnɪʃl/
intense /ɪnˈtens/
latter ⚷ /ˈlætə(r)/
metric /ˈmetrɪk/
modern-day /ˈmɒdn ˌdeɪ/
organic /ɔːˈɡænɪk/
passionate /ˈpæʃənət/
pioneering /paɪəˈnɪərɪŋ/
pre-measured /ˈpriː ˌmeʒəd/
questionable /ˈkwestʃənəbl/
seasonal /ˈsiːzənl/
spicy ⚷ /ˈspaɪsi/
sustainable /səˈsteɪnəbl/
typical ⚷ /ˈtɪpɪkl/

Adverbs

environmentally /ɪnˌvaɪrənˈmentəli/
primarily ⚷ /praɪˈmerəli/
significantly ⚷ /sɪɡˈnɪfɪkəntli/
traditionally ⚷ /trəˈdɪʃənəli/

Expressions and idioms

eat my words /ˌiːt ˌmaɪ ˈwɜːdz/
fish out of water /ˌfɪʃ ˌaʊt əv ˈwɔːtə(r)/
fishy /ˈfɪʃi/
have her cake and eat it /ˌhæv ˌhɜː ˌkeɪk ən ˈiːt ˌɪt/
in contrast ⚷ /ˌɪn ˈkɒntrɑːst/
in other words ⚷ /ˌɪn ˈʌðə ˌwɜːdz/
lose (some) weight ⚷ /ˌluːz (səm) ˈweɪt/
make a meal of it ⚷ /ˌmeɪk ə ˈmiːl əv ˌɪt/
ranging from sth to sth ⚷ /ˈreɪndʒɪŋ frəm/
realize a dream ⚷ /ˌriːəlaɪz ə ˈdriːm/
sour grapes /ˌsaʊə ˈɡreɪps/
to put it another way ⚷ /tə ˌpʊt ˌɪt əˈnʌðə ˌweɪ/
what a shame ⚷ /ˌwɒt ə ˈʃeɪm/

Phrasal verb

consist of ⚷ /kənˈsɪst əv/

Preposition

besides /bɪˈsaɪdz/

Nouns

attire /əˈtaɪə(r)/
background 🔑 /ˈbækɡraʊnd/
bus stop /ˈbʌs ˌstɒp/
business associate 🔑 /ˈbɪznəs əˌsəʊʃiət/
camaraderie /ˌkæməˈrɑːdəri/
deference /ˈdefərəns/
degree 🔑 /dɪˈɡriː/
error 🔑 /ˈerə(r)/
escalator /ˈeskəleɪtə(r)/
etiquette /ˈetɪket/
exception 🔑 /ɪkˈsepʃn/
extent 🔑 /ɪkˈstent/
gear 🔑 /ɡɪə(r)/
gender /ˈdʒendə(r)/
guideline /ˈɡaɪdlaɪn/
hardship /ˈhɑːdʃɪp/
heap /hiːp/
instructor /ɪnˈstrʌktə(r)/
local authority /ˌləʊkl ɔːˈθɒrəti/
masters course /ˈmɑːstəz ˌkɔːs/
metaphor /ˈmetəfɔː(r)/
meter 🔑 /ˈmiːtə(r)/
norm /nɔːm/
overgeneralization /ˌəʊvədʒenrəlaɪˈzeɪʃn/
passage (of time) 🔑 /ˈpæsɪdʒ (əv ˌtaɪm)/
personal space 🔑 /ˌpɜːsənl ˈspeɪs/
photo album /ˈfəʊtəʊ ˌælbəm/
physical contact 🔑 /ˌfɪzɪkl ˈkɒntækt/
pitch 🔑 /pɪtʃ/
plethora /ˈpleθərə/
prosperity /prɒˈsperəti/
rapport /ræˈpɔː(r)/
remote 🔑 /rɪˈməʊt/
renewal /rɪˈnjuːəl/
rugby /ˈrʌɡbi/
semester /sɪˈmestə(r)/
session 🔑 /ˈseʃn/
shrine /ʃraɪn/
status 🔑 /ˈsteɪtəs/
taxi stand 🔑 /ˈtæksi ˌstænd/
turn taking 🔑 /ˈtɜːn ˌteɪkɪŋ/
typo /ˈtaɪpəʊ/
variation 🔑 /ˌveəriˈeɪʃn/

Verbs

bash /bæʃ/
characterize /ˈkærəktəraɪz/
chat 🔑 /tʃæt/
differ /ˈdɪfə(r)/
discuss 🔑 /dɪsˈkʌs/
distinguish 🔑 /dɪˈstɪŋɡwɪʃ/
dribble /ˈdrɪbl/
enrol /ɪnˈrəʊl/
gossip /ˈɡɒsɪp/
grab 🔑 /ɡræb/
illustrate 🔑 /ˈɪləstreɪt/
interrupt 🔑 /ˌɪntəˈrʌpt/
mutter /ˈmʌtə(r)/

overcharge /ˌəʊvəˈtʃɑːdʒ/
overlap /ˌəʊvəˈlæp/
protest 🔑 /prəˈtest/
reflect 🔑 /rɪˈflekt/
resemble /rɪˈzembl/
signal 🔑 /ˈsɪɡnəl/
socialize /ˈsəʊʃəlaɪz/
strike 🔑 /straɪk/
symbolize /ˈsɪmbəlaɪz/
tackle 🔑 /ˈtækl/
toss /tɒs/
wave 🔑 /ˈweɪv/
whisper 🔑 /ˈwɪspə(r)/
whistle 🔑 /ˈwɪsl/

Adjectives

appropriate 🔑 /əˈprəʊpriət/
automatic 🔑 /ˌɔːtəˈmætɪk/
conversational /ˌkɒnvəˈseɪʃənl/
customary /ˈkʌstəməri/
discourteous /dɪsˈkɜːtiəs/
extensive 🔑 /ɪkˈstensɪv/
homesick /ˈhəʊmsɪk/
intercultural /ˌɪntəˈkʌltʃərəl/
lively 🔑 /ˈlaɪvli/
navigational /ˌnævɪˈɡeɪʃənl/
pharmaceutical /ˌfɑːməˈs(j)uːtɪkl/
procedural /prəˈsiːdʒərəl/
reticent /ˈretɪsnt/
spontaneous /spɒnˈteɪniəs/
strict 🔑 /strɪkt/
uncomfortable 🔑 /ʌnˈkʌmftəbl/

Adverbs

simultaneously /ˌsɪməlˈteɪniəsli/
somewhat 🔑 /ˈsʌmwɒt/

Expressions and idioms

absence makes the heart grow fonder
/ˌæbsəns ˌmeɪks ðə ˌhɑːt ˌɡrəʊ ˈfɒndə(r)/
actions speak louder than words 🔑
/ˌækʃnz ˌspiːk ˌlaʊdə ðən ˈwɜːdz/
clothes make the man 🔑
/ˌkləʊðz ˌmeɪk ðə ˈmæn/
don"t judge a book by its cover 🔑
/ˌdəʊnt ˌdʒʌdʒ ə ˌbʊk ˌbaɪ ˌits ˈkʌvə(r)/
form a queue /ˌfɔːm ə ˈkjuː/
jump the queue /ˌdʒʌmp ðə ˈkjuː/
he who hesitates is lost 🔑
/ˌhiː ˌhuː ˌhezɪteɪts ˌɪz ˈlɒst/
hit it big 🔑 /ˌhɪt ˌɪt ˈbɪɡ/
hit it off 🔑 /ˌhɪt ˌɪt ˈɒf/
hit the buffers /ˌhɪt ðə ˈbʌfəz/
hit the ground running 🔑
/ˌhɪt ðə ˌɡraʊnd ˈrʌnɪŋ/
hit the hay /ˌhɪt ðə ˈheɪ/
hit the nail on the head 🔑
/ˌhɪt ðə ˌneɪl ˌɒn ðə ˈhed/
hit the road 🔑 /ˌhɪt ðə ˈrəʊd/

hit the roof 🔑 /ˌhɪt ðə ˈruːf/
hold the floor 🔑 /ˌhəʊld ðə ˈflɔː(r)/
in terms of 🔑 /ˌɪn ˈtɜːmz əv/
it just isn't done 🔑 /ˌɪt ˌdʒʌst ˌɪznt ˈdʌn/
look before you leap /ˌlʊk bɪˌfɔː juː ˈliːp/
many hands make light work 🔑
/ˌmeni ˌhændz ˌmeɪk ˌlaɪt ˈwɜːk/
on silent 🔑 /ˌɒn ˈsaɪlənt/
on the blink /ˌɒn ðə ˈblɪŋk/
open the conversation 🔑
/ˌəʊpən ðə kɒnvəˈseɪʃn/
out of order 🔑 /ˌaʊt əv ˈɔːdə(r)/
out of sight, out of mind 🔑
/ˌaʊt əv ˈsaɪt ˌaʊt əv ˈmaɪnd/
the pen is mightier than the sword
/ðə ˌpen ˌɪz ˌmaɪtiə ðən ðə ˈsɔːd/
too many cooks spoil the broth
/ˌtuː ˌmeni ˌkʊks ˌspɔɪl ðə ˈbrɒθ/
wait your turn 🔑 /ˌweɪt jɔː ˈtɜːn/

Literature Corner

bosom (n) /ˈbʊzəm/
by degrees (idm) 🔑 /ˌbaɪ dɪˈɡriːz/
cannon (n) /ˈkænən/
captivity (n) /kæpˈtɪvəti/
chamber (n) /ˈtʃeɪmbə(r)/
cleave (v) /kliːv/
contradict (v) /ˌkɒntrəˈdɪkt/
convey (v) /kənˈveɪ/
crest (n) /krest/
dash (to pieces) (v) /ˌdæʃ (tə ˈpiːsɪz)/
extremity (n) /ɪkˈstreməti/
famished (adj) /ˈfæmɪʃt/
firmament (n) /ˈfɜːməmənt/
foaming (adj) /ˈfəʊmɪŋ/
fortress (n) /ˈfɔːtrəs/
fugitive (n) /ˈfjuːdʒətɪv/
gild (v) /ɡɪld/
governor (n) 🔑 /ˈɡʌvənə(r)/
harbour (n) /ˈhɑːbə(r)/
imposing (adj) 🔑 /ɪmˈpəʊzɪŋ/
inanimate (adj) /ɪnˈænɪmət/
majesty (n) /ˈmædʒəsti/
pass muster (idm) /ˌpɑːs ˈmʌstə(r)/
pretext (n) /ˈpriːtekst/
prow (n) /praʊ/
pursue (v) 🔑 /pəˈsjuː/
spectacle (n) /ˈspektəkl/
strive (v) /straɪv/
tempest (n) /ˈtempɪst/
turnkey (n) /ˈtɜːnkiː/
wretched (adj) /ˈretʃɪd/

/p/ pen	/d/ dog	/tʃ/ beach	/v/ very	/s/ speak	/ʒ/ television	/n/ now	/r/ radio
/b/ big	/k/ can	/dʒ/ job	/θ/ think	/z/ zoo	/h/ house	/ŋ/ sing	/j/ yes
/t/ two	/g/ good	/f/ food	/ð/ then	/ʃ/ she	/m/ meat	/l/ late	/w/ we

Nouns

adverse effect /ˌædvɜːs əˈfekt/
air conditioner /ˈeə kənˌdɪʃənə(r)/
air conditioning /ˈeə kənˌdɪʃənɪŋ/
air travel ☛0 /ˈeə ˌtrævl/
appliance /əˈplaɪəns/
belongings /bɪˈlɒŋɪŋz/
bench /bentʃ/
bungalow /ˈbʌŋɡələʊ/
breeze /briːz/
calculation ☛0 /kælkjuˈleɪʃn/
capital city ☛0 /ˌkæpɪtl ˈsɪti/
caravan /ˈkærəvæn/
carbon footprint /ˌkɑːbən ˈfʊtprɪnt/
characteristic ☛0 /kærəktəˈrɪstɪk/
chemical ☛0 /ˈkemɪkl/
climate ☛0 /ˈklaɪmət/
committee ☛0 /kəˈmɪti/
construction ☛0 /kənˈstrʌkʃn/
consumption /kənˈsʌmpʃn/
corporation /kɔːpəˈreɪʃn/
degrees centigrade /dɪˌɡriːz ˈsentɪɡreɪd/
demand ☛0 /dɪˈmɑːnd/
demographic trend /deməˌɡræfɪk ˈtrend/
detached house /dɪˈtætʃt ˌhaʊs/
dioxin /daɪˈɒksɪn/
emission /iˈmɪʃn/
energy ☛0 /ˈenəʤi/
environmental group ☛0
  /ɪnvaɪrənˈmentl ˌɡruːp/
generator /ˈʤenəreɪtə(r)/
government agency ☛0
  /ˈɡʌvnmənt ˌeɪʤənsi/
greenhouse gas /ˌɡriːnhaʊs ˈɡæs/
humidity /hjuːˈmɪdəti/
incentive /ɪnˈsentɪv/
laboratory /ləˈbɒrətri/
ladder /ˈlædə(r)/
landfill /ˈlændfɪl/
light bulb /ˈlaɪt ˌbʌlb/
limitation /lɪmɪˈteɪʃn/
living space ☛0 /ˈlɪvɪŋ ˌspeɪs/
location ☛0 /ləʊˈkeɪʃn/
loft /lɒft/
mansion /ˈmænʃn/
married couple ☛0 /ˌmærid ˈkʌpl/
material ☛0 /məˈtɪəriəl/
medical facilities /ˈmedɪkl fəˌsɪlətiz/
modern conveniences
  /ˌmɒdn kənˈviːniənsɪz/
natural resources ☛0 /ˌnætʃrəl rɪˈzɔːsɪz/
orchard /ˈɔːtʃəd/
period ☛0 /ˈpɪəriəd/
place setting /ˈpleɪs ˌsetɪŋ/
plastic ☛0 /ˈplæstɪk/
plateau /ˈplætəʊ/
portability /pɔːtəˈbɪləti/
professor ☛0 /prəˈfesə(r)/
purchase ☛0 /ˈpɜːtʃəs/

quality ☛0 /ˈkwɒləti/
range ☛0 /reɪnʤ/
season ☛0 /ˈsiːzn/
semi-detached house /ˌsemi dɪˈtætʃt ˌhaʊs/
solar heating /ˌsəʊlə ˈhiːtɪŋ/
solar panel /ˌsəʊlə ˈpænl/
square metre ☛0 /ˌskweə ˈmiːtə(r)/
terraced house /ˈterəst ˌhaʊs/
toxic waste /ˌtɒksɪk ˈweɪst/
variety ☛0 /vəˈraɪəti/
wildlife habitat /ˈwaɪldlaɪf ˌhæbɪtæt/

Verbs

accommodate /əˈkɒmədeɪt/
assemble /əˈsembl/
classify /ˈklæsɪfaɪ/
construct ☛0 /kənˈstrʌkt/
donate /dəʊˈneɪt/
downsize /daʊnˈsaɪz/
equip /ɪˈkwɪp/
entertain ☛0 /entəˈteɪn/
evaporate /ɪˈvæpəreɪt/
locate ☛0 /ləʊˈkeɪt/
range ☛0 /reɪnʤ/
reduce ☛0 /rɪˈdjuːs/
withstand /wɪðˈstænd/

Adjectives

accessible /əkˈsesəbl/
adequate ☛0 /ˈædɪkwət/
atmospheric /ætməsˈferɪk/
available ☛0 /əˈveɪləbl/
biodegradable /baɪəʊdɪˈɡreɪdəbl/
daily ☛0 /ˈdeɪli/
disposable /dɪˈspəʊzəbl/
durable /ˈdjʊərəbl/
eco-friendly /ˌiːkəʊ ˈfrendli/
economical /iːkəˈnɒmɪkl/
elevated /ˈelɪveɪtɪd/
empirical /ɪmˈpɪrɪkl/
energy efficient ☛0 /ˌenəʤi ɪˈfɪʃnt/
energy-saving ☛0 /ˈenəʤi ˌseɪvɪŋ/
exorbitant /ɪɡˈzɔːbɪtənt/
experimental /ɪksperɪˈmentl/
fold-out /ˈfəʊld ˌaʊt/
fold-up /ˈfəʊld ˌʌp/
incapacitated /ɪnkəˈpæsɪteɪtɪd/
inept /ɪˈnept/
inexplicable /ɪnɪkˈsplɪkəbl/
insignificant /ɪnsɪɡˈnɪfɪkənt/
integral /ˈɪntɪɡrəl/
intrepid /ɪnˈtrepɪd/
mass-market /ˈmæs ˌmɑːkɪt/
material ☛0 /məˈtɪəriəl/
negative ☛0 /ˈneɡətɪv/
portable /ˈpɔːtəbl/
pre-assembled /ˈpriː əˌsembld/
quality ☛0 /ˈkwɒləti/
regular ☛0 /ˈreɡjələ(r)/

significant ☛0 /sɪɡˈnɪfɪkənt/
tiny ☛0 /ˈtaɪni/
toxic /ˈtɒksɪk/
trivial /ˈtrɪviəl/
uncanny /ʌnˈkæni/
undaunted /ʌnˈdɔːntɪd/
unimaginable /ʌnɪˈmæʤɪnəbl/
unwieldy /ʌnˈwiːldi/
widespread /ˈwaɪdspred/
wind-powered /ˈwɪnd ˌpaʊəd/

Adverbs

currently ☛0 /ˈkʌrəntli/
full-time /ˌfʊl ˈtaɪm/
namely /ˈneɪmli/
primarily ☛0 /praɪˈmerəli/
respectfully /rɪˈspektfəli/
seldom /ˈseldəm/
typically ☛0 /ˈtɪpɪkli/
worldwide /wɜːldˈwaɪd/

Expressions and idioms

little do we realize ☛0
  /ˈlɪtl ˌduː ˌwiː ˌriːəlaɪz/
on behalf of sb/sth ☛0 /ˌɒn bɪˈhɑːf əv/
on standby /ˌɒn ˈstændbaɪ/
under no circumstances ☛0
  /ˌʌndə ˈnəʊ ˌsɜːkəmstɑːnsɪz/

Phrasal verbs

break down ☛0 /ˌbreɪk ˈdaʊn/
charge up ☛0 /ˌtʃɑːʤ ˈʌp/
get rid of ☛0 /ˌɡet ˈrɪd əv/
grow up ☛0 /ˌɡrəʊ ˈʌp/
pack up ☛0 /ˌpæk ˈʌp/

Conjunction

whereas ☛0 /weərˈæz/

Nouns

aluminium /ˌæljəˈmɪnɪəm/
anthem /ˈænθəm/
aptitude /ˈæptɪtjuːd/
arithmetic /əˈrɪθmətɪk/
audience 🔑 /ˈɔːdɪəns/
base camp /ˈbeɪs ˌkæmp/
behaviour 🔑 /bɪˈheɪvjə(r)/
boarding school /ˈbɔːdɪŋ ˌskuːl/
buzzer /ˈbʌzə(r)/
cameraman /ˈkæmərəmən/
composer /kəmˈpəʊzə(r)/
concert hall 🔑 /ˈkɒnsət ˌhɔːl/
conductor /kənˈdʌktə(r)/
deal 🔑 /diːl/
enthusiasm 🔑 /ɪnˈθjuːzɪæzəm/
executive 🔑 /ɪgˈzekjutɪv/
fabric /ˈfæbrɪk/
flute /fluːt/
genius /ˈdʒiːnɪəs/
honour 🔑 /ˈɒnə(r)/
houseboat /ˈhaʊsbəʊt/
impediment /ɪmˈpedɪmənt/
legal age /ˈliːgl ˌeɪdʒ/
mid-court /ˈmɪd ˌkɔːt/
murmur /ˈmɜːmə(r)/
non-profit organization
  /ˌnɒn ˌprɒft ɔːgənaɪˈzeɪʃn/
opera /ˈɒprə/
orchestra /ˈɔːkɪstrə/
ovation /əʊˈveɪʃn/
overtime /ˈəʊvətaɪm/
pianist /ˈpɪənɪst/
performance 🔑 /pəˈfɔːməns/
pressure 🔑 /ˈpreʃə(r)/
primary school /ˈpraɪməri ˌskuːl/
psychologist /saɪˈkɒlədʒɪs/
recital /rɪˈsaɪtl/
recording contract 🔑 /rɪˈkɔːdɪŋ ˌkɒntrækt/
special needs 🔑 /ˌspeʃl ˈniːdz/
stardom /ˈstɑːdəm/
summit /ˈsʌmɪt/
symphony /ˈsɪmfəni/
symphony orchestra /ˈsɪmfəni ˌɔːkɪstrə/
synthesizer /ˈsɪnθəsaɪzə(r)/
tie 🔑 /taɪ/
trailer /ˈtreɪlə(r)/
two-digit multiplication
  /ˌtuː ˌdɪdʒɪt mʌltɪplɪˈkeɪʃn/
victory 🔑 /ˈvɪktəri/
violin /vaɪəˈlɪn/
violinist /vaɪəˈlɪnɪst/
virtuoso /vɜːtʃuˈəʊsəʊ, -ˈəʊzəʊ/
yurt 🔑 /jɜː/

Verbs

anchor /ˈæŋkə(r)/
augment /ɔːgˈment/
blog (about) /blɒg/
call upon 🔑 /ˈkɔːl əˌpɒn/

cherish /ˈtʃerɪʃ/
equip /ɪˈkwɪp/
launch 🔑 /lɔːntʃ/
withdraw (from) 🔑 /wɪðˈdrɔː/

Adjectives

academic 🔑 /ækəˈdemɪk/
accelerated /əkˈseləreɪtɪd/
acclaimed /əˈkleɪmd/
accomplished /əˈkʌmplɪʃt/
adamant /ˈædəmənt/
alternative 🔑 /ɔːlˈtɜːnətɪv/
classical /ˈklæsɪkl/
conclude 🔑 /kənˈkluːd/
felt-like /ˈfelt ˌlaɪk/
gifted 🔑 /ˈgɪftɪd/
impressive 🔑 /ɪmˈpresɪv/
intellectual /ɪntəˈlektʃuəl/
level-headed /ˌlevl ˈhedɪd/
low-income /ˌləʊ ˈɪnkʌm/
mediocre /miːdiˈəʊkə(r)/
multi-million-dollar /ˈmʌlti ˌmɪljən ˌdɒlə(r)/
nomadic /nəʊˈmædɪk/
portable /ˈpɔːtəbl/
preparatory /prəˈpærətri/
prestigious /preˈstɪdʒəs/
remedial /rɪˈmiːdɪəl/
semi-detached /ˌsemi dɪˈtætʃt/
temporary 🔑 /ˈtemprəri/
troubled 🔑 /ˈtrʌbld/
underprivileged /ʌndəˈprɪvəlɪdʒd/
unprecedented /ʌnˈpresɪdentɪd/

Adverbs

essentially 🔑 /ɪˈsenʃəli/
onstage /ɒnˈsteɪdʒ/
permanently 🔑 /ˈpɜːmənəntli/
significantly 🔑 /sɪgˈnɪfɪkəntli/
stereotypically /steriəˈtɪpɪkli/
successfully 🔑 /səkˈsesfəli/

Expressions and idioms

act dumb /ˌækt ˈdʌm/
award a contract 🔑 /əˌwɔːd ə ˈkɒntrækt/
even more so 🔑 /ˌiːvn ˈmɔː ˌsəʊ/
get rid of sth 🔑 /ˌget ˈrɪd əv/
get to grips with sth /ˌget tə ˈgrɪps ˌwɪð/
get to the bottom of sth 🔑
  /ˌget tə ðə ˈbɒtəm əv/
resolve the situation 🔑
  /rɪˌzɒlv ðə sɪtʃuˈeɪʃn/
show an interest (in) 🔑 /ˌʃəʊ ən ˈɪntrəst/
smart move 🔑 /ˌsmɑːt ˈmuːv/
smart set 🔑 /ˈsmɑːt ˌset/
struck dumb /ˌstrʌk ˈdʌm/
under pressure 🔑 /ˌʌndə ˈpreʃə(r)/
with ease 🔑 /ˌwɪð ˈiːz/

Phrasal verbs

back away (from) 🔑 /ˌbæk əˈweɪ/
call off 🔑 /ˌkɔːl ˈɒf/
chip in with 🔑 /ˌtʃɪp ˈɪn ˌwɪð/
come in for 🔑 /ˌkʌm ˈɪn fə/
come up with 🔑 /ˌkʌm ˈʌp ˌwɪð/
draw up 🔑 /ˌdrɔː ˈʌp/
dumb down /ˌdʌm ˈdaʊn/
get across 🔑 /ˌget əˈkrɒs/
get along with sb 🔑 /ˌget əˈlɒŋ ˌwɪð/
get at sb 🔑 /ˈget ət/
get by 🔑 /ˌget ˈbaɪ/
get into 🔑 /ˌget ˈɪntuː, ˈɪntə/
get over 🔑 /ˌget ˈəʊvə(r)/
get up to 🔑 /ˌget ˈʌp ˌtuː, tə/
go back on 🔑 /ˌgəʊ ˈbæk ˌɒn/
hand over sth to someone 🔑
  /ˈhænd ˌəʊvə/
opt for /ˈɒpt ˌfɔː(r), fə(r)/
originate with /əˈrɪdʒɪneɪt ˌwɪð/
pick up (on) 🔑 /ˌpɪk ˈʌp ˌ(ɒn)/
sign up 🔑 /ˌsaɪn ˈʌp/
smart from sth 🔑 /ˈsmɑːt frəm/
take on 🔑 /ˌteɪk ˈɒn/
take over 🔑 /ˌteɪk ˈəʊvə(r)/
turn down 🔑 /ˌtɜːn ˈdaʊn/
wait out 🔑 /ˌweɪt ˈaʊt/

Literature Corner

absurd (adj) /əbˈsɜːd/
beseech (v) /bɪˈsiːtʃ/
commendable (adj) /kəˈmendəbl/
corpse (n) /kɔːps/
courtier (n) /ˈkɔːtiə(r)/
dejected (adj) /dɪˈdʒektɪd/
denote (v) /dɪˈnəʊt/
eternity (n) /ɪˈtɜːnəti/
filial (adj) /ˈfɪliəl/
impart (v) /ɪmˈpɑːt/
impious (adj) /ˈɪmpiəs/
intent (n) /ɪnˈtent/
mourning (n) /ˈmɔːnɪŋ/
obligation (n) /ɒblɪˈgeɪʃn/
obsequious (adj) /əbˈsiːkwiəs/
obstinate (adj) /ˈɒbstɪnət/
peevish (adj) /ˈpiːvɪʃ/
preserve (v) 🔑 /prɪˈzɜːv/
retrograde (adj) /ˈretrəgreɪd/
solemn (adj) /ˈsɒləm/
take sth to heart (idm) 🔑 /ˌteɪk ... tə ˈhɑːt/
throne (n) /θrəʊn/
trappings (n, pl) /ˈtræpɪŋz/
unfortified (adj) /ʌnˈfɔːtɪfaɪd/
unprevailing (adj) /ʌnprɪˈveɪlɪŋ/
visage (n) /ˈvɪzɪdʒ/
vulgar (adj) /ˈvʌlgə(r)/
woe (n) /wəʊ/

/p/ pen	/d/ dog	/tʃ/ beach	/v/ very	/s/ speak	/ʒ/ television	/n/ now	/r/ radio
/b/ big	/k/ can	/dʒ/ job	/θ/ think	/z/ zoo	/h/ house	/ŋ/ sing	/j/ yes
/t/ two	/g/ good	/f/ food	/ð/ then	/ʃ/ she	/m/ meat	/l/ late	/w/ we

IRREGULAR VERB LIST

Base form	Past simple	Past participle
be	was/were	been
beat	beat	beaten
become	became	become
begin	began	begun
bend	bent	bent
bite	bit	bitten
blow	blew	blown
break	broke	broken
bring	brought	brought
build	built	built
burn	burnt	burnt
buy	bought	bought
can	could	been able to
catch	caught	caught
choose	chose	chosen
come	came	come
cost	cost	cost
cut	cut	cut
deal	dealt	dealt
do	did	done
draw	drew	drawn
drink	drank	drunk
drive	drove	driven
eat	ate	eaten
fall	fell	fallen
feed	fed	fed
feel	felt	felt
fight	fought	fought
flee	fled	fled
find	found	found
fly	flew	flown
forget	forgot	forgotten
get	got	got
give	gave	given
go	went	gone/been
grow	grew	grown
hang	hung	hung
have	had	had
hear	heard	heard
hide	hid	hidden
hit	hit	hit
hold	held	held
keep	kept	kept
know	knew	known
lay	laid	laid
lead	led	led
learn	learnt/-ed	learnt/-ed
leave	left	left
lend	lent	lent
lose	lost	lost

Base form	Past simple	Past participle
make	made	made
mean	meant	meant
meet	met	met
overcome	overcame	overcome
pay	paid	paid
put	put	put
read	read	read
ride	rode	ridden
ring	rang	rung
run	ran	run
say	said	said
see	saw	seen
sell	sold	sold
send	sent	sent
set	set	set
shake	shook	shaken
shine	shone	shone
shoot	shot	shot
show	showed	shown/-ed
shut	shut	shut
sing	sang	sung
sink	sank	sunk
sit	sat	sat
sleep	slept	slept
smell	smelt/-ed	smelt/-led
speak	spoke	spoken
spell	spelt/-ed	spelt/-led
spend	spent	spent
spill	spilt/-ed	spilt/-led
split	split	split
spread	spread	spread
spring	sprang	sprung
stand	stood	stood
steal	stole	stolen
swim	swam	swum
take	took	taken
teach	taught	taught
tear	tore	torn
tell	told	told
think	thought	thought
throw	threw	thrown
understand	understood	understood
wake	woke	woken
wear	wore	worn
win	won	won
write	wrote	written

OXFORD
UNIVERSITY PRESS

Great Clarendon Street, Oxford OX2 6DP

Oxford University Press is a department of the University of Oxford.
It furthers the University's objective of excellence in research, scholarship,
and education by publishing worldwide in

Oxford New York

Auckland Cape Town Dar es Salaam Hong Kong Karachi
Kuala Lumpur Madrid Melbourne Mexico City Nairobi
New Delhi Shanghai Taipei Toronto

With offices in

Argentina Austria Brazil Chile Czech Republic France Greece
Guatemala Hungary Italy Japan Poland Portugal Singapore
South Korea Switzerland Thailand Turkey Ukraine Vietnam

OXFORD and OXFORD ENGLISH are registered trade marks of
Oxford University Press in the UK and in certain other countries

© Oxford University Press 2011

ISBN: 978 0 19 445317 2

Printed in China
This book is printed on paper from certified and well-managed sources.

ACKNOWLEDGEMENTS

*The authors and publisher are grateful to those who have given permission to reproduce
the following extracts and adaptations of copyright material:* p.20 *Leisure* by William
Henry Davies. Reproduced by kind permission of Dee & Griffin Solicitors; p.38
from *Adventures of Tom Sawyer* by Mark Twain, edited by Peter Stonely © Oxford
University Press 2008. Reproduced by permission of Oxford University Press;
p.56 from *Lost World* by Arthur Conan Doyle, edited by Ian Duncan © Oxford
University Press 2008. Reproduced by permission of Oxford University Press;
p.74 from *Count of Monte Cristo* by Alexandre Dumas, edited by David Coward
© Oxford University Press 2008. Reproduced by permission of Oxford
University Press; p.92 from *Hamlet* by William Shakespeare, edited by G. R.
Hibbard © Oxford University Press 2008. Reproduced by permission of Oxford
University Press.

Sources: p.76 www.tumbleweedhouses.com; p.82 www.wikipedia.com; p.84
www.rickyrubio9.com

Grammar Reference and Builder pages by: Eileen Flannigan

The publisher would like to thank the following for permission to reproduce photographs:
Alamy Images pp.4 (Skiers/imagebroker), 4 (Spanish farmhouse/David Askham),
5 (Elephant herd walking past tourists/Gerald Hinde), 8 (Ice hotel lobby/Chad
Ehlers), 8 (Deluxe hotel suite/Jochen Tack), 8 (Youth hostel/Archimage),
8 (Backpacker/PhotoStock-Israel), 9 (First class travel/Tony Hobbs), 9 (Economy
travel/Tom King), 10 (Paris/D A Barnes), 15 (Teens at counter/conmare GmbH),
15 (Businessman at hotel reception/View Stock), 16 (Apple Macintosh iMac/
Finnbarr Webster), 16 (Video game screen/Jamaway), 16 (Family portrait/Sergey
Galushko), 18 (Cable section of the Bank of London/Hans Wild/Time & Life
Pictures), 20 (Beach/Anna Stowe), 21 (Portrait of author Chingiz Aitmatov/Ulf
Andersen), 21 (Wild horses at river/Robert Harding Picture Library Ltd), 21 (Local
store/Mark Dyball), 22 (Kirby-Bauer antibiotic sensitivity test/Phototake),
22 (Illustration of Uranus/Gunter Hofer), 26 (Illustration of a orbiting satellite/
Paul Fleet), 26 (Microwave/D.Hurst), 26 (iPhone/ICP-UK), 26 (Mobile phone/
Dunca Daniel Mihai), 26 (Microwave meal/mediablitzimages (uk) Limited),
26 (Satellite navigation/ICP), 27 (Side view of the Ford Model T/Car Culture),
30 (Center Parcs villa/T.M.O.Buildings), 30 (Trainers/mediablitzimages (uk)
Limited), 32 (Billboard/Robert Landau), 33 (Online shopping/Mirjam Kleine
Staarman), 35 (Blackberry mobile phone/David J. Green - technology), 40 (Willow
tree/Birgit Hergert), 40 (Cinchona bark/Zena Elea), 41 (Foxglove/Arco Images
GmbH), 44 (Snail/David Cole), 44 (Aromatic herbs/Bon Appetit), 44 (Spa
treatment/Leszek Gadula), 44 (Walking across hot coals/Stewart Tilger),
45 (Pharmacy/Janine Wiedel Photolibrary), 45 (Chinese traditional herbalist/
Derek Webb), 48 (Boys playing in garden/PBimages), 48 (Men on farm/LatinStock
Collection), 57 (American diner/Robert Harding Picture Library Ltd),
57 (London bus and taxi cab/Eric Nathan), 57 (Beefeater at the Tower of London/
Travelshots.com), 58 (Basket of food/Bon Appetit), 58 (Burger meal/Fabian
Gonzales Editorial), 58 (Coffee beans/Sue Cunningham Photographic), 58 (Prince
William on Duchy Home Farm with Prince Charles/Tim Graham), 58 (Sugar
cane plantation/Peter Horree), 60 (Okra/Keith Leighton), 60 (Pomegranates/
Lew Robertson/FoodPix), 60 (Parsley/Lisa Romerein/Botanica), 60 (Bay leaves/
Tom Grill/Iconica), 60 (Cinnamon sticks/Tom Grill/Iconica), 62 (Colander/
Nikreates), 62 (Cast iron cooking pot/Geoffrey Kidd), 62 (Potato peeler/
studiomode), 62 (Pestle and mortar/Art Directors & TRIP), 63 (Man lifting lid
off tajine/Marko MacPherson/The Image Bank), 63 (Moroccan spicy bean soup/
Lisa Linder/Dorling Kindersley), 64 (hotpot/MBI), 66 (Men playing basketball/
Jupiterimages), 70 (The Roman Empire senate/Lebrecht Music and Arts Photo
LIbrary), 71 (Ginza district of Tokyo/Chad Ehlers), 71 (London Underground
escalator/Ashley Cooper), 72 (Oxford Street, London/Mike Stone), 75 (Japanese
girls in kimonos/Malcolm Fairman), 78 (Pollok House, Scotland/John McKenna),
78 (Detached modern house/bobhderring), 78 (Semi-detached houses/Barry
Mason), 79 (Energy efficient light bulb/ng), 80 (Deforestation/Cre8tive Studios),
80 (Dead trees/Buschkind), 81 (Man at computer workstation 1970/f8 Imaging/
Hulton Archive), 82 (Downtown Amman Jordan/Peter M.Wilson), 84 (Portrait
of violinist Midori/Marianne Barcellona//Time Life Pictures), 85 (Basketball
player/Jose Luis Surralles/Euroleague Basketball), 88 (Classroom bullying/ACE
STOCK LIMITED), 88 (School class/Neil McAllister), 89 (Mountain climber
Samantha Larson/Evan Agostini), 90 (Family tension/Catchlight Visual Services),
93 (A yurt/Olivier Renck/Aurora), 93 (Narrowboat/Chris Cooper-Smith); Corbis
pp.28 (Inventor Thomas Alva Edison/Library of Congress - digital ve/Science
Faction/), 44 (Drilling through stone/Jonathan Blair), 60 (Root Ginger/Maximilian
Stock Ltd/photocuisine), 60 (Tangerines/Joel Glenn/AgStock Images), 66 (Rugby
scrum/Franck Seguin), 70 (Cricket match/Anthony Phelps/Reuters), 70 (Omayyad
Mosque chapel/YOSHIO TOMII/amanaimages), 70 (Astrolabe by Elias von Lennep/
Austrian Archives), 75 (New Year's Ball Dropping in Times Square/Alan Schein
Photography), 78 (Terraced housing/Arcaid), 84 (Boy using laptop in classroom/
Peter M.Fisher); Getty Images p.93 (Mobile home park/Wayne Eastep/Riser);
iStockphoto pp.16 (Plasma TV/Dmitry Kutlayev), 16 (Waitress/Sean Locke),
27 (Light bulb/Wei Ti Ng), 35 (Blackberries/Valentyn Volkov); Oxford University
Press pp.7 (Beach/Digital Vision), 8 (Businesswoman/Radius Images), 16 (Bowl
of fruit salad/Photodisc), 20 (Snowdonia National Park/Digital Vision), 22 (DNA
molecules/Comstock), 44 (Cupcakes/Photodisc), 46 (Tropical beach/Photodisc),
46 (Hong Kong at night/Corbis/Digital Stock), 52 (Smiling woman/Stockbyte),
57 (Big Ben and Houses of Parliament/Photodisc), 62 (Metal whisk/Ingram),
71 (Taxis in New York/image100); Photolibrary pp.7 (Beach in the Maldives/
Mauritius), 8 (Senior couple smiling outdoors/OJO Images), 8 (Businessman at
airport/Ariel Skelley/Blend Images), 21 (Beach on rocky seashore/Polka Dot
Images), 51 (School girls walking home/Image100), 52 (Portrait of man/Radius
Images), 54 (Portrait of two girls/Design Pics Inc), 61 (Curry/Tim Hill/Fresh
Food Images), 62 (Ladle/White), 67 (Bowling/Spike Mafford/Uppercut Images),
69 (Two men using laptop at cafe/Chase Jarvis/White), 75 (New Year Celebrations/
Britain on View), 78 (Bungalow/Dominic Whiting), 79 (Smart Fortwo city car/
imagebroker.net), 80 (Landfill burning/Superstock), 87 (Boy playing piano/
moodboard), 89 (Base camp at Mount Everest/imagebroker.net); PunchStock
pp.22 (Apple falling out of sky/UpperCut Images), 60 (Artichokes/Photodisc),
62 (Wok/Dorling Kindersley), 62 (Food processor/Dorling Kindersley), 62 (Garlic
crusher/Dorling Kindersley); Rex Features p.46 (Oxygen bar, Tokyo/Sutton-
Hibbert); Ronald Grant Archive p.43 (Mary Poppins, Ed Wynn, Dick Van Dyke/
Walk Disney PIctures); Science Photo Library pp.25 (Coloured SEM of hooks
and loops material/Eye of Science), 27 (Engraving on a press); SuperStock
p.78 (Holiday caravan/Robert Harding Picture Library); The Advertising
Archives pp.30 (McDonald's advert), 30 (Nintendo advert); Tumbleweed Tiny
House Company pp.76, 77.

Cover: Photolibrary (Glider flying/Michael Turek/White)

Main illustrations by: Carl Pearce

Other illustrations by: Simon Gurr pp.38, 56, 74, 92